Reading *The Waste Land*

READING *THE WASTE LAND*

Modernism and the Limits of Interpretation

JEWEL SPEARS BROOKER AND JOSEPH BENTLEY

THE UNIVERSITY OF MASSACHUSETTS PRESS / AMHERST

Library of Congress Cataloging-in-Publication Data
Brooker, Jewel Spears, 1940–
Reading The waste land : modernism and the limits of interpretation /
Jewel Spears Brooker and Joseph Bentley.
p.   cm.
ISBN 0-87023-692-X
1. Eliot, T. S. (Thomas Stearns), 1888–1965. Waste land. 2. Modernism
(Literature) I. Bentley, Joseph, 1932–1988. II. Title.
PS3509.L43W3634   1990
821'.912—dc20   89-36484

British Library Cataloguing in Publication data are available.

Acknowledgment is made for permission to reprint from the following material under copyright:

"The Waste Land" and excerpts from "The Love Song of J. Alfred Prufrock," "Mr. Apollinax," "Gerontion," and "Sweeney Agonistes" in *Collected Poems 1909–1962*, by T. S. Eliot, copyright 1936 by Harcourt Brace Jovanovich, Inc. and copyright © 1963, 1964 by T. S. Eliot, are reprinted by permission of Harcourt Brace Jovanovich, Inc. and Faber and Faber Ltd.

Excerpts from "Burnt Norton," "East Coker," "The Dry Salvages," and "Little Gidding" from *Four Quartets*, by T. S. Eliot, copyright 1943 by T. S. Eliot and renewed 1971 by Esme Valerie Eliot, are reprinted by permission of Harcourt Brace Jovanovich, Inc., and Faber and Faber Ltd.

Excerpts from "The Metaphysical Poets," "Baudelaire," "Francis Herbert Bradley," "Dante," and "Ben Jonson" in *Selected Essays*, by T. S. Eliot, copyright 1950 by Harcourt Brace Jovanovich, Inc. and renewed 1978 by Esme Valerie Eliot, are reprinted by permission of the publisher.

Excerpts from *The Waste Land: A Facsimile and Transcript of the Original Drafts*, by T. S. Eliot, edited by Valerie Eliot, copyright © 1971 by Valerie Eliot, are reprinted by permission of Harcourt Brace Jovanovich, Inc. and Faber and Faber Ltd.

Excerpts from *Knowledge and Experience in the Philosophy of F. H. Bradley*, by T. S. Eliot, © 1964 by T. S. Eliot, are reprinted by permission of Faber and Faber Ltd and Farrar, Straus and Giroux, Inc.

Excerpts from the Introduction to Savonarola, from *Vanity Fair*, February 1924, and "Ulysses, Order and Myth," November 1923, by T. S. Eliot, are reprinted by permission of Mrs. Valerie Eliot and Faber and Faber Ltd.

Frontispiece: Oskar Kokoschka, *London, Large Thames View I*, 1926, oil on canvas, 35¼ × 51¼". Courtesy Albright-Knox Art Gallery, Buffalo, N.Y. Room of Contemporary Art Fund, 1941.

For H. Ralph Brooker and Mary Ann Bentley

The finest tact after all can give us only an interpretation, and every interpretation, along perhaps with some utterly contradictory interpretation, has to be taken up and reinterpreted by every thinking mind and by every civilization.

—T. S. Eliot, *Knowledge and Experience in the Philosophy of F. H. Bradley*

Contents

Acknowledgments

Our debts are many. The first is to Eliot himself. For longer than we can remember, we have been fascinated by the special quality of his poetic intelligence and by the combination of tradition and modernity his art represents. We are also indebted to the many Eliot critics from the 1930s to the 1980s and acknowledge special debts to those mentioned in our Introduction. We do not summarize or catalog criticism in the pages that follow, but we do wish to acknowledge our appreciation for all scholars working in the field. In a general way, we should also like to acknowledge an indebtedness to the theorists who have been writing since the middle of the century. They have made it possible to read all texts in new and refreshing ways. Although we have reservations about some of this work and deplore the divisive tone used in some of it, we realize that our reading of *The Waste Land* would have been poorer without it.

We take this opportunity to acknowledge the patience and support of our spouses—H. Ralph Brooker and Mary Ann Bentley—over the three years we spent on this manuscript; and we are indebted to our children—Emily Hope Brooker, Mark Spears Brooker, and Janet Bentley—for the endless inspiration they provided. We are also grateful to our students. We could not have finished this book without the support of the National Endowment for the Humanities, who in 1987 awarded Jewel Spears Brooker a Fellowship for College Teachers, and without the goodwill of Dr. Lloyd Chapin of Eckerd College, who supported Professor Brooker in her research efforts. We are grateful to Mrs. Valerie Eliot, for permission to quote from Eliot's work, and to Dr. Michael Halls of King's College (Cambridge University), the staff at the Houghton Library (Harvard University), the New York Public Library, and the Ransom Humanities Research Center at the University of Texas. Others who helped in various capacities include Carolyn Johnston, Jeffrey Perl, and Grover Smith.

SPECIAL NOTE: Several months after this book was completed, but long before it was published, Joseph Bentley was smitten with cancer. He discovered this devastating illness in midsummer 1988, and on September 28, he died. His death came two days after the hundredth anniversary of T. S. Eliot's birth. Professor Bentley, a brilliant teacher and scholar at the height of his powers at the time of his death, was to have been a participant in several of the Eliot centennial celebrations. *Reading "The Waste Land"* meant much to him, and although he died on the day the acceptance letter arrived, he had seen the readers' reports and was pleased by its warm reception at the University of Massachusetts Press.

Reading *The Waste Land*

Introduction

The Waste Land was published in 1922, and by the 1930s it was being treated by many as the poem of the century, as a text that serious readers could not ignore. The history of discussions of *The Waste Land* can be divided into roughly three dispensations, the first extending from the thirties through the fifties, the second from the sixties to the eighties, and the third beginning in the eighties.

The first period was dominated by scholars loosely called the New Critics. Many of these scholars knew Eliot personally, many admired him intensely, and although a number of individual voices were negative about his work, virtually all acknowledged his importance. These critics tended to read texts closely and carefully, and their work is still indispensable for an understanding of *The Waste Land*. The second period was in large part a reaction against the first. Dominated by figures interested primarily in literary theory, it was a period in which many younger scholars validated their credentials as Newer Critics by rejecting both the methods and the canon of their elders. Most abandoned close reading altogether in favor of metacritical discourse, and many were open in their hostility to Eliot. In the background, meanwhile, foundations of a new era in Eliot studies were taking shape. The poet's early philosophical writings began to appear, and the original drafts of *The Waste Land*, edited by Valerie Eliot, were published.[1] A new dispensation of Eliot studies, greatly enriched by an awareness of the new primary materials and also by an increased appreciation of the relevance of theoretical concerns with language, emerged in the eighties.

The best of the New Critics were masters of close readings. Cleanth Brooks, for example, in 1937 wrote a detailed commentary on *The Waste Land* which is still a model of critical helpfulness.[2] The fact that certain basic insights in the past generation have originated as reactions against Brooks and his colleagues does not in any way diminish their excellence. What is usually perceived as a repudiation of them, in fact, can best be understood as part of a dialogue that would have been impossible without them. One problem with the work of the New Critics was that their close readings, no matter how brilliant, could not deliver all they seemed to promise. The emphasis on the text itself as a reservoir of meaning gave the impression that a text could be confronted and overcome through close reading, that questions could be answered in authoritative and final ways. The best of the New Critics never made such claims, but some of their enthusiastic disciples were insufficiently aware of the open-ended nature of modernist masterpieces such as *The Waste Land*. In the late fifties, in a general demoralized retreat from close reading, many critics simply gave up on *The Waste Land*, a work which had remained intransigent to their best efforts.

The decline of sustained close reading of Eliot is also related, ironically, to the emergence of historical scholarship regarding sources and allusions. The major figure here is Grover Smith, who in the midfifties published an encyclopedic study of Eliot's sources.[3] The mere existence of Smith's scholarly tome changed the shape of close readings of Eliot. The poet's allusions and sources moved to the foreground of concern, and although most readers of Eliot's poetry and plays benefited from Smith's work, others found themselves frustrated by the weight of the intellectual backgrounds. William Arrowsmith's close readings of Eliot's Sweeney poems marry the interpretative brilliance of Brooks with the comprehensive learning of Smith.[4] Such readings as Arrowsmith's by their very excellence tend to move in opposing directions. They convey, by their exhaustiveness, an impression that everything that can be said has been said. At the same time, by their creativeness, they convey an impression that the text invites an unlimited range of interpretative activities.

The sixties began what many admirers of Eliot would consider a bleak period. The anxiety of influence of the profession at large seemed to inspire quick and increasingly uninformed dismissals of Eliot, and these repeated denigrations produced, predictably, a generation of students with vague and inaccurate impressions about his poetry and ideas. But there is a bright side to Eliot studies of the last quarter century. The general retreat from Eliot coincided with the beginning of basic and important work on his ideas, especially on his early philosophical writings. His intellectual development during the *Criterion* years (1922–39) was chronicled by John D. Margolis.[5] More fundamentally, Eliot's dissertation and several of his early papers, edited by Anne C. Bolgan,[6] appeared in the mid-sixties, as did some notes, edited by Grover Smith, from his 1913–14 graduate seminar with Josiah Royce.[7] Some critics, notably Lewis Freed, have virtually devoted their careers to following up the leads in these basic primary materials.[8] In the meantime, several scholars, including one of the authors of this book, began to visit research collections and to read Eliot's unpublished graduate school papers. The interest in his graduate work in philosophy has continued and has issued in several exceptionally helpful studies of his ideas. For example, Piers Gray's *T. S. Eliot's Intellectual and Poetic Development, 1909–1922*, based in part on a careful reading of unpublished materials, appeared in 1982.[9] William Skaff's *Philosophy of T. S. Eliot* appeared in 1986, and though Skaff does not work from unpublished materials, he brings together and discusses with special insight most of Eliot's early reading.[10] A number of critics, such as Jeffrey Perl, have written helpful articles based on their readings of the graduate school papers.[11] Cleo McNelly Kearns's *T. S. Eliot and Indic Traditions*, published in 1987, also breaks new and important ground regarding the shape of Eliot's mind and art.[12]

The period of general neglect of Eliot's poetry was one in which a revolution was occurring in the theory of interpretation. Existentialist, phenomenologist, structuralist, psychoanalytic, feminist, and poststructuralist theories appeared and stimulated dazzling conversations about how texts mean. Bloom, Miller, Poulet, Gadamer, Foucault, Lacan, Kristeva, and Derrida are just a few of the critics who have contributed to these conversations. These studies have enormous value for critics interested in Eliot. In the first place, they have popularized insights about language which are central in Eliot's poetry from "The Love Song of J. Alfred Prufrock" to *Four Quartets*. Anyone who doubts this should read Derrida's "Structure, Sign, and Play in the Discourse of the Human Sciences"[13] and follow up with a reading of part 5 of each of *Four Quartets*. In the second place, the studies in theory have created an audience that will be able to appreciate Eliot's dissertation and early philosophical work, an audience unthinkable a generation ago. One remembers that even philosophers—Richard Wollheim comes to mind—declined to make sense of Eliot's philosophical work.[14] The increasing availability of Eliot's philosophical papers and the increasing sophistication of readers hold high promise for Eliot studies in the coming decades.

Few books have appeared that show both an informed appreciation of Eliot and an awareness of contemporary theory. Marianne Thormählen's *"The Waste Land": A Fragmentary Wholeness* (1978) is an insightful study that makes use of phenomenology.[15] Gregory Jay's *T. S. Eliot and the Poetics of Literary History* (1983) attempts to place Eliot in contemporary criticism.[16] Harriet Davidson's *T. S. Eliot and Hermeneutics* (1985) summarizes some of the relevant contemporary literary theory and relates postexistentialist hermeneutics to an overview of *The Waste Land*. Her book is valuable, but it focuses on contemporary theory itself and does not include a close reading of the poem.[17] Calvin Bedient's *He Do the Police in Different Voices: "The Waste Land" and Its Protagonist* (1986) is the one close reading that has appeared.[18] Bedient's study is suggestive, but his controlling assumption that the poem has a single protagonist is one which, for reasons that will be evident in our study, we cannot accept.

Our book is a return to close reading, a return characterized by an awareness of the scholarship on Eliot's philosophy and also an awareness of the new critical theories. Because our main interest is the poem itself, we move quickly through the philosophical backgrounds and try to avoid the language theorists have developed for talking among themselves. Readers who know such figures as Lévi-Strauss, Derrida, and Gadamer, however, will be able to see that Eliot in his philosophical work arrived at theories before 1916 that have much in common with contemporary insights. Like Lévi-Strauss and Derrida, he saw every text as *bricolage*—work with tools known to be "always already" fallen into imprecision. The hallmark of his major poetry is the use of language that is conscious of itself and of its finitude and thus is designed to put itself under erasure. A major subject of *The Waste Land*, we shall argue, is the contingency of language.

Like Gadamer, Eliot saw interpretative activity as a never-ending process, yet a process that must be subjected to the limitations imposed by knowledge of the text's origins and intertextual relations. Gadamer insisted that interpretation should proceed only after we have done the research necessary to arrive at the text's required "preunderstandings." As Gadamer and his master Heidegger conceive hermeneutics, interpretation must be preceded by a search for all the text "wants" us to know. In basic agreement with this principle, we have taken the time to find out what Eliot was thinking about Bradley, Royce, Frazer, and several other figures during the years when he was contemplating the series of fragments that eventually became *The Waste Land*. As a practical matter, we cannot do justice to all of these figures and have chosen to focus on Bradley. Eliot was absorbed in Bradley's thought during the two years in which he conceived and wrote his dissertation, and we believe that an awareness of Eliot's work in Bradley is especially helpful in understanding *The Waste Land*.

In the first chapter, we will attempt to identify the context or, to borrow a term from Foucault, the *episteme* or epistemological field in which Eliot and *The Waste Land* arose. We will discuss certain aspects of early-twentieth-century Western civilization which were attracting the attention of emerging artists, philosophers, and scientists, and we will indicate how avant-garde artists responded to the collapse of epistemological models in science and philosophy. Some of the currents brought together in this survey of modernism will be familiar to some of our readers, but since these materials are vital to our argument, we offer the review as a preparation for the reading that follows. In the second chapter, we will note the personal and philosophic foundations of this leviathan poem and point to specific ideas in Bradley and, to a lesser extent, in Frazer, which have helped us in reading *The Waste Land*. The importance of Eliot's studies can hardly be overestimated, for in them he discovered paradigms which suggested that it might be possible to achieve a transcendent perspective from which things could be imagined more holistically, a sort of platform from which the artist could gain a unique perspective on his material. After establishing the general and specific contexts for *The Waste Land*, we will devote several chapters to a section-by-section reading of the poem.

The close reading of *The Waste Land* is the heart of our book. In approaching the text by way of Eliot's philosophical writings, we hope to suggest and to illustrate that the text is self-limiting, but in a way different from that conceived of by earlier critics. The poem, in our view, calls attention to itself as a text about reading. Like several other modernist texts, it can be read with profit as a set of guide- lines, rather analogous to a musical score, on how to read, or perform into actuality, the complete artistic experience. One clear hint that the process of reading is one of the poem's major subjects is the simple and widely recognized fact that it is unreadable by ordinary methods. Eliot calls attention to the nature of reading by virtually eliminating transitions. As an undisputed master of prose, in full knowledge of what he was doing, he left out the signals that normally move the reader from sentence to sentence and paragraph to paragraph. These transitions, in traditional texts, reveal how parts are related to each other. Their absence in *The Waste Land* insures that readers will be conscious of reading, that critics will be self-conscious, that readings will unfold unpretentiously as read- ings and not as another thing. The poem, of course, is about many subjects, including, as Harriet Davidson says, the subject of "ab- sence."[19] Our way of putting it is that the poem is in part about "loss," not only the loss of community but the loss of the text itself, which occurs in the process of reading it. In respecting Eliot's location of his subject in the reading process itself, we became increasingly aware of the fruitfulness of grounding a close reading of the text in insights about reading it. The importance of this matter is the main reason we call this book *Reading "The Waste Land."*

Our subtitle *Modernism and the Limits of Interpretation* is also re- lated to the fact that texts like *The Waste Land* present themselves primarily as linguistic structures. They tend to displace attention from the meaning of words to the meaning of meaning, from the end of interpretation to the process. As for the limits of interpreta- tion, it is true in one way that the only limit on interpretation is the imagination of the interpreter, that reading a text such as *The Waste Land* sets in motion a ceaseless and never-ending activity. This activity, paradoxically, leads to the discovery that all interpretation is essentially and severely limited in what it can achieve, that the value of interpretation is related more to something gained en route than to something waiting at the end. Interpretation is limited in its usefulness, in its applicability, in its temporality. No interpretation is good for all seasons, and some interpretations seem incoherent and virtually useless to everyone except the person who formulated them. One of the issues we address in this book is this tension between the limitations and the unlimitedness of interpretation. We believe that the most useful interpretations are those in which the interpreter is self-conscious about the nature of interpretation and utilizes principles that impose limits on interpretative activity. Our principles are relatively simple.

Our first principle is that interpretation must take account of what Bradley calls the systematic nature of judgment.[20] This means that every judgment involves contexts and that every judgment produces and complicates relations between part and part and between part and whole. Reading must show an informed awareness of intellectual contexts and, in particular, of the poet's own epistemological field, of his episteme, as Foucault might say. Accordingly, we begin our study by unfolding a background of general ideas that were of special interest for Eliot and other artists in the early years of this century, and then focus on Bradley and Eliot's graduate studies. Our emphasis on contexts should not be taken as an indication that we believe that Eliot was the ideal reader of his own poem or as evidence that we subscribe to a theory of authorial intent. No critic, regardless of energy and competence, can reconstruct Eliot's mind during the years in which he was writing *The Waste Land*. On the other hand, any critic can learn specific things about that mind and can use what he or she knows as a set of boundaries for the process of reading. Such boundaries, of course, will not prevent misreadings, and indeed such concepts as "true reading" are not helpful or even meaningful. We offer our interpretations not as true or false but as contributions to the exchange of ideas that is needed in the community of those who study *The Waste Land*.

Our second principle is that readers must distinguish between internal and external interpretations. By internal interpretation, we mean one made within the poem itself, and by external, one made by the reader of the poem. Take, for example, the opening of "The Love Song of J. Alfred Prufrock."

> Let us go then, you and I,
> When the evening is spread out against the sky
> Like a patient etherised upon a table[21]

These lines are an interpretation made by someone within the poem; they are an internal interpretation. In making sense of the poem, the reader has to interpret this interpretation, a task which is external to the poem. Reading a poem consists in large part of interpreting interpretations. Another important point is that neither the internal nor the external interpretation should be equated with Eliot's interpretation. We cannot say that the poet says that the evening resembles a patient under ether on a surgery table; we can only say that he presents us with a heterocosm in which a character sees the world in this way. In interpreting Prufrock's interpretation, we are not interpreting Eliot's, which is another thing altogether and irrecoverable.

Our third principle derives from the special importance in Eliot's poetry of literal meanings and from the puzzling fact that many commentators seem not to have read the text itself with care. Perhaps they move too quickly to *symboliste* suggestiveness or to metaphor because of Eliot's descent from the French symbolists and his association with T. E. Hulme and Ezra Pound. The movement beyond the literal is important, of course, but it should be restrained until account has been taken of precise and straightforward meanings. Eliot's use of simple words with literal accuracy or of philosophical terms with precision often disconcerted his friends and critics. He was fully aware of this; it was, in fact, a playful part of his sense of irony. For example, when I. A. Richards spoke of the disillusionment of a generation, Eliot spoke of their illusion of being disillusioned. That seemed clever to the point of being oracular, but all it said was that no one is ever free from some kind of illusion. And in the notes to *The Waste Land*, when he says that "what Tiresias *sees*, in fact, is the substance of the poem," he is using words with technical precision, as we shall show in the course of our study. Literal meanings are important in the poetry too. The fruitfulness of privileging the literal can be illustrated by recalling Prufrock's rejection of comparisons to Hamlet.

> No! I am not Prince Hamlet, nor was meant to be;
> Am an attendant lord, one that will do
> To swell a progress, start a scene or two,
> Advise the prince; no doubt, an easy tool,
> Deferential, glad to be of use,
> Politic, cautious, and meticulous;

> Full of high sentence, but a bit obtuse;
> At times, indeed, almost ridiculous—
> Almost, at time, the Fool.

Countless annotators have declared that Prufrock is like Polonius. Others have noted that Shakespeare's fools are invariably masters of language and thus possessed of the skills Prufrock needs most. Even subtler readings have appeared in textbooks, but no reading that we have seen notes the passage's plain, literal message. Prufrock says that, unlike Hamlet, he is a secondary character in the story of his own life, a means but never an end, a peripheral presence in a psychic complex where the central position is either vacant or occupied by a fantasy. This is precisely what the passage says. It says much more, of course, but that "much more" is available only if the interpretative process begins with an acknowledgment of the obvious.

Our fourth principle is related to the fact that, somewhat in the manner of modern painters, Eliot forces multiperspectivism upon his readers. As Picasso and Braque juxtapose several perspectives on canvas, so Eliot juxtaposes many perspectives of the same idea or object, thus causing us to be aware of the limits of every perspective and of the desirability of moving from one perspective to another and, finally, of comprehending many perspectives at once. The female portrait at the center of *The Waste Land*, for example, is a cubist portrait, comprehending facets of Cleopatra, a nervous contemporary woman at her dressing table, a pub gossip, and many others.

Our fifth principle involves an openness to texts that both insist upon and defeat interpretation. Eliot often demands that we interpret at the same time that he trivializes or undermines any interpretation we can construct. When Madame Sosostris tells her client to "Fear death by water," the reader trying to make sense of a poem about a waste land cannot fail to be drawn into the interpretative process. At the same time, however, the reader will probably notice that every interpretation is trivialized by its association with a paranoid fortune-teller with a bad cold.

A final principle involves recognition of a certain circularity involved in reading difficult texts. *The Waste Land* and many other texts force us through interpretative exercises not, as one might expect, to reward us with some final truth but to bring us back to the words from which our interpretative journey began. When we read "April is the cruellest month," we immediately move away from the text in an attempt to figure out what it means. In this process of interpretation, we automatically push the text aside. But we discover multiple and inconclusive results which are insufficient or aesthetically less desirable than the initial textual fact. This leads us to abandon our interpretations and refocus on "April is the cruellest month." We have moved outside, found and weighed various meanings, considered them, and returned to the text. But it is a return with a difference, a difference made by the process of trying to interpret. We call this journey which begins and ends with the text a "hermeneutical loop," a journey which finally takes us beyond hermeneutics, leaving us in a posthermeneutical state.

We will follow our reading of *The Waste Land* with an interpretative postscript in which we speculate about possible foundations of the poem in the poet's early life. The inspiration behind these speculations comes from Jean Piaget, whose theories of genetic epistemology bear a striking resemblance to certain epistemological notions outlined by Bradley and endorsed by Eliot. In *The Construction of Reality in the Child*,[22] Piaget discusses the infantile mind in ways that are congruous not only with Eliot's theories but also with his practice as evidenced by *The Waste Land*. The discussion of Piaget is meant to be suggestive only. Bringing Piaget to bear on *The Waste Land* resituates some of the philosophical issues raised by Bradley and his fellow philosophers, putting them into the more universal context of infantile epistemology. The Piagetan materials suggest the possibility of a holistic theory of the structure of Eliot's poem and a metatheory of modernism itself.

We do not wish to claim, in conclusion, that our attention to the books Eliot read, the papers he wrote, and the critics he inspired gives us privileged access to his mind from his own point of view. At the same time, we believe that our research has enabled us to construct an interpretative environment, however imperfect, and to suggest a version of Eliot's mind, however inadequate, that we can use and that we can share in the reading process. By decoding *The Waste Land*'s instructions on how it is to be read, we hope to contribute to the renewal and enrichment of dialogue on this great text which after sixty-five years still appears to be the poem of the century.

1 / A Wilderness of Mirrors

Perspectives on the Twentieth Century

[Seen] from the right height everything comes together: the thoughts of the philosopher, the work of the artist, and good deeds.—F. Nietzsche, "The Philosopher"

In his 1923 review of James Joyce's *Ulysses*, T. S. Eliot focused on one of his generation's recurrent anxieties—the idea that art might be impossible in the twentieth century. The reasons that art seemed impossible are many and complex, but they were all related to the collapse of ways of knowing that had served the Western mind at least since the Renaissance and that had received canonical formulation in the seventeenth century in the science of Newton and the philosophy of Descartes. In both science and philosophy, the crisis was essentially epistemological; that is, it was related to radical uncertainty about how we know what we know about the real world. This crisis, disorienting even to specialists, was at once a cause of despair and an incentive for innovation in the arts.

This study is rooted in the complicated but necessary relationship between the way that artists "know" the external world and the form that develops in their art. Creative activity requires, whether the artist is aware of it or not, some sort of theory of knowledge as backdrop. Admittedly, a number of contemporary philosophers, for example, Richard Rorty in *Philosophy and the Mirror of Nature*, have subverted the very idea of epistemology. And admittedly, many artists consider philosophical inquiry to be unprofitable. An anti-epistemology, however, is in a real sense another epistemology. And since knowing is part of being human, an unconscious epistemology is an epistemology no less. Simply to function as a human being (even more so, to function as a philosopher or an artist) in the world is to work within a context of how and to what extent reality can be known. Eliot makes this point in the concluding chapter of his dissertation. He claims that the act of theory formation in epistemology is an important practical step in the process of knowing, even if the theory turns out to be invalid.[1] He makes a similar point in part 5 of "East Coker" when he speaks of the importance of trying to use words, even though one is aware that each attempt is "a different kind of failure," "a raid on the inarticulate/With shabby equipment always deteriorating." Like many philosophers, scientists, and artists in the first quarter of this century, Eliot was preoccupied with both the impossibility and the inevitability of epistemology.

The use of epistemology as a reference point in the discussion of art is one which Eliot himself might have found objectionable. He denounced the use of the word in his dissertation, but in the same document he also defended its use, taking the point of view of the psychologist in his denunciation of epistemology and the point of view of the epistemologist in his attack on psychology.[2] Clearly, though, he distrusted professional epistemological inquiry, for like his mentor F. H. Bradley he associated it with discredited assumptions inherited from previous centuries, with methodologies that arbitrarily divided the world into subject and object. In 1916, after five intense years of graduate study in philosophy, he concluded that epistemology was a pseudoscience and that the search for ultimate Meaning was ultimately meaningless, comparable to tying knots in the wind. He argued in chapter 4 of his dissertation that epistemology as an intellectual enterprise depends on the division of the world into subject and object and on the assumption that the subject can describe the object from without and, further, on the assumption that both subject and object are stable entities unaffected by the process of knowing and the process of explaining. Eliot claims, however, that separating the explainer, the explanation, and the explained is an impossible dream. His doctoral dissertation for Harvard University consists of an out-and-out assault on philosophy, especially on epistemology. His attack on epistemology does not mean, of course, that he had no theory of knowledge. It means, rather, that his reflections on the nature of language led him to believe that epistemological inquiry was unfruitful and that his reflections on the problems of philosophy led him to abandon the dualism (analysis in terms of subjects and objects) that had dominated epistemology since Descartes.

Eliot's focus on the problem of language and the related problem of dualism is consistent with the focus of other artists and scientists in his moment of history. A number of modern thinkers who have analyzed Western history into epistemological dispensations have characterized the twentieth century in terms that parallel those operating in Eliot's art. Historians of the human sciences, such as Michel Foucault, characterize the twentieth century in terms of theories of language and interpretation; historians of the natural sciences, such as Gerald Holton and Thomas Kuhn, and of philosophy, such as A. O. Lovejoy, discuss the twentieth century as a period of the collapse of dualism. These historians, though differing in striking ways from each other, have in common the view that in most periods of history (however defined) there tends to be an overarching epistemology or way of knowing which most people unconsciously accept and use in going about the business of life (and, of course, the business of art). Their analyses are helpful in establishing the context for Eliot and his work.

In *Les Mots et les choses* (translated as *The Order of Things: An Archaeology of the Human Sciences*), Foucault argues that large blocks of history can profitably be approached by attention to their *episteme*, which he defines as the "epistemological field . . . in which knowledge . . . grounds its positivity and thereby manifests a history which is . . . that of its conditions of possibility."[3] Foucault, who calls himself an archaeologist in the human sciences (in some circles called the behavioral sciences), maintains that certain identifiable principles undergird the thought that occurs in any one period. Speaking of the classical period, he maintains that, "unknown to themselves, the naturalists, economists, and grammarians employed the same rules to define the objects proper to their own study, to form their concepts, to build their theories. It is these rules of formation, which were never formulated in their own right, but are to be found only in widely differing theories, concepts, and objects of study," that Foucault calls the period's *episteme*.[4] The purpose of Foucault's study is to reveal this level of positive but *unconscious* knowledge which is shared by people in many fields at once; his goal, in other words, is to develop a geography of that epistemological space which eludes consciousness but grounds discourse in different periods.

In the broadest terms, Foucault sees two great periods in the episteme of Western culture. He defines the first (or classical) episteme as a dispensation running from the Greeks through the middle of the seventeenth century; he defines the second (or modern) episteme as beginning in the late eighteenth century, a period which in other terminologies might be called the post-Renaissance period. In working out his analysis of the history of nonformal but systematic knowledge, Foucault argues that the history of the second period can be understood in terms of three shifting epistemological dynasties: the biological, the economic, and the linguistic. In the first period (roughly the romantic age), the biological model reigns; perception is in terms of the organic, and analysis proceeds in terms of function. In the next dispensation, the economic model reigns supreme; perception and analysis, whether conscious or unconscious, proceed in terms of conflict. In the present dispensation, the philological model assumes the throne; perception and analysis are in terms of language; interpretation moves to the foreground.[5] Foucault insists that all of these models are present and interlinked in all periods but that one or another has the ascendancy. This movement from biology through economics to language, from an emphasis on function to an emphasis on conflict to, finally, an emphasis on signification or interpretation, tends to marginalize or remove questions of value. Eliot's graduate studies at Harvard focus on many of the figures used in Foucault's analysis of the modern episteme, for example, Lévy-Bruhl and Durkheim in sociology and Janet and Freud in psychology.

Epistemological dispensations can also be profitably understood in terms of a rejection of the dualism that ruled the Western mind from the Renaissance until the early twentieth century. From the seventeenth century to the twentieth, the Western world assumed that the knower and the known could be sharply separated and that the subject could observe, understand, and describe the object. This pervasive epistemology is everywhere evident in art. Most painters, for example, assumed that there is a real world "out there" and that they as artists (subjects) can stand apart from it and without significant distortion represent it on the canvas. In the late nineteenth and early twentieth centuries, scientists, philosophers, and other specialists came to believe that the subject and object are tightly coupled and that the subject cannot see (much less, describe and transmit) an object without changing it in fundamental ways.

The disquieting views involved disorientation about space and time, and even before the turn of the century these views were being popularized in magazines and in science fiction. Artists of the first decades of this century responded by trying to find new ways of seeing, new models of knowing. These new ways have in common an assumption that the subject and object cannot be arbitrarily separated, that the artist is a part of the world that he sees. In the visual arts, experiments included abandoning rules of perspective, and in literature, abandoning a fixed point of view.

The idea that the late nineteenth and early twentieth centuries constitute a watershed in intellectual history has been popularized by such figures as Jacob Bronowski, figures who preside over public television specials on the arts and sciences and write intellectual histories for the general reader. In *The Common Sense of Science*, Bronowski divides intellectual history into three giant dispensations, each of which is undergirded by an idea about the nature of things, an idea so pervasive and so unconscious that it might be said to describe the mentality of the entire era.[6] Bronowski's first dispensation runs from the Greeks to the Renaissance. Its archetypal thinker is Aristotle, and its basic idea is order or hierarchy, an idea taken for granted in science, religion, and other fields. Bronowski's second dispensation runs from Copernicus to Einstein. Its archetypal thinker is Newton, and its basic assumption is causality, a principle unconsciously used at every level of society. His third dispensation begins around the turn of the twentieth century. Its representative thinker is Niels Bohr, and its principal assumption is chance. Bronowski's thesis is one version of an account of Western history which is included in standard textbooks in various fields. His book, in some ways quite helpful, is misleading in that it takes insufficient notice of the collapse of dualism and the receding of the subject. More sophisticated versions of this dispensational idea may be found in Kuhn's *Structure of Scientific Revolutions*, Holton's *Thematic Origins of Scientific Thought*, and Lovejoy's *Revolt against Dualism*.[7]

Holton, like Foucault, maintains that periods are characterized by epistemological configurations that are largely unconscious. Holton's thesis is that dispensations in science are defined by a few basic underlying ideas and mental habits, which he calls themata.[8]

17

In each dispensation, scientists depend on themata which are not in themselves scientific but which are part of the unconscious givens of the age. Holton includes in his themata both the model for reality used by an age (for example, the universe as a machine) and also its assumption about how reality may be known. He argues that each of the three major dispensations in the history of science can be described in terms of a single underlying epistemological assumption, that is, by an attitude that the age has toward the relation between the subject and the object, the knower and the known. And he argues that this assumption, far from being merely theoretical, makes all the difference in what people can think and do in everyday life. The ancients, with their theories of emission and emanation, believed that the observer and the observed are closely bound and reciprocally influential. A major breakthrough in science occurred when Kepler in his *Dioptrics* (1611) showed how lenses really work, thus removing the connection between subject and object. The most dazzling achievements from the early Renaissance to the late nineteenth century were based on the confident assumption that the subject and object were separable, that the subject could stand outside the object and from that position could describe, analyze, and understand it. The third major dispensation in the history of science was precipitated by the realization that the subject and object are tightly coupled, that they are part of a single system, and that the subject cannot observe the object without changing and distorting it. According to Holton, this inseparability of subject and object is the distinctive assumption of most of the great theories of modern physics, including Einstein's relativity, Bohr's complementarity, and Heisenberg's uncertainty theories.

Lovejoy's *Revolt against Dualism* describes early-twentieth-century philosophical activity in parallel terms. His thesis is that twentieth-century philosophy is primarily a rebellion against seventeenth-century philosophy, more particularly a rebellion against Locke and Descartes.[9] Locke and Descartes, like Newton, assumed that the subject and object are separable, that objectivity is possible and necessary for understanding the world. Lovejoy shows that modern philosophers have joined in an attempt to escape from this dualism of subject and object, and from the parallel dualism of mind and matter. In this dethronement of Locke and Descartes, philosophers came to see that the subject and object were connected in a systematic relationship and that mind and matter were aspects of a single world. An understanding of the revolt against dualism described by Lovejoy can lead to an immediate clarification of the confusing proliferations of intellectual revolutions around the turn of the century. Most of the makers of the twentieth-century mind, figures such as Freud, Heisenberg, Picasso, Joyce, and Eliot, have in common an about-face on the subject–object question and the mind–matter question; they all reject the dualism that arbitrarily and irreversibly splits the world into pieces. This rejection of dualism and the corresponding reach for monism are of the essence in understanding the revolutionary nature of twentieth-century science and art.

The period between dispensations in intellectual history is without exception a period of insecurity and crisis. In *Man and Crisis*, José Ortega y Gasset outlines a notion of crisis based on this very idea.[10] He maintains that there are basically two types of change in history. The first and normal type of change is that from generation to generation within dispensations, a change in which "the profile of the world which is valid for one generation is succeeded by another and slightly different profile. . . . the skeleton framework of the world remains in force throughout that change."[11] The second type of change is that from dispensation to dispensation, a change characterized by massive epistemological disorientation in which the backbone of the universe gives way.[12] The change consists in the fact that the basic model of reality, the system of convictions that had served many generations, suddenly collapses, and for a while there is no new model. This collapse of the most fundamental ideas which had enabled people to live and act leads to a sense of disorientation and panic as they stand on the terra incognita dividing two worlds. Ortega y Gasset argues that the catastrophic type of change occurred in the early Renaissance with the Copernican revolution, and again at the beginning of the twentieth century with the Einsteinian. In the latter crisis, the epistemological skeleton inherited from Newton, Locke, and Descartes collapsed, dropping us into an epistemological vacuum. "We do not know

19

what is happening to us, and that is precisely the thing that is happening to us—the fact of not knowing what is happening to us."[13]

Heidegger has described the early twentieth century in similar terms. He calls this time between the collapse of Newton's God and the appearance of his not-yet-apparent successor (the rough beast Yeats imagined as slouching toward Bethlehem) a great "between."[14] The feeling of being between two somethings is one thing, but the feeling of being between something and nothing is quite another. If this abstract "betweenness" is related to how we know what we know (in technical terms, to epistemology), it produces profound anxiety or uneasiness. In the early twentieth century, the awareness of living in an epistemological limbo was not restricted to physicists and philosophers. Intellectuals in many fields in the period around the turn of the century had this consciousness of being caught between dispensations in history. A dispensational consciousness pervades the theories of Freud, Mallarmé, T. E. Hulme, Spengler, Pound, Joyce, Wyndham Lewis,[15] and the many scientists and philosophers discussed by Holton, Kuhn, and Lovejoy.

The relation of the general epistemology of an age to the form in its art is always (and inevitably) immediately apparent in the visual arts. The necessary relation between epistemology and artistic form, with focus on the modern period, is the subject of *Abstraction and Empathy* by Wilhelm Worringer, first published as a doctoral dissertation in art history in 1908.[16] Worringer's thesis is enormously helpful in understanding the history of art in all media. He argues that in periods when people have a more or less settled epistemology with which they are content (that is, when they are confident about their world and their ways of knowing it), they tend to produce representational art. Art of this sort is controlled by what Worringer calls "empathy," an impulse to identify with one's object and to trust its appearances as reality, or, at least, as indicative of a congruent and manageable reality. Form is representational with emphasis on curvilinear and organic shapes which call forth feelings of sympathy or identification. Worringer's examples include Greek, Renaissance, and romantic painting and sculpture. On the other hand, in periods when people tend to lack an epistemology that makes their world manageable (in periods of "be-tweenness"), they tend to produce abstract art. Art of this sort is controlled by "abstraction," an impulse to withdraw from the ap-pearances of a world they neither trust nor understand and to take refuge in pure form. Form is abstract and rectilinear and tends to create emotional distance and detachment. Worringer's examples include both primitive and modern art. In primitive art, abstraction is due to a lack of knowledge about the world and the fear that comes from not knowing; in modern art, abstraction is due to an excess of knowledge and the radical skepticism that comes from knowing too much.

Worringer's thesis is congruent with that of many other intellec-tual historians. Ortega y Gasset, for example, expounds a comple-mentary thesis in his famous essay "The Dehumanization of Art."[17] Another essay by Ortega y Gasset, "On Point of View in the Arts," deals more specifically with the relation of assumptions about see-ing to form in art.[18] He argues that the evolution of Western paint-ing from the Renaissance to the present (he was writing in 1949) can be seen as an adjustment in the relation of subject and object, an adjustment in which the object goes from a solid existence in itself to an existence inside the head of the subject. From focus on the object itself in the Renaissance, the artist moved to focus on the experience of seeing in impressionism, and finally to focus on sub-jective states or ideas in modern art. In the first, the subject and object are assumed to be separate; in the last, they are assumed to be inseparable.

The idea that the late nineteenth and early twentieth centuries constitute a bridge between dispensations in Western intellectual history involves the recognition that a mentality or paradigm ac-cepted for several centuries had been destroyed or supplanted in the early twentieth century by an antithetical paradigm. In the behavioral sciences, as Foucault says, the supplanted paradigm was economic. In the natural sciences, as Bronowski, Kuhn, and Holton make abundantly clear, the supplanted paradigm was the assump-tion of causality (and continuity) inherent in Newtonian physics. In philosophy, as Lovejoy makes clear, the supplanted paradigm was the assumption of dualism inherent in Cartesian and Lockean phi-losophy. The dispensational idea in the history of art, similarly,

21

involves the recognition that a long-standing aesthetic had been supplanted. The prevailing aesthetic for several centuries before the twentieth had been expressed in canonical form in the eighteenth century by the German literary critic Gotthold Ephraim Lessing in *Laocoön* (1766), a work with the subtitle *The Limits of Painting and Poetry*.[19]

The context for *Laocoön* is the Renaissance practice of comparing paintings and poems, a practice supposedly authorized by Horace's phrase "ut pictura poesis" ("as is a painting, so is poetry"). The immediate occasion of *Laocoön* was Lessing's irritation with a comparison that the art critic Johann Winckelmann had made between the celebrated Greek sculpture *Laocoön* and Virgil's *Aeneid*. Winckelmann contrasted the noble stillness and restrained grandeur in the countenance of the Laocoön of the Greek sculpture with the agonized movement and unrestrained cry of the Laocoön in the Latin epic. Lessing was taken aback by this disapproving glance at the great epic poet, and in the process of vindicating Virgil he articulated the underlying principles of form in both the visual and the literary arts. The difference in the sculpture and the poem is not one of quality, for the two works are in different media governed by different rules and cannot be compared in the way that Winckelmann was comparing them. The visual arts are spatial; that is, they imitate bodies or forms that exist in space, and they use forms and colors that are organized in space. Poetry, on the other hand, is temporal; that is, it imitates actions or events that occur in time, and it uses language that consists of words that follow one after another in time. Further, the visual arts are by definition static, and the literary arts by definition dynamic. Since sculpture cannot represent movement in time, it must choose a single moment to depict. Poetry, on the other hand, can show continuous actions moving through time but cannot show fullness of bodies. The noble stillness on the face in the Greek sculpture is related to the fact that the sculptor was limited to one pregnant moment, a moment (whether serene or agitated) forever frozen in space by the medium. The agitated violence of Virgil's Laocoön is related to the fact that the poet was able to show an entire series of actions, actions of both stillness and agitation which move through time with the medium of language.

22

Lessing outlines his conclusions on the limits of the visual and literary arts in chapter 16 of *Laocoön*. He uses the vocabulary of epistemology. Form in art, he says, is intimately related to the manner in which an artist perceives his object. The visual artist perceives an object in space and imitates it by organizing his material in space. The resulting art object is then perceived in space by the critic. The literary artist perceives an action in time and imitates it by arranging one word after another in time. The poem is then perceived by a reader who reads one word after another in time. In both the visual and the literary arts, being a good artist depends to a great extent on the ability of the artist (or subject) to separate himself from the object he is imitating.

Lessing's description fits the arts in a general way until around the beginning of the twentieth century. And then, in both the visual and the literary arts, there was a period of disorientation about Lessing's categories, followed by an attempt, conscious on the part of many artists, to reverse them. Artists in the visual arts started trying to avoid the presentation of three-dimensional space. As Worringer argued as early as 1908, modern painting is agoraphobic; that is, it fears space, its natural medium, and avoids the presentation of space. Most painters since the Renaissance had constructed their paintings so that, in viewing such art, the spectator seems to be looking through a window at objects organized in space. But most modern painters have constructed their paintings so that the viewer is forced to abandon the illusion that he is looking through a window. The viewer is forced to look at and not through the painting, as one would look at a decorated opaque screen. And this evasion of space or depth is accompanied by an attempt to portray movement in time. A traditional painter might have painted a nude on a stair but not, as Marcel Duchamp did, a *Nude Descending a Staircase*, for descending is an action that takes place in time. Both in trying to shun the presentation of space and in trying to achieve a temporal dimension, these artists were redefining the limitations of their medium. Their efforts, like those of Einstein or Heisenberg, involve a repudiation of a principle that had been dominant for centuries, or perhaps, as Lessing claims, a principle that goes all the way back to Homer.

The visual artist avoided the presentation of space by abandoning

23

the rules of perspective that had governed painting since the Renaissance. The parallel in the literary arts is an evasion of time, and this is attempted by abandoning the principles governing point of view and by abandoning narrative. Joyce's attempts to circumvent Lessing's principles form part of the plot in both *Stephen Hero* and *Portrait of the Artist*, in which Stephen expresses irritation with Lessing's rules and offers an alternative aesthetic. The critic who first described modern literature in terms of an assault on Lessing's principles is Joseph Frank. In "Spatial Form in Modern Literature" (1945), Frank argues that, just as modern painters had shunned space and tried to achieve a temporal dimension, so modern writers had undercut narrative and tried to achieve a spatial dimension.[20] Frank's thesis is vulnerable on a number of fronts, but nevertheless it has been invaluable in stimulating discussion on form in the arts. His proof texts include Joyce's *Ulysses* and Eliot's *Waste Land*, works designed to subvert the idea of a beginning, middle, and end. These works cannot be read, according to Frank. They can only be reread, for the entire work, including the last lines, must be in the reader's mind before he can understand the first lines. Frank argues that these writers are trying to force their readers to perceive the work all at once, in mental space. Frank does not argue, and we do not wish to suggest, that the modernist quarrel with Lessing has invalidated his principles. On the contrary, as critics of Frank's provocative thesis have pointed out, form in literature is inevitably temporal, and for the very reasons of perception suggested long ago by Lessing. Reflection on the analogy between form in the visual arts and form in literature, nevertheless, is helpful in understanding both media. The value of the analogy is evident in Jo-Anna Isaak's long article on *Ulysses*, to which we are indebted.[21] Some of her arguments could be applied with equal validity to *The Waste Land*. In both works, the writers were consciously trying to invent new ways of seeing the world, new ways demanded by the fact that the old assumptions about the knower and the world that is known had been fatally undermined by the new physics.

The centrality of cubism in the twentieth-century revolution in the arts is virtually undisputed. In the years from 1907 to 1914, Picasso, Braque, and their fellow artists radically altered the way that artists formalized the world on canvas. Although Picasso and

Braque did not themselves make many claims for cubism, they were surrounded by writers who publicly associated their paintings with the dawn of a new dispensation in physics and philosophy and with such concepts as the fourth dimension. The cubist group in Paris included several poet critics who spent much time in Picasso's studio, who clearly recognized that he and other cubists were challenging the assumptions that had governed Western art for centuries, and who set out to explain this to the world. Two of these writers, Guillaume Apollinaire and André Salmon, were art critics for important newspapers and covered the cubist exhibitions with enthusiastic and highly informative reviews. Apollinaire and Salmon early set themselves up as historians of the movement, both publishing histories of the movement in 1912.[22] Albert Gleizes and Jean Metzinger, two other members of the cubist group, also wrote a history of the movement, published in 1912.[23]

The cubist revolution has long been associated with developments in science, particularly with relativity theory in physics. In the past decade, however, it has become clear that cubism owes little or nothing to Einstein's work. The documents associated with the cubist activities from 1907 to 1914 show that these artists were searching for an epistemology; that is, they were consciously trying to figure out how reality can be known. As their writings make abundantly clear, the cubists believed that the traditional idea that reality is "out there," inherent in the object or the objective world, is simply a mistake, and they knew that the traditional practice of privileging one perspective on reality actually limits the artist in his struggle to see the world as it is. Their speculations about these matters, however, were made not in terms of relativity theory but in terms of non-Euclidean geometry and, even more, in terms of ideas about the so-called fourth dimension. In *The Fourth Dimension and Non-Euclidean Geometry in Modern Art* (1983), Linda D. Henderson describes the emergence of the idea of a fourth dimension in late-nineteenth-century mathematics and science and documents the ubiquity of this idea in the first decade of this century.[24] She then shows from the writings of the cubists themselves that they were searching not so much for an understanding of the nature of reality as for a "place" or perspective from which they would have a chance to "see" reality, and that their epistemological speculations were focused on the notion of the fourth dimension, a dimension which would enable them to dodge the consequences of the collapse of traditional models by providing them with a platform for seeing things as they really are.

The idea of a higher dimension from which it would be possible to see things as they are can be seen as part of philosophic idealism and in the late nineteenth century was associated with Plato's allegory of the cave and Kant's "thing-in-itself." Significantly, it emerged in the late nineteenth century as part of the dissatisfaction with materialism and with dualism. It was a response to the realization that division of the world into mind and matter and into subject and object is arbitrary and false, and to the realization that the subject and the object are bound together in a system and that there is no perspective from which the subject can perceive the truth about the object. Henderson reveals that the idea of a dimension from which the thing-in-itself would be revealed was used in some of the most popular fiction of the late nineteenth century, including E. A. Abbott's *Flatland: A Romance of Many Dimensions by a Square* (1884), H. G. Wells's science fiction stories, and George MacDonald's fantasy novels. The idea of a fourth dimension became a standard part of the fashionable interest in theosophy, with Madame Blavatsky herself as one of its expositors. The popularity of this notion reached its zenith in 1909, when *Scientific American* sponsored a contest for the best essay explaining the fourth dimension and, according to Henderson, received entries from all over the world. The *Scientific American* contest indicated that the idea of a fourth dimension was an extremely loose one, for definitions ranged from the Platonic ideal and the Christian heaven to technical explanations of contemporary geometrical puzzles such as "curved space." What most or all of these explanations have in common, however, is the idea of a new perspective which would get us outside of ourselves and outside of our systems and from which we could see reality in its wholeness.

Direct references to the fourth dimension appear in the writings of the cubists before 1910, and also in the early histories by Apollinaire and by Gleizes and Metzinger. Apollinaire explained in 1913 that the new painters were preoccupied with the new possibilities of spatial measurement offered by the fourth dimension. He describes it as the "dimension of the infinite," as springing from the three dimensions and "eternalizing itself in all directions at any given moment," as a dimension that enables the artist to restore the object to wholeness.[25] Max Weber's 1913 painting *Interior of the Fourth Dimension* is one obvious attempt to capture the fourth dimension on canvas. Metzinger's 1911 *Cubist Landscape* is also an experiment with notions of "curved space" and the fourth dimension. As late as 1952, Metzinger was still talking about the cubists and the fourth dimension: "ideas in painting necessitated more than the three dimensions, since these show only the visible aspects of a body at a given moment. Cubist painting . . . needed a dimension greater than the Third to express a synthesis of views and feelings toward the object. This is possible only in a 'poetic' dimension in which all the traditional dimensions are superseded."[26]

Henderson's thesis is particularly relevant to our study. Citing Ortega y Gasset and Heidegger, we have associated the many revolutions in the first part of this century with the disorientation created by the collapse of old theories and with the uneasiness created by being between dispensations. The nineteenth-century idea of a fourth dimension in space, coming between Newtonian and Einsteinian physics, is a between-times theory, and the cubists' interest in it underscores the connection of their innovations to the disorientation created by being stranded between epistemologies, stranded without a perspective on the world. The literary parallel to the cubist preoccupation with space, to return to Lessing's aesthetics, would be time. And it is significant that late-nineteenth-century writers such as H. G. Wells thought of the fourth dimension not in terms of a place from which it would be possible to "see" things as they are but as a time from which it would be possible to understand things as they are, as a means of reaching another era from which it would be possible to comment on contemporary society. In *The Time Machine* (1895), Wells has his "Time Traveller" explain that, in addition to the three dimensions of space, there is a fourth dimension of time, from which it is possible to move around in time as one moves around in space. The real revolution in literary form, however, occurred not from the use of this concept as a topic

27

or as part of a traditional plot but from its later use (consciously or unconsciously) by writers such as Eliot and Joyce in liberating themselves from traditional concepts of plot and structure.

There can be no doubt that Eliot followed the analogy between the fourth dimension and the search for a new perspective in the arts and that he thought of the fourth dimension in relation to literary form. In a 1919 review of a book on Ben Jonson, he defends Jonson's art by distinguishing it from the art of Swift, which consists of a criticism of the actual world, and from the art of Shakespeare, which consists of the generation of a "third dimension" of the actual world by creating a "network of tentacular roots reaching down to the deepest terrors and desires."[27] Jonson's art, unlike that of Swift and Shakespeare, finds its source not in any relation to the actual world but in the imaginative projection of an alternative world which forms a platform for seeing or criticizing the actual world. Eliot continues: "the worlds created by artists like Jonson are like systems of non-Euclidean geometry. They are not fancy, because they have a logic of their own; and this logic illuminates the actual world, because it gives us a new point of view from which to inspect it."[28] Eliot's contrast of Shakespeare and Jonson, incidentally, is at bottom a contrast between empathy and abstraction.

Eliot did not write much about modern art, and it is possible that he paid little attention to it. Certainly, it would be a mistake simply to group him with the cubists, futurists, or even with the vorticists. At the same time, it is important to note that he shared the dispensational mentality of these artists, and even more than they, he realized that traditional notions of reality were no longer valid and that traditional models of knowing were inadequate. And, of course, Eliot was exactly contemporary with these artists. He was a graduate student in Paris in 1910–11, the very years in which the startling experiments in the arts were part of the daily news.

Eliot's first recorded close contact with the new painters dates from his first year in London, 1914–15, when through Ezra Pound he came into contact with Wyndham Lewis. Early in 1915, Eliot sent Lewis some poems for consideration in the second issue of his magazine *Blast*. *Blast* was the sensational interdisciplinary brainchild of Pound and Lewis, who used it to blast the end of the old dispensation in the arts and to bless the dawn of the new era and, more particularly, to launch vorticism, the English approximation of cubism and futurism. Eliot's first published poems (apart from those in school magazines) appeared in *Blast* in 1915. "Preludes" and "Rhapsody of [*sic*], a Windy Night" appeared in the second issue of *Blast*, an issue featuring a sample of Lewis's vorticist art on the cover and including Charles Nevinson's *On the Way to the Trenches*. Like Duchamp's *Nude Descending a Staircase*, Nevinson's painting shows movement through time as the soldiers move toward death in the trenches. Eliot's poems were sandwiched between "A Review of Contemporary Art," in which Lewis in plain and provocative language explains the principles underlying the revolution in painting, and "Progression," a vorticist design by Etchells. It is worth noting that the two poems published in *Blast* are striking not only as harbingers of a new attitude in poetry but as evidence that Eliot was working his way around the limitations of traditional literary structure. "Preludes" consists of four juxtaposed views of city life, and "Rhapsody on a Windy Night" is in part an experiment based on Bergson's latest theories about time. It is also worth noting that these poems date from 1909–11 and that both owe something to Eliot's presence in Paris, the hotbed of cubism. Facts such as these underscore the obvious but often overlooked point that Eliot did not arrive in London in August 1914 as a blank slate and simply pick up the theories of Pound and Lewis; the essentials of his breakthrough in style and structure are clearly evident in the poems of 1909–11.

A number of critics have commented on the relevance of experiments in modern art to Eliot's poetry, especially to his work in *The Waste Land*. Joseph Frank discussed Eliot in his historic essay on spatial form in modern literature. In a brief essay (1960), Jacob Korg suggested several parallels between the techniques of modern painters and the techniques used in *The Waste Land*.[29] Korg expanded his discussion of *The Waste Land* and modern art in an essay in *Approaches to Teaching Eliot's Poetry and Plays* (1988).[30] The parallel revolutions in the visual and the literary arts have been discussed in a general way by Hugh Kenner in *The Pound Era*, by Wylie Sypher in *Rococo to Cubism in Art and Literature*, by Roger Shattuck in *The Banquet Years*, and by Marjorie Perloff in *The Futurist Moment*.[31] Gertrude Patterson's 1971 study of Eliot is based partially on an understanding of developments in the visual arts.[32] And in a 1980 essay in *Twentieth Century Literature*, David Tomlinson discussed Eliot and the cubists.[33] We are indebted to all of these studies, and although in our reading of *The Waste Land* we will focus on Eliot's philosophical studies, we cannot but take note of the fact that his innovations in form are parallel to those taking place in the visual arts and that, in both the visual arts and Eliot's poetry, the central issues can be stated in terms of epistemological reorientation.

The emphasis on idealism in cubism is especially relevant to our study. The concept of the fourth dimension is idealist through and through. In fact, most of the techniques in the twentieth-century revolution in the arts stem from a conscious rejection of materialism (the notion that reality has to do with matter) and a conscious adoption of idealism (the notion that reality has to do with the mind). Gleizes and Metzinger, in their 1912 history of the movement, maintain that "objective knowledge" is "chimerical" and natural appearances merely conventional. A true realist is not one who copies matter but one who fashions the real in his mind.[34] This loss of faith in appearances and this turn to idealism are fundamental to modern artists in all media, and especially to Eliot, who spent a decade examining idealist perspectives on the twentieth century.

The uncertainty about appearances, as Worringer and Frank have pointed out, leads to reflexivity in art, to a displacement of attention from what is depicted to the medium that is used to depict it. Painting becomes self-referential, calling attention to itself as paint and lines on canvas instead of pointing beyond itself to something else. Literature becomes self-referential, calling attention to itself as language, to words as words instead of words as signifiers. This self-referentiality in art is clearly a rejection of dualism, a collapse of the object into the subject. The no-longer-separate subject and object are deemed to be part of a single system, an idea which is thoroughly idealistic. This systematic coupling of the subject and object means that any action or movement on the part of the subject changes the system of which both subject and object are a part. In regard to art, the space between the artist and his object collapses. In regard to audience, the space between the viewer (or reader) and the art object also disappears. In twentieth-century painting and literature, a role is built in for the viewer or reader, who must collaborate with the artist in achieving the work of art, which can exist in wholeness only in the mind of a reader collaborator.

The most conspicuous feature of cubist form is the abandonment of single perspective. The cubists weighed and found wanting the Renaissance assumption that artists stand in one place and view objects that exist apart and can be accurately represented by their appearances at one particular moment in their history. In 1912, Gleizes and Metzinger argued that cubism assumes an artist who is "moving around an object to seize from it several successive appearances, which, fused into a single image, reconstitute it in time."[35] The single-perspective theory was part of the invalid view that reality exists somewhere "out there" and that it can be captured on a canvas and passed along intact to viewers or readers. Early-twentieth-century artists knew that no single perspective is privileged, that no one perspective captures the truth, and they responded by presenting many perspectives at once. Jean Metzinger, for example, in *Tea Time* (1911) and Juan Gris in *Portrait of Picasso* (1912) created cubist portraits consisting of overlapping shapes and planes. This mode of formalizing reality suggests that the only point of view or perspective that could capture the whole truth would be a transcendent one, analogous to another dimension in space or time. This multiperspectivism suggests that the many appearances in the world are less "true" than the abstract design produced by their juxtaposition. The proliferation of perspectives obvious in cubism is also basic to Eliot's poetry. As in "Preludes" Eliot simply juxtaposes slices or fragments of city life, so in *The Waste Land* he presents many broken perspectives on many cities in and out of time. The juxtaposition of these many partial fleeting perspectives leads to the formation of an abstract city (the real "Unreal City") in the mind of his reader collaborator.

Perspective in cubism is not only multiplied but destabilized as the viewer is put into motion. The relation between the subject and object goes from fixity to fluidity. And in *The Waste Land* there is a continuous instability in which images dissolve, re-form, melt, and overlap. Related to the multiplication and the destabilization of perspectives is an assumption that any glimpse of the object is partial. The traditional assumption of wholeness is abandoned, as the artist uses not objects but bits and pieces of objects arranged in various patterns. Any presentation of wholeness would have to be made from a transcendent point of view. The need for a transcendent point of view is one reason that artists of this period found primitive art so fascinating, and also a reason that they found the work of Frazer so useful and the work of contemporary sociologists so stimulating. Primitives were not dualistic; they did not sharply separate the subject or knower from the object. Frazer, the great chronicler of primitive life, must also be seen as reaching beyond dualism; he had worked his way backward through layers of myth to a monistic vision, one that indicated an underlying unity in human history, one that included a mythic platform for seeing all history more comprehensively.

That the process of reading generates a type of platform in space-time forms part of the argument in our book. We will suggest that reading initiates a series of transcendences which finally include the reader and which point by implication to the reader's reader. As Grover Smith has pointed out in regard to the visual arts, the viewer of any painting necessarily adds a time dimension to it, simply by viewing it in time. Smith points to the example of ancient Egyptian tomb paintings that recapitulate a life and career on a single wall space, and to the undeniable fact that the passing of time is an element added by the spectator as serial observer. Thus, in such a work as Duchamp's *Nude Descending a Staircase*, there are the three dimensions suggested by conventional rules of perspective, the "fourth dimension" of time added by the artist's use of overlapping images, and the "fifth dimension" of space-time added by the observer. Smith suggests that the spectator's addition of the time dimension to a painting, a spatial work, is analogous to the projector's conversion of a film strip to a moving picture.[36]

The intellectual context in which Eliot began work on the "long poem" that was to become *The Waste Land* has much to tell us about formal aspects of his poem. Certainly it reveals something of the problem any artist would have had in finding a perspective on the twentieth century. Emphasis on context, however, should not be taken as an assertion of specific influence. It should not be assumed that Eliot was consciously trying to adjust his presentation of reality to conform with the presentations in science or in the visual arts or even that he was greatly influenced by any specific scientific theory or any aesthetic manifesto. Without a doubt, he was aware of what was happening in science, in philosophy, and in the other arts. And without a doubt, he created structures in art which show his sensitivity to his age and which are formally analogous to structures created by other artists. He arrived, however, not by following anyone but by trying to find his own way. He spent most of the decade before writing *The Waste Land* as a close student of philosophy, comparative religion, and Buddhism, and his understanding of these subjects is part of the basic context of his art.

Reading *The Waste Land*, then, is in part reading about reading in the early twentieth century. The crisis in epistemology brought on by the discrediting of objectivity is especially relevant to understanding the poem, because the problem of knowledge is itself one of its major subjects. Like Joyce, Valéry, and other contemporary writers, Eliot consciously adds a dimension in which his work is self-reflexive, a dimension in which it refers to itself and its nature as a linguistic structure, a dimension which incorporates the larger subject of the crisis in Western culture into the process of reading. *The Waste Land* contains, in addition to its many other gifts, a partial set of instructions on how to read in the twentieth century. We believe and shall try to demonstrate that Eliot's poem, in one of its aspects, is a brief and striking primer, a *McGuffey's Eclectic Reader* for the twentieth century.

2 / Unifying Incompatible Worlds

The Sibyl of Cumae and Tiresias

The life of a soul does not consist in the contemplation of one consistent world but in the painful task of unifying (to a greater or less extent) jarring and incompatible ones, and passing, when possible, from two or more discordant viewpoints to a higher which shall somehow include and transmute them.—Eliot, *Knowledge and Experience*

Eliot and many other artists of his generation were fascinated by contemporary accounts of the primitive mind. According to Frazer and other social scientists, the primitive mind, unlike the modern mind, tended to be nondualistic, to work holistically. The contrast between primitive consciousness and contemporary scientific consciousness can be clarified by considering two examples, one from a major background text of Eliot's poem and the other from *The Waste Land* itself. In *Heart of Darkness*, from which Eliot took his original epigraph for *The Waste Land*, Conrad's narrator Marlow speaks of Africans who were taught to tend a steam boiler on a riverboat.[1] The first Africans were taught the simple physics of steam boilers, namely, that steam boilers build up dangerous pressures. They were instructed to open the pressure valves when the gauge reached a certain point and that, if they did not, the boiler could explode and kill them. Fully aware of these facts, several Africans nevertheless perished when they allowed boilers to explode. The Europeans finally condescended to instruct the Africans in native terms. The boiler, they explained, is a god. It signals its demand to be worshiped by moving its gauge needle to a certain point. The prescribed rite of worship is opening the pressure valves. If the god does not receive this form of reverence, it will visit instant wrath and destroy all within its range. Africans so instructed had a faultless record with the boilers.

The Africans, Marlow realized, were not at all inept or unintelligent. They simply had a nondualistic imagination and thus could not see themselves as subjects and the boiler as an object.

Having had no experience with the kind of thinking that assigns actions to nonvolitional objects, they could not associate cause-and-effect relations with mere matter. In short, even though they knew what to do, they were too emotionally remote to perform as instructed. By deifying the boiler, they invested it with (or recognized its) subjectivity and thus made possible a series of personal interactions with it. By treating it like a god, they recognized it as another albeit mysterious subject, one who could strike them dead if they neglected their duties. They acknowledged, in fact, one of the fundamental insights of modern science and philosophy, namely, that everything is connected to everything else, or, in technical terms, they acknowledged that reality is one and, therefore, that all relations are internal.

A complementary example of dualistic or modern consciousness is provided by the last sequence of "The Burial of the Dead." This is one of the "Unreal City" passages in *The Waste Land*. The unreal city is specifically identified as London, but the passage contains allusions and details that juxtapose contemporary London and the Vestibule of Dante's Hell. This juxtaposition automatically associates the crowds flowing over London Bridge and down King William Street with the dead who have become denizens of Ante-Hell, the place reserved for those who did not qualify for either heaven or hell, those who in life did not choose between good and evil. A nameless member of the crowd sees a familiar face and accosts him with the following speech.

> There I saw one I knew, and stopped him, crying: "Stetson!
> "You who were with me in the ships at Mylae!
> "That corpse you planted last year in your garden,
> "Has it begun to sprout? Will it bloom this year?
> "Or has the sudden frost disturbed its bed?
> "Oh keep the Dog far hence, that's friend to men,
> "Or with his nails he'll dig it up again!
> "You! hypocrite lecteur!—mon semblable,—mon frère!"

The speech to Stetson is particularly appropriate for someone who has never dealt with issues of good or evil, someone who, in a moral sense, has never been alive. It is an utterance carefully confined to the codes of contemporary cognition, as carefully stated for Stetson by the nameless modern speaker as the mythic explanation of steam boilers was stated for Conrad's Africans. In many time-honored religions, death and burial are part of a cycle that includes rebirth and new life. In the myths behind Eliot's poem, death and burial are part of a ritual that lifts a curse from the hero's land and people. Such rituals are as unimaginable to Stetson and the speaker, who think in terms of cause and effect, as modern physics is to Conrad's Africans. The two meeting in contemporary London seem to have asked themselves the following question: "How can a dead man, whether he was god, hero, or peasant, restore fertility to the land?" And consciously or unconsciously, they have answered the question. The only way for a dead man to restore fertility to a garden is for him to remain buried in that garden. He can there decompose and serve as fertilizer. A corpse is, after all, only a corpse, and nature is only another manifestation of what Pynchon calls the "politics of bacteria." To make sure the corpse releases its chemicals properly into the soil, it must be kept buried. At all costs, therefore, the dog must not be allowed to dig it up, for that would be to preclude its beneficial effect upon the land.

The Stetson passage is an allusion to Frazer's theory in *The Golden Bough* that religion originated as agricultural engineering. Through a grotesque process of literalization, all of the dying gods and heroes in *The Golden Bough*, along with Christ and the Fisher King, are transferred from mythic to modern consciousness (Frazer himself was an unabashed positivist) to be made explicable in scientific terms as fertilizer. In his adaptation of lines from Webster, Eliot changes "wolf" to "Dog" and "foe" to "friend." In Webster's day, it was the wolf who dug up corpses. But in our day it is a friendly dog. *Dog* is *god* spelled backward, a coincidence picked up not only by Eliot but by several modern writers. The dog "that's friend to men" suggests a modern god substitute which seemed to be a friend but which has become in numerous senses a destroyer. Eliot is here concerned with a rampantly reductive scientism (including that practiced by Frazer) that demythologizes myth by digging up the buried god or hero and revealing its nature. A myth, one might say, can function only when it is approached with reverence. The process that leads to digging it up destroys it and makes it impossible to test its validity. The speech to Stetson ends by identifying him as a Baudelairean "hypocrite lecteur" whose pretense of uniqueness is

36

rejected by the speaker who insists that he is a double, precisely like all who now find themselves incapable of religious consciousness. The questions and the accusation he throws at Stetson reveal that the speaker is someone who knows what transcendent knowledge is but who also knows he has lost it.

Eliot's own reflections on the primitive mind as a model for nondualistic thinking and on the nature and consequences of different modes of consciousness were informed by an excellent education in the social sciences and philosophy. As a prelude to our guided tour of the text of *The Waste Land*, we now turn to a brief survey of some of his intellectual preoccupations in the decade before he wrote it, preoccupations which in our view are enormously helpful in understanding the form of the poem. Eliot entered Harvard as a freshman in 1906 and finished his doctoral dissertation in 1916, with one of the academic years spent at the Sorbonne and one at Oxford. At Harvard and Oxford, he had as teachers some of modern philosophy's most distinguished individuals, including George Santayana, Josiah Royce, Bertrand Russell, and Harold Joachim; and while at the Sorbonne, he attended the lectures of Henri Bergson, a philosophic star in Paris in 1910–11. Under the supervision of Royce, Eliot wrote his dissertation on the epistemology of F. H. Bradley, a major voice in the late-nineteenth-, early-twentieth-century crisis in philosophy. Eliot extended this period of concentration on philosophical problems by devoting much of his time between 1915 and the early twenties to book reviewing. His education and early book reviewing occurred during the period of epistemological disorientation described in our first chapter, the period of "betweenness" described by Heidegger and Ortega y Gasset, the period of the revolt against dualism described by Lovejoy.[2]

Eliot's personal awareness of the contemporary epistemological crisis was intensified by the fact that while he was writing his dissertation on Bradley he and his new wife were actually living with Bertrand Russell. Russell as the representative of neorealism and Bradley as the representative of neoidealism were perhaps the leading expositors of opposite responses to the crisis discussed in our first chapter. Eliot's situation was extraordinary. He was a close student of both Bradley and Russell; he had studied with Bradley's friend and disciple Harold Joachim and with Russell himself. And in 1915–16, while writing a dissertation explaining and in general defending Bradley against Russell, Eliot found himself face to face with Russell across the breakfast table. Moreover, as the husband of a fragile wife to whom both men (each in his own way) were devoted, Eliot must have found life to be a kaleidoscope of brilliant and fluctuating patterns.[3]

In the two years that he spent reading Bradley, Eliot encountered in philosophy most of the issues discussed in our first chapter, and, moreover, in following Bradley's arguments he encountered a formal and elegant defense of the positions that undergird modernism in the arts and sciences. Bradley was an unflinching leader in the revolt against dualism; and from the beginning of his career he was a radical skeptic who insisted that true objectivity is a chimera. Like all idealists, he believed that everything is connected to everything else in a systematic way and that everything is part of a single comprehensive whole. He believed, consequently, that all relations are internal relations and that every perspective is partial and incomplete and thus is unreal, an appearance. He believed that experience (knowledge) begins in unity, falls into fragments, and, of special importance for our study, he believed in the possibility of a recovery of unity, in the possibility of forming new wholes. In all of these areas and others as well, he provided Eliot with a philosophic statement of positions that were enormously useful for a poet living in a time of epistemological confusion.

To say that Bradley is undeniably important in understanding Eliot is not to say that he is all-important, that he is the "source" of Eliot's insights or technique. In the great poems of 1910–11, several years before studying Bradley, Eliot had already arrived at many Bradleian insights. Most of the issues presented in Bradley's *Appearance and Reality* and *Essays on Truth and Reality* were, in one form or another, in the air in the early part of the century. Moreover, Eliot did not accept Bradley's ideas uncritically. His dissertation is no mere summary but a critique. Clearly, he agreed with Bradley's general position, but at the same time he disagreed with a number of Bradley's ideas and was explicit about points of disagreement.[4] All of this said, the fact remains that Eliot spent years immersed in Bradley; and further, in spite of the closest personal and intellectual involvement with a formidable realist (Russell), he defended many of Bradley's ideas in his dissertation. Moreover, there are traces of Bradley's ideas in Eliot's poetry from the quatrain poems of 1917–19 through *Four Quartets*, and clear indications of Bradley's influence in his literary criticism. Eliot's graduate education in philosophy also includes special attention to the social sciences and to the implications of the new and quasi-scientific methods of the social scientists. He studied psychology, sociology, and, of special interest for our study, anthropology as it was developed in the work of Frazer and other scholars in myth and religion.

Eliot's dissertation, as we have mentioned, is focused on Bradley's epistemology. Bradley divided cognition into three stages/levels. The first exists prior to (and beneath) consciousness of consciousness, the second consists of consciousness of consciousness, and the third involves a transcendence of consciousness of consciousness. The movement from the immediate experience of the first level to the intellectual experience of the second is accompanied by the intrusion of language, by the rise of objects, and by the fragmentation of reality. The movement from the second to the third level involves a transcendence of brokenness and a return on a higher level to the unity of the first level. Both in his dissertation and in his literary criticism, Eliot often refers to the first level as feeling, the second as thought, and the third as a unification of the first two. It is not possible to identify the lines between the stages in any precise way, and the progression from one stage to another is a transcendence comprehending rather than banishing the previous stages.

These levels of knowing are also levels of being. The first level dissolves almost as it arises, the second persists throughout most of waking life, and the third occasionally comes, either as a gift or as the reward of special effort and discipline. None of these levels is characterized by complete knowledge. In the first, there is actually no such thing as knowledge, as knower and known. In the second, there is specific but limited knowledge, with special distortion caused by the fact that the knower is imprisoned in his own perspective and receives only a few bits and pieces of experience, all of which are filtered through language.[5] In the third, there is a special ideal knowledge which comes from passing beyond diffusion to a higher many-in-one unity. In his essay on the metaphysical poets, Eliot uses these levels to describe the poetry of the seventeenth century, in which both sensuous and intellectual experiences were known immediately, and that of the eighteenth and nineteenth, in which feeling and thought were compartmentalized. And he uses it to suggest that a poet should have a mind that goes beyond both feeling and thought, a mind that enfolds both into a unity.[6]

Eliot's reflections on lost but still felt unity, on entrapment in language and in intellect, and on the promise of transcendence are of central importance in all of his poetry and criticism, including *The Waste Land* and *Four Quartets*. His clearest discussion of these matters is to be found in the first chapter of his dissertation "On Our Knowledge of Immediate Experience," in large part an exposition of a chapter by the same name in Bradley's *Essays on Truth and Reality*.[7] Eliot argues that "we are forced, in building up our theory of knowledge, to postulate something given upon which knowledge is founded."[8] That something is "immediate experience," which Bradley, in the essay that is the *locus* for Eliot's first chapter, defines in the following way.

> We in short have experience in which there is no distinction between my awareness and that of which it is aware. There is an immediate feeling, a knowing and being in one, with which knowledge begins; and, though this in a manner is transcended, it nevertheless remains throughout as the present foundation of my known world.[9]

As an example of immediate experience, Eliot describes being so absorbed in viewing a painting that one has no consciousness of self or subject, on the one side, and of painting or object, on the other.[10] This directly experienced nonrelational many-in-one is not the viewer's experience, for he as subject and the painting as object do not yet exist. When he becomes aware of his experience and of the painting as other than himself, then immediate experience has dissolved or "melted" into Bradley's second stage of knowing, which Brooker in a 1979 essay named "relational experience."[11]

Immediate experience can only be known because it breaks up into a dualistic or intellectual stage. This happens automatically because the mind, existing heretofore as an undifferentiated part of

40

a totality, assumes dominance and analyzes the whole into self and other, mind and matter, subject and object, time and space, and numerous other categories. It should not be imagined that immediate experience is totally absent from this intellectual stage. As Bradley (in a passage quoted by Eliot) says, immediate experience

> is not a stage which shows itself at the beginning and then disappears, but it remains at the bottom throughout as fundamental. And further, remaining, it contains in itself every development which in a sense transcends it. Nor does it merely contain all developments, but in its own way it acts as their judge.[12]

Immediate experience, however much transcended, "both remains and is active."[13] It exists before consciousness of consciousness and can only be known as an inference after it has been transcended. But in remaining as an object of inference and as a felt background of wholeness, it becomes both a judge of dualism and a hint that it can be transcended.

This brings us to Bradley's third stage of knowing. By reflecting on the nature of immediate experience and by somehow reclaiming its felt residue and transforming it on a higher plane, one moves beyond it. As Bradley says in another passage which is part of the background of Eliot's dissertation, "From such an experience of unity below relations we can rise to the idea of a superior unity above them. Thus we can attach a full and positive meaning to the statement that Reality is one."[14] All knowing is self-transcendent in nature. Immediate experience is transcended by relational experience constantly and over and over again, and relational is or can be transcended. The end of all transcendences is the Absolute, an all-comprehensive whole which we are logically forced to project. To use Eliot's language, "We are led to the conception of an all-inclusive experience outside of which nothing shall fall."[15] Eliot concludes the first chapter of his dissertation by summarizing Bradley's three stages of cognition and by unequivocally stating his concurrence.

> If anyone object that mere experience at the beginning and complete experience at the end are hypothetical limits, I can not say a word in refutation for this would be just the reverse side of

> what opinions I hold. And if anyone assert that immediate
> experience, at either the beginning or end of our journey, is
> annihilation and utter night, I cordially agree.[16]

We should note that, in this passage in the last paragraph of the first
chapter of his dissertation, Eliot is referring to both epistemology or
cognitive process and to metaphysics or the nature of reality. In
doing so, he is following Bradley, who merges the study of epistemology with the study of being. In our study, however, we are more
concerned with lesser transcendences than we are with transcendence to the all-encompassing Absolute.

One other point must be made in regard to Eliot's discussion of
cognition in the first chapter of his dissertation. He repeatedly
warns of what we might call the "language trap." The problem is
that language and conscious cognition can occur only in the relational or dualistic phase, and consequently language inevitably
carries dualistic assumptions which distort any description of either
immediate or transcendent experience. As Eliot says, "In describing
immediate experience we must use terms which offer a surrep-
titious suggestion of subject or object."[17] It is almost impossible to
think of experience, for example, without thinking of "my" experience or of somebody's experience. But immediate experience is
nobody's experience; it is not something experienced by an experiencer but pure experience without the categories and relations that
intrude themselves simply because we have to use words when we
describe it. Language, to put it another way, cannot occur before the
fall from unity and cannot survive the transcendence of dualism.

Eliot's reflections on lost unity, on dualism and its consequences,
and on transcendence are related to his studies of the social sciences. Bradley, in the essay that served as the basis of Eliot's opening chapter, suggested a possible parallel to immediate experience
in both anthropology and psychology.

> Was there and is there in the development of the race and the
> individual a stage at which experience is merely immediate?
> And, further, do we all perhaps at moments sink back to such a
> level? . . . I think it probable that such a stage of mind not only,
> with all of us, comes first in fact, but that at times it recurs even
> in the life of the developed individual.[18]

In the growth of the race, primitive experience would be analogous to immediate experience, and in the growth of the individual, infancy would be the corresponding stage. Eliot maintains that earlier and lower stages are not purely immediate,[19] that indeed immediate experience and transcendent experience exist only as necessary abstractions. They must be postulated in order to think about how we can know anything. He does concede, however, that there are states of minds, such as those associated with animals or infants or ourselves when mentally inactive, in which one perceives more immediately because less consciously. Some critics, notably William Skaff, have pointed out the analogy between immediate experience and the collective unconscious, an analogy which seems obvious and which is highly suggestive.[20] Eliot, however, says in his dissertation that immediate experience is not the same as the unconscious, that the unconscious can only exist in contrast to the conscious, whereas immediate experience is independent (i.e., it simply exists).[21]

An awareness of the difference between relational and transcendent experience explains to some extent why Eliot first chose and later defended the following passage from *Heart of Darkness* for his epigraph to *The Waste Land*.[22]

> Did he live his life again in every detail of desire, temptation, and surrender during that supreme moment of complete knowledge? He cried in a whisper at some image, at some vision—he cried out twice, a cry that was no more than a breath—
> "The horror! The horror!"[23]

Heart of Darkness is the story of Mr. Kurtz, a connoisseur of knowledge who undertakes an exploration of the primitive mind. A cultivated European idealist in flight from the modern world, he pursues lost unity by crossing boundaries into the unknown, geographically, intellectually, and most of all, spiritually. It is one thing to return to live with primitives, however, and quite another to recover a primitive mind. Conrad leads us to believe that Kurtz never escapes the dualism of the modern mind. As he is dying, however, he does achieve, in a way, his goal of unity, of complete knowledge. In the passage quoted in Eliot's epigraph, Kurtz experiences a transcendent moment, a complete vision, a vision at once from his own perspective but also, it seems, from an outside perspective, from the boundary between life and death. And in what we can perhaps think of as the underside of transcendent experience, he glimpses the horror, the heart of darkness. Ezra Pound, to whom Eliot submitted his manuscript for suggestions, objected to using the passage on Kurtz's moment of knowledge as an epigraph, saying that the passage was not weighty enough. Eliot defended it as both "the most appropriate I can find, and somewhat elucidative."[24]

Further consideration led Eliot to remove the epigraph from Conrad and substitute the passage from Petronius which now stands at the head of the poem. His new choice is also concerned with knowledge and knowing, but it introduces additional considerations, considerations which force us to attend to the importance of mythic consciousness in *The Waste Land*. Eliot's alternative was chosen meticulously, with the entire poem in his mind, with Pound's objection in mind, and perhaps even more than the Conrad passage, it is appropriate and elucidative.

> Nam Sibyllam quidem Cumis ego ipse oculis meis vidi in ampulla pendere, et cum illi pueri dicerent: Σίβυλλα τί θέλεις; respondebat illa: ἀποθανεῖν θέλω.
>
> [With my own eyes, I saw the Sibyl at Cumae hanging in a bottle; and when the boys said to her: "Sibyl, what do you want?" she would always respond, "I want to die."]

This passage occurs in chapter 48 of the *Satyricon* by Petronius, a work which Eliot had studied as an undergraduate at Harvard and from which he had also chosen the epigraph to *The Sacred Wood*, published in 1920, two years earlier than *The Waste Land*.

The words Eliot quotes are from a section usually called "Trimalchio's Feast." Spoken by a vulgar Roman named Trimalchio at a dinner and intended to impress his friends, they could be called "Trimalchio's Boast," for they are Trimalchio's contribution to a boasting contest. Trimalchio's boast is that with his own eyes he has seen the Sibyl of Cumae, who like Tiresias is an ancient seer and a gatekeeper of the underworld. She is best introduced in the *Aeneid*, where Virgil presents her as the divinity consulted by Aeneas when he lands in Italy. She tells him of the Trojans' future and then leads him on a tour of the underworld where he consults his father Anchises, who prophesies the future of the Roman people. The Sibyl is taken up a century later by Petronius in the passage quoted by Eliot, the passage in which the narrator Encolpius quotes Trimalchio's boast that he has seen the Cumaean Sibyl. Trimalchio's story is an incredible one, for he says that the Sibyl, having eternal life without eternal youth, has shrunk to the size of an insect and is confined in a bottle. The episode reveals, moreover, that she is on display for the amusement and the sport of drunken boys; an incarnation of the logos, she has been reduced to the level of a character in a circus freak show.

Commentators on *The Waste Land* customarily note that the Sibyl exists in Eliot's poem as a symbol of death-in-life and life-in-death or as an example of prolonged depression. Sometimes, following Dante G. Rossetti's mistaken translation of *ampulla*, critics discuss the Sibyl as suspended in a cage. They often note, too, that Trimalchio is a gross fool and drunkard who hopelessly garbles myth and history and that he is also a parvenu with no stable place in society; and they point out the obvious appropriateness of placing such a character at the head of *The Waste Land*.

These customary readings are helpful but should be refined to take account of a number of nuances. First, in spite of his vulgar behavior, Trimalchio knows enough Greek to suggest that he is not an uneducated oaf. Second, most of his listeners give no sign that they are capable of understanding any Greek at all. Petronius's suggestion seems to be that Trimalchio is deliberately presenting himself as an uneducated person and deliberately garbling myth. The passage is even more convoluted when we realize that, although Cumae was a Greek colony, it was in Italy and the Cumaean Sibyl is a Roman figure. We are left with a Roman telling other Romans an anecdote in which a Roman prophetess speaks Greek in response to questions asked in Greek. This is analogous to Americans telling stories to other Americans and quoting Buffalo Bill or John Wayne in French.

One of the most startling things about Trimalchio's picture is that it presents a seer confined within the closed system of a jar or bottle. A mythic seer like the Sibyl of Cumae or Tiresias differs from ordinary human beings in not being restricted to a single perspective at a single moment. The usual human situation, as we have pointed out, is one Bradley calls relational experience. The knower is limited to a single perspective, and although the perspective changes from moment to moment, it is single in any given moment. He perceives the world not as a whole but as a constantly shifting array of patterns, with images continuously appearing and dissolving, forming and re-forming in the air. The perspective changes even if the knower stays in the same spot, for he is in time, and the world around him is in time. Because all of the perspectives in an endless series of perspectives are within a system, the series is bound to generate a feeling of disorder. As Eliot puts it in his dissertation, the knower does not have the luxury of contemplating one consistent world; he has, rather, "the painful task of unifying (to a greater or less extent) jarring and incompatible ones, and passing, when possible, from two or more discordant viewpoints to a higher which shall somehow include and transmute them."[25] Eliot's parenthetical "to a greater or less extent" underscores the fact that even our transcendent experiences are still within a system; that is, they may be more comprehensive, but they are never complete, never equivalent to a god's-eye view. And Eliot's "when possible" indicates that, unlike immediate experience and unlike relational experience, transcendent experience is not automatic, not a given for ordinary mortals. These Bradleian levels of being and knowing have much in common with experiences Eliot deals with in *Four Quartets*. In "The Dry Salvages," part 5, for example, the poet indicates that although "most of us" will know only the unity that comes with something similar to immediate experience, a few extraordinary beings will achieve (or receive as a gift) a perspective from the intersection of time and timelessness, a perspective similar to that associated with Bradley's transcendent experience.

> But to apprehend
> The point of intersection of the timeless
> With time, is an occupation for the saint—
> No occupation either, but something given
> And taken, in a lifetime's death in love,
> Ardour and selflessness and self-surrender.
> For most of us, there is only the unattended
> Moment, the moment in and out of time,

> The distraction fit, lost in a shaft of sunlight,
> The wild thyme unseen, or the winter lightning
> Or the waterfall, or music heard so deeply
> That it is not heard at all . . .

Figures such as the Sibyl of Cumae and Tiresias, of course, cannot be classed with "most of us," nor can they be classed with extraordinary people such as saints. They are mythic creatures, with experience in several realms of knowing and being. On the level on which they interact with humans, they enter into relational experience, much as Christ incarnated as Jesus entered into relational experience. On another level, however, they are outside both time and space. In the *Aeneid*, for example, the Sibyl can grasp the history of Rome in a single picture, either before or after it happens. She can move between this world and Hades and can know both at once. Mythic seers have a binary perspective; that is, they enjoy both a mythic and a relational mode of knowing and being and, moreover, enjoy both at once. They can see from the inside, part to part, but also from the outside, part to whole.

In Trimalchio's story, the Sibyl has been deprived of her binary perspective, maimed in her visionary powers. She is still immortal and has memory and holds history in her imagination. But she has lost her mythic perspective and is imprisoned in a jar; like finite beings, she has been reduced to a single perspective and deprived of her ability to see systems and eras and situations from both inside and outside. In Bradley's terms, she is trapped within the dualisms of relational knowledge. That entrapment seems to be the reason she wants to die. The knowledge that her knowledge is limited to a single perspective destroys her will to live. Later, in "The Burial of the Dead," Eliot will introduce another maimed sibyl, Madame Sosostris. This modern seer, the "wisest woman in Europe," has poor vision and a bad cold to boot. She worries about what she cannot see, but, taking precautions to keep the horoscope out of the wrong hands ("One must be so careful these days"), she nevertheless goes about her business. We will deal with the contemporary sibyl in another chapter.

To return to Eliot's epigraph from Petronius: when we combine the content of Trimalchio's anecdote with its manner of presentation, we arrive at a vivid rendering of a concentric arrangement of closed systems. Eliot presents to English readers a quotation from Petronius's fabrication of Encolpius's account of Trimalchio's presentation of Latin and Greek to Latin speakers concerning the debilitating effects of knowledge from a limited point of view. With awesome economy, Eliot establishes not only his mythic and epistemological stance but also his procedure of calling attention to multiple perspectives by using multiple languages. In the poem to follow, characters speak from their own limited perspectives in their own languages; moreover, birds, a cock, and the thunder speak from specific countries and use the language of those countries, underscoring the idea that all knowing is filtered through a place and a time and a language.

Trimalchio, to approach our subject from a slightly different angle, is an individual talent and the Sibyl is an aspect of his tradition which his presentation alters. Encolpius, the narrator who relates the episode, is a mind that contains both his knowledge of tradition and his knowledge of how Trimalchio and others alter it in their individual and unique ways. Encolpius presents history as an array of varying and mutually exclusive interpretations, some of them deliberately distorted and some of them unintentionally distorted. But regardless of intent, as Eliot argued in his graduate paper on interpretation of primitive ritual and in his dissertation, and as he remarked in his introduction to *Savonarola*, interpretations are always distortions, and yet interpretations are all that we have.[26] Petronius created Encolpius as the creator of others who would multiply interpretations in a way that would preclude a synthesis of meanings that could add up to something a reader might feel to be true. Eliot adds another layer to this palimpsest of vivid confusion by quoting it at the beginning of his poem, and in adding our observations and interpretations we are adding still another dimension to what must be a never-ending process of multiplying variety in a wilderness of mirrors.

Eliot's use of the Sibyl of Cumae brings us to his indebtedness to Frazer's massive encyclopedia of religion and myth, *The Golden Bough*. Frazer's magnum opus was inspired by his curiosity about the myth of the golden bough, a myth featuring the Sibyl as a central character. She is the prophetess who instructs Aeneas to pluck the golden bough before descending with her to the underworld in his quest for knowledge. *The Golden Bough* captured the imagination of many artists in the early twentieth century. Eliot, certainly, was immersed in it, discussing it familiarly in his graduate school papers and book reviews and constantly alluding to it in his art. The most straightforward advice he offers to readers of *The Waste Land* (given in the notes to the poem) is, in paraphrase, that any serious reader of the poem must take into consideration modern scholarship in myth and anthropology, especially Frazer's *Golden Bough* and Jessie Weston's *From Ritual to Romance*. The poet says that he is indebted to this scholarship for his title, his plan, his symbolism, and many of his references to ancient religion and society. His claim about the title, taken from the monomyth of Frazer and Weston, his claim about the symbolism, associated with the birth-death-rebirth cycles of the myths, and his claim about the miscellaneous undergirding references have been discussed by Grover Smith and other scholars.[27] We wish to focus more on Eliot's claim about being indebted to Frazer for the plan of the poem. We believe it refers, at least in part, to Frazer's use of the comparative method and to his practice of assembling many perspectives and allowing these perspectives to make his point.

It must be noted at once that Eliot was quite selective in his admiration of Frazer. For example, he did not admire Frazer's positivism. Frazer put his faith in science and celebrated what he called the evolution from magic to religion to science.[28] Nor did Eliot share Frazer's conclusions. In his 1913 paper on the interpretation of primitive ritual, he says that Frazer's interpretations of specific myths (the myth of the dying god is his example) are almost certainly mistaken.[29] But Eliot did admire Frazer's erudition and his increasingly nontheoretical presentation of many angles of vision which in themselves tend to generate an overarching abstract primitive vision. In 1924, on the occasion of the publication of a condensed edition of *The Golden Bough*, Eliot wrote a review in which he lauded Frazer for having "extended the consciousness of the human mind into as dark a backward and abysm of time as has yet been explored."[30] Eliot argues that Frazer's importance for artists is in his exemplary withdrawal from speculation, his adoption of the absence of interpretation as a positive modus operandi. "With every fresh volume of his stupendous compendium of human superstition and folly, Frazer has withdrawn in more and more cautious abstention from the attempt to explain. . . . The absence of speculation is a conscious and deliberate scrupulousness, a positive point of view."[31] Eliot's reason for admiring Frazer's withdrawal from interpretation may be seen in the following comment, made the same year (1924) as the above remarks in the review.

> *no* interpretation of a rite could explain its origin. For the meaning of the series of acts is to the performers themselves an interpretation; the same ritual remaining practically unchanged may assume different meanings for different generations of performers; and the rite may even have originated before "meaning" meant anything at all.[32]

The reference to a stage before "meaning" meant anything at all is also interesting in that it indicates that Eliot is thinking about the primitive mind in terms of Bradley's epistemology, namely, in terms of an analogue of immediate experience. These points were first made by Eliot in graduate school.[33] In one of his seminar papers, he insists that the meaning of ancient rituals cannot be reconstructed out of abstractions torn from our sophisticated theories, that the best we can do is what Frazer has done, simply to accumulate as many points of view (or "facts," which Eliot defines as a point of view from a single aspect) as possible.[34]

Eliot's most explicit discussion of the importance of Frazerian studies to modern artists may be found in his 1923 review of Joyce's *Ulysses*.[35] Eliot argues that Frazer's work makes possible the use of the mythical method and that this method makes the modern world possible for art. Many critics misquote Eliot as saying that the mythical method makes art possible in the modern world. But Eliot, who generally uses words with precision, says that this method does something to the modern world, alters it in some way beneficial to artists. This curious and somewhat oracular utterance, to which we shall return, needs to be understood in the context of Eliot's preoccupation with history. In the introduction to *Savonarola*, Eliot says that every period of history is seen differently by itself and by every other period, and "the past is in perpetual flux, although only the past can be known."[36] As in "Tradition and the Individual Talent," he indicates that we know the past in a way that it could not have known itself because we can see it from the outside, but that in other ways we cannot know it as it knew itself because we cannot see it from the inside (except in a limited way by reading surviving documents).[37] Eliot is concerned here with the problems involved in perceiving objects from a perspective within a system. Just as it is impossible to form an accurate idea of a house from a position within it, or of the universe from any position inside it, it is impossible to understand history or to perceive and judge one's life because one is always looking from within. Far from a new motion, this is an ancient concept which forms part of the famous conclusion to *Oedipus Rex*. As the wretched and miserable king leaves the stage, the chorus moralizes:

> Men of Thebes: look upon Oedipus.
>
> This is the king who solved the famous riddle
> And towered up, most powerful of men.
> No mortal eyes but looked on him with envy.
> Yet in the end ruin swept over him.
>
> Let every man in mankind's frailty
> Consider his last day; and let none
> Presume on his good fortune until he find
> Life, at his death, a memory without pain.[38]

The term translated "good fortune" is *eudaimon*, a word that has no simple translation but carries connotations of having been accompanied throughout one's life by a good *daimon* or friendly guardian deity or, sometimes, of having led a life full of good luck (or fate).[39] The end of Sophocles' play is an assertion that no life can be judged until it is complete, until it can be seen as a whole. The actor cannot be in the play and see it at the same time.[40] Nietzsche made a similar point in *Twilight of the Idols* when he noted that the value of life cannot be assessed by the living since they are all interested parties. It cannot be assessed by the dead either—"for a different reason."[41]

Eliot's theory of history, like Bradley's,[42] is an elaboration of the doctrine of internal relations and is directly relevant to our concern with perspectivism. From a perspective within any aggregate of phenomena all objects will seem structured, but as internal points of view change, objects assume a sequence of variant structures. What we call disorder is a sequence of diverse orders emerging as the perspective on events changes. Thus, when Eliot in the *Ulysses* review calls the modern world an "immense panorama of futility and anarchy," he is not simply complaining. He is speaking with philosophical precision about the instability of all relations when they are perceived from inside a closed system. From one point of view, all of history is a closed system, a house with many "cunning passages" and "contrived corridors," as he puts it in "Gerontion."[43] But by moving (or by trying to move) to a higher view, we (to a greater or less extent) can discover order. In "Tradition and the Individual Talent," for example, he urges us to do the necessary work to construct the entire literary tradition into a single, simultaneous, ideal system. But he recognizes that in most situations the contemporary world is our closed system and that most of our experiences are received and evaluated from a position within it.

And now we come to what we consider a special importance of Frazer. One way of passing beyond the restrictions of relational experience, one way of manufacturing a synthetic perspective, a place from which the feeling of seeing from the outside can be juxtaposed with the problem of being trapped on the inside, is by alluding to ancient myths. Alluding without explanation to many myths generates an abstraction, something outside ourselves in both time and space.[44] It makes the modern world possible for art by enabling it to be seen or perceived from an ideal or imagined position similar in some ways to a fourth dimension. The modern world is altered to make it viable matter for art by inventing a perspective on it. Myth provides the raw materials out of which the synthetic transcendent perspective is manufactured. In explaining the points of similarity among myths by proposing a common origin, Frazer comes up with an abstract first myth, a monomyth. This myth provides a common ground, a sort of fourth dimension, from which viewers can look at the contemporary world from a sufficient distance to make that world appear to have an order. At the same time—or in rapid alternation—viewers are observing the contemporary world from their various perspectives within it. By simultaneously or in alternation occupying both an ideal mythic platform and a real position within the house of history, the poet permits binary vision.

With this idea in mind, we can better understand Eliot's note on Tiresias:

> Tiresias, although a mere spectator and not indeed a "character," is yet the most important personage in the poem, uniting all the rest. Just as the one-eyed merchant, seller of currants, melts into the Phoenician Sailor, and the latter is not wholly distinct from Ferdinand Prince of Naples, so all the women are one woman, and the two sexes meet in Tiresias. What Tiresias *sees*, in fact, is the substance of the poem.

Tiresias defines a binary perspective that serves as the point of view of the poem. He is a figure from the ideal order of myth; yet he is spying on the sordidly historical typist and clerk. By saying that Tiresias is spying on all the characters, Eliot is suggesting that the reader make an effort to perceive them in an equivalent way, from both internal and external perspectives. From a position inside the modern world, the characters are distinct and separate, but from the Tiresias or mythic position, the characters "melt" into each other.

A common misunderstanding is the notion that Eliot regarded certain historical periods with idealizing nostalgia while despising his own time. Those who hold this opinion fail to note the logical rigor involved in Eliot's thought. If you consider an epoch from a position outside it, it will appear as a coherent whole. The act of reading that epoch's major documents, however, will transfer you to a position partially within it, from which it is chaotic, and partially outside it, from which it is ordered. It follows that Eliot's statement that the modern world is an "immense panorama of futility and anarchy" could be said about any period in history by a person who is experiencing it from the interior.

Bradley's concept of the Absolute is also relevant here. In contrast to Hegel, Bradley does not conceive of the Absolute as a metaphysical concept. Bradley, in fact, is an empiricist who regards the Absolute as an inventory of experiences. Put simply, the Absolute is the sum total of all experiences. There have been and will be an uncountable number of experiencing minds in the universe, so the Absolute not only cannot be known by a single experiencer but also does not yet exist. Like the *eudaimon* of a person, it can come into being only at the instant when it is finished, when it ceases to exist. This apparent paradox is not at all metaphysical. It only states the tautology that nothing is complete until it is complete. After that completion, however, the experiences are finished. Thus the Absolute of all experiences will exist only in the moment when the last experience is over.

With this idea in mind, what is the status of the "seeing" Eliot attributes to Tiresias and—by implication—to the viewer attempting to share his view? Tiresias does not "see" in a literal sense because he is blind, but he "sees" in some suprasensory mode that is the gift of Zeus. It is necessary, if we follow Eliot's concern with both Bradley and Frazer, to conclude that Tiresias perceives the contemporary world in the poem from a perspective outside space and time altogether. He is thus not only one side of a binary perspective; he is also the suggestion that the reader must try to imagine that *The Waste Land* is a phenomenon to be viewed from the perspective of the Absolute, or at least from a more comprehensive perspective. Tiresias functions as Eliot's "higher" viewpoint which will include and transmute the figures in *The Waste Land* and also, perhaps, include and transmute reader as subject and text as object. This specifies the kind of collaboration readers are asked for, a subsumption of themselves under the aspects of a binary perspective.

The most striking claim in Eliot's note on Tiresias is that what Tiresias sees is the "substance" of the poem. As Anne Bolgan has said, "This could not be more misleading if it were intended by its author as a deliberate piece of obfuscation and that, I would suggest, is precisely what it is."[45] Bolgan is one of several perceptive critics who have failed to see that Eliot is using the term "substance" in its philosophical sense as unitive essence. His attribution of substance to the poem from Tiresias's point of view is a warning that the poem has no substantial unity from any other point of view. We as readers are obliged to experience the poem in two ways at once: from a perspective in our own time where its lack of clear order is its distinguishing characteristic and from a synthetic or imagined perspective from which it has a metaphysical substance. This is not the kind of doubleness that leads to irony, paradox, or parody; it is the doubleness implicit in Bradley's doctrine of transcendent experience. In that doctrine we are asked to accept the difficult task of living in the commonsense realm of unstable relations where subject and object fail to cohere, while at the same time attempting to fabricate a nondualistic viewpoint from which subject and object are mere adjectives modifying a larger whole which is that fabricated nondualistic viewpoint. We are asked to accept the inevitability of enduring incompatible and jarring worlds, while at the same time attempting to unify them through occasional moments of transcendence.

Transcendent experience is a difficult concept. To see more clearly how it works in *The Waste Land*, let us turn to the scene in "The Fire Sermon" where Tiresias appears and describes a scene from contemporary London.

> At the violet hour, when the eyes and back
> Turn upward from the desk, when the human engine waits
> Like a taxi throbbing waiting,
> I Tiresias, though blind, throbbing between two lives,
> Old man with wrinkled female breasts, can see
> At the violet hour, the evening hour that strives
> Homeward, and brings the sailor home from sea,
> The typist home at teatime, clears her breakfast, lights
> Her stove, and lays out food in tins.
> Out of the window perilously spread
> Her drying combinations touched by the sun's last rays,
> On the divan are piled (at night her bed)
> Stockings, slippers, camisoles, and stays.
> I Tiresias, old man with wrinkled dugs,
> Perceived the scene, and foretold the rest—
> I too awaited the expected guest.
> He, the young man carbuncular, arrives,
> A small house agent's clerk, with one bold stare,
> One of the low on whom assurance sits
> As a silk hat on a Bradford millionaire.
> The time is now propitious, as he guesses,
> The meal is ended, she is bored and tired,
> Endeavours to engage her in caresses
> Which still are unreproved, if undesired.
> Flushed and decided, he assaults at once;

Exploring hands encounter no defence;
His vanity requires no response,
And makes a welcome of indifference.
(And I Tiresias have foresuffered all
Enacted on this same divan or bed;
I who have sat by Thebes below the wall
And walked among the lowest of the dead.)
Bestows one final patronising kiss,
And gropes his way, finding the stairs unlit . . .

She turns and looks a moment in the glass,
Hardly aware of her departed lover;
Her brain allows one half-formed thought to pass:
"Well now that's done: and I'm glad it's over."
When lovely woman stoops to folly and
Paces about her room again, alone,
She smoothes her hair with automatic hand,
And puts a record on the gramophone.

Within the narrated scene, the typist is the subject, or experiencing center, and the clerk is the object, or person experienced. These designations are assigned simply because the focus is on the typist. She is present at the beginning, middle, and end of the episode, and her mind is directly rendered: "Well now that's done: and I'm glad it's over." The clerk's mind is inferred from his behavior: "His vanity requires no response/And makes a welcome of indifference." The scene, viewed from a contemporary and nonmetaphysical perspective, dramatizes the failure of sex to create even a temporary relationship beyond the merely physical plane. Copulation is an activity in which the failure of subject and object to merge for a nondualistic moment is especially pointed and poignant. It is the form of love without the function of love.

Typist and clerk are examples of subject and object failing to merge. The reader who is ignoring Tiresias as narrator experiences only that failure. But when readers consent to the mediation of Tiresias as both narrator and voyeur, their points of reference are multiplied. In his dissertation on Bradley and in his graduate school papers, Eliot frequently addresses the need for a transcendent point of view. In one paper, written at Harvard between 1912 and 1914, he notes the insufficiency of locating reality in either mind or matter, in either the observer's consciousness or the object that is observed, and indicates the desirability of finding a larger reality, some transcendent point or platform that would permit a comprehensive view.[46] In the scene at hand, the typist is the observer's consciousness on a contemporary plane (inside the closed system of her life), and the clerk is the observed object. The reality that subsumes both is the mind of Tiresias, in which subject and object exist as aspects of that mind. They are thus from his perspective fused, "melted" into each other. Bradley's transcendent experience is the simultaneity of dualism within a sphere with monism outside that sphere.

The preceding observations are open to the objection that Tiresias himself judges the transactions of typist and clerk as a failed relation. His perception is the same as the strictly contemporary view with which his perspective supposedly is contrasted. How, to put it briefly, can he provide a transmuting viewpoint when what he sees is precisely what is seen from a mundane viewpoint? This difficulty vanishes when we note that Tiresias is forced to report on an event in time by adjusting his position to a point within contemporaneity. He defines his condition as "throbbing between two lives," clearly a reference to his periods as male and female but also to his position as a mediator between a timeless perspective and a time-bound one. After designating his own situation "between," he focuses on a specific "evening hour," then foretells the clerk's visit, then announces that he has "foresuffered all" sexuality from both male and female perspectives, then recalls his ancient past and visit to the realm of the dead. Though his narrative function traps him in time, he injects into the narrative frequent reminders of his temporal versatility, his competence in perceiving from several viewpoints in time. Our impression of the episode as a whole is of a woman experiencing a man and at the same time of an androgyne experiencing them both with a single perception. One aspect of that unitive perception is that the "lovers" do not aspire to any kind of unity.

It is plain now that the "continuous parallel between contemporaneity and antiquity" mentioned in Eliot's review of *Ulysses* is not the presentation of a simple set of polarities. It is permissible to regard the contemporary world as existing on one level as a single class of entities, but the same simplicity cannot reasonably be applied to the mythic world cited in the poem. Frazer's dying god is one type of figure referred to, Perceval the questor who must prepare the god or king to die is another type, clearly distinguished from the first because he is only an enabling adjunct to the savior whose death will regenerate the barren land. Tiresias, along with the Sibyl of Cumae, is a third type who neither dies nor prepares another to die but merely sees, and Prajapati, lord of the thunder, is still another type, a transcendent messenger who is not of this earth at all. Other classifications can be easily made, but for our purposes it is sufficient to consider these four—saviors, their adjuncts, seers, and transcendent messengers. The first two are mortal, and the second two are immortal.

Mortality is the condition of existing on a straight time line beginning at conception and ending at death. The limited and definitive nature of mortality stresses the separateness and individuality of the person. Immortality is the condition of existing on a circular time line that endlessly repeats the cycles of nature. Insofar as a mythic hero dies, he is an individual, a unique event, but insofar as he is a symbol of the optimum functioning of nature, its fertility and endlessly repeatable health, he is a representative of immortality. He is thus a paradoxical synthesis of life and death, circular and rectilinear vectors of time. In regard to what we have called the savior type, the synthetic perspective from myth or contemporaneity is itself a synthesis. Where we are looking at the events of the poem from the viewpoint of the Fisher King, for example, we are looking from a perspective that must be imagined as the nexus or point of intersection between two kinds of time, the once-and-once-only pattern of a person and the over-and-over-again pattern of the nature that person's unique career has optimized. The habit of not seeing this type of time fusion as paradoxical is what must be called mythic consciousness. If we insist that this coexistence of straight and circular cannot exist, we have a modern or, as Bradley put it, a relational consciousness.

We can now sum up what has so far been stated. Bradley divided experience into three phases: immediate, relational, and transcendent. Immediate experience is pure consciousness; it is consciousness but consciousness of nothing; it comes prior to intellectual consciousness. It is a state in which subject and object have not yet separated into related entities. Relational experience is intellectual consciousness, the state in which structuring activities must be continued from moment to moment entirely from within the closed system of one's experiencing consciousness. Transcendent experience is the result of a mode of consciousness capable of perceiving both diffusion and unity by contriving a unifying point of view.

Mythic consciousness exists under the category of transcendent experience and in *The Waste Land* functions as a counterpoise to the relational cognitions upon which secular knowledge depends. In using such figures as the Sibyl of Cumae and Tiresias, Eliot is trying to provide a means for the reader to transcend jarring and incompatible worlds, to move to a higher viewpoint that both includes and transcends the contemporary world. Like any scene viewed from the inside, the contemporary world is a panorama of futility and anarchy. But the contemporary world is anarchic for a further reason—it is trapped in a relational mentality because it happens to be a culture based upon the assumptions that the transcendent either does not exist or is irrelevant to its principal concerns. And like Blake, Eliot deplores "single vision and Newton's sleep."[47]

3 / Relational Consciousness
and Transcendent Reading

"The Burial of the Dead"

A relational way of thought—any one that moves by the machinery of terms and relations—must give appearance, and not truth. It is a makeshift, . . . most necessary but in the end indefensible. We have to take reality as many, and to take it as one, and to avoid contradiction. . . . And we succeed, but succeed merely by shutting the eye, which if left open would condemn us; or by a perpetual oscillation and a shifting of the ground, so as to turn our back upon the aspect we desire to ignore.—F. H. Bradley, *Appearance and Reality*

"The Burial of the Dead" consists of a brief introductory lyric, in which an oracular voice describes essential features of Eliot's waste land, and five episodes, each concerned with varying problems of knowledge and interpretation and each introducing a motif that will later be expanded. In the first episode, Marie comments on the cycles of nature and ways of interpreting them. She also reveals the concern with language and national identity by quoting the line, "Bin gar keine Russin, stamm' aus Litauen, echt deutsch." In the second episode, a voice asks questions and informs the "son of man" that he has no chance of answering them until, from a perspective in shadow, he listens to an answer. In the third episode, the poet introduces the motif of communication between lovers and shows the failure of the hyacinth girl and her lover within a contrived perspective of Wagner's *Tristan und Isolde*. In the fourth episode, Madame Sosostris, a contemporary equivalent of the Cumaean Sibyl and Tiresias, appears as a seer who depends on the sortilege of tarot cards designed to defeat interpretations by multiplying them. In the last episode, briefly discussed in our previous chapter, the city is seen as hell's vestibule, and contemporary urban attitudes about life and death are related to positivistic interpretations of mythic patterns. These sections correspond to Eliot's verse paragraphs, both in the original drafts and in the published poem.

In the first verse paragraph, an impersonal voice introduces a

60

world where humans are out of phase with the seasons and other cycles, and then a personal voice emerges and substantiates life out of rhythm with nature.

> April is the cruellest month, breeding
> Lilacs out of the dead land, mixing
> Memory and desire, stirring
> Dull roots with spring rain.
> Winter kept us warm, covering
> Earth in forgetful snow, feeding
> A little life with dried tubers.
> Summer surprised us, coming over the Starnbergersee
> With a shower of rain; we stopped in the colonnade,
> And went on in sunlight, into the Hofgarten,
> And drank coffee, and talked for an hour.
> Bin gar keine Russin, stamm' aus Litauen, echt deutsch.
> And when we were children, staying at the archduke's,
> My cousin's, he took me out on a sled,
> And I was frightened. He said, Marie,
> Marie, hold on tight. And down we went.
> In the mountains, there you feel free.
> I read, much of the night, and go south in the winter.

The formal and impersonal opening voice makes a universal statement about the waste land, then modulates into a choral voice from within the waste land, and then to an individual voice clearly identified as that of Marie. "Winter kept us warm" continues the oracular tone of the first four lines but, by introduction of the personal pronoun and by the parallelism with "Summer surprised us," is seen to be a particularization of the opening voice. This opening episode reveals a general present where April is cruel, a specific present in which the speaker cannot sleep at night and migrates to avoid seasonal cycles, and a recent past in which winter was perceived as providing warmth and summer as a surprising occurrence. The speaker recalls her childhood, however, as a time when she was in tune with the seasons, as a time when she overcame her winter fears instead of avoiding them by moving south. Two perspectives exist and contend within Marie's mind. Her present in the waste land involves a partially successful evasion of natural cycles, but her past, still present in memory, includes an acceptance of circularity as the form of straight-line growth. "And down we went," she says, recalling a descent in winter which constituted an ascent beyond fear to freedom. As a child, Marie had lived in a largely nondualistic world in which she accepted contradictions because she did not perceive them as contradictions; as an adult, she lives in a world of intolerable paradoxes created by her compulsion to perceive up and down, fear and security, circular and straight, as contraries. She sees paradoxes as openings onto vistas of chaos. Like all inhabitants of the waste land, she interprets April as cruel because it breeds life from death, because it brings endless circularity and unavoidable paradox. The opening voice suggests that Marie's interpretation issues from mixing memory and desire, past and future. Memory is vividly presented in the image of a childhood experience, but desire is left vague. Marie is portrayed as stretched between a past which was in special ways unconscious and carefree and a future which may in some way correspond to that childhood condition. She perceives the dualistic and paradoxical present as cruel because, in remembering the past and intuiting the future, she is left with a vacuum in the present moment, an absence in the middle of her life.

In Bradley's terms, Marie is trapped in relational knowledge. The ideal unity of immediate experience, in which space, time, and self do not exist, has broken down into a jungle of contending dualisms in which the self exists only to perceive its instability. Transcendent experience would be possible for her if she could accept the simultaneity of her condition in the curvilinear time of nature and the rectilinear time of her isolated uniqueness. But that paradox defeats her precisely because she cannot avoid seeing it as a paradox, a failure of relations to melt into unity.

To put it in Frazerian terms, she cannot experience the mythic mode of perception in which the centers of all existence are metonymic mergers of the individual with his lord. Mythic heroes live and die like those who revere them; but unlike ordinary mortals, they transcend death because their suffering is part of a springtime (April, usually) ritual that lifts a curse from nature. The secret of well-being in myth is an epistemology that accepts both individual and general life, that sees no contradiction between death for the one and rejuvenation for the other, between the finitude of the hero's biography and the infinity of the cycles of nature his biography represents. If Marie could tap into this epistemology, she could construct a point of view from which she could accept paradox and perceive the world as one. But she cannot imagine such a mode of knowing.

Marie, then, although discontent (because of memory) with relational experience and nudged (by desire) toward her first world, cannot return to that world or to that mode of knowing. Another gate to a world beyond dualism would be a surrender to love, to love of another person or to love of God. In Eliot's work, from beginning to end, waste lands are related to failures of love,[1] to failures of individuals to transcend their separate spheres and become complements in a comprehensive and mutually nourishing unity. But Marie, Eliot suggests, is as incapable of love as of mythic consciousness and will never escape from her trap, will always experience April as cruel.

As a transition to our discussion of the second episode of "The Burial of the Dead," we would like to emphasize that our reading process is not direct interpretation. It is a process most accurately understood as metahermeneutics: interpretation of interpretations and of their denial. For example, we interpret Eliot's decision to have Marie (if Marie is the narrator of the first lines) interpret April as cruel, and we also interpret his presentation of situations in which meanings multiply into mutually canceling arrays of meanings. An awareness of Eliot's focus on the process of reading and the nature of interpretation is often missing in commentaries in *The Waste Land*. The famous issue of what the thunder really said is a case in point. The first "command of the thunder" is given in lines 400–410.

> Then spoke the thunder
> DA
> *Datta*: what have we given?
> My friend, blood shaking my heart
> The awful daring of a moment's surrender
> Which an age of prudence can never retract
> By this, and this only, we have existed
> Which is not to be found in our obituaries

> Or in memories draped by the beneficent spider
> Or under seals broken by the lean solicitor
> In our empty rooms

Books have been written in an attempt to decipher the message of the thunder, but in fact, as this passage and those relating the second and third commands clearly show, the thunder has no message; the thunder says nothing at all. The command *"Datta"* (its rough equivalent is "give") is said not by the thunder god but by a person who hears a thunderclap. And certainly, the images that follow are said not by the thunder but by a persona of Eliot's poem. The action of the passage becomes the hermeneutic effort to interpret (1) an impersonal and natural noise "DA," the conventional Indian onomatopoeic sound for a thunderclap, equivalent to "Boom" in English; (2) a word that comes to mind because it begins not with the same sound but with the same letter; (3) a question suggested by the word *"Datta"*; and (4) an intensely personal and sophisticated answer to the question. The passage shows interpreters assigning meaning, and our task is to interpret the interpretations of the sound of the thunder. Since we have only interpretations of interpretations, there is no way for us to slice through layers of commentary and arrive at a pure or essential utterance. This situation is analogous to the way in which Russell and Whitehead conceived of entities in the *Principia Mathematica*. Objects are only "bundles" of qualities and functions. Peeling away the surface qualities reveals, at every layer, only another bundle of qualities. At no point can an analysis arrive at the pure entity modified by the bundles of adjectival qualities. This way of thinking is what the *Principia* calls the Theory of Descriptions.[2] In Eliot's poetry, it is clearer to call it the theory of interpretations. The poem is a bundle of meanings that merely coexist. They cannot be analyzed into a pure message, and that is the poem's pure message.

These ideas are directly applicable to the second episode in "The Burial of the Dead," for in a special way the passage is an exercise in the hazardous activity of interpreting interpretations.

> What are the roots that clutch, what branches grow
> Out of this stony rubbish? Son of man,
> You cannot say, or guess, for you know only

> A heap of broken images, where the sun beats,
> And the dead tree gives no shelter, the cricket no relief,
> And the dry stone no sound of water. Only
> There is shadow under this red rock,
> (Come in under the shadow of this red rock),
> And I will show you something different from either
> Your shadow at morning striding behind you
> Or your shadow at evening rising to meet you;
> I will show you fear in a handful of dust.

This episode begins by posing two seemingly profound questions, and then by addressing the "son of man" and saying that he has no hope of answering them. The reason for his helplessness is that his experience is limited to a realm of broken images where he can see only his own shadow, where deadly heat and barren dryness keep him from knowing or guessing the answer to the original questions, where the light is so blinding and debilitating that he cannot even imagine answers. The speaker informs the son of man that relief from the heat is available under the shadow of a red rock and invites him to come into this shelter. If the son of man is willing to shift his viewpoint to the realm of shadow cast by the red rock, he will be able to see something different from his own shadows; he will see fear in a handful of dust.

The passage is rich in associations, and satisfying, in part because it provides what Eliot's title promised: a waste land. But on examination, it proves to be curious and unsettling. The familiar shift in perspective is from light to shadow as a means of seeing what can only be felt: fear. This association of fear and dust points to a powerful emotion and to the matter from whence we come and to which we go and thus arguably to the substance of the son of man in contrast to his silhouette. But it is important to note that this response is in no way an answer to the original questions. The questions asked for an identification of rocks and branches growing from "stony rubbish," whereas the answer refers to dust as a conventional metaphor of human physicality. After recognizing that questions and answer do not match, readers will quickly find a way of fabricating a mental perspective in which they do match. This is accomplished by bringing the trope of metonymy into play. Roots and branches thus merge with their ground, and the son of man becomes specifically identified with his ground, literally his soil, in which fear resides. If we do not go through the process, first, of seeing the irrelevance of answer to question and, then, of consciously constructing a metonymic relevance, we are not experiencing the passage as it stands. That process reveals, among other things, the artificiality of metonymic associations.

Metonymy, as we have noted, is a crucial aspect of myth. In the grail legends assembled by Jessie Weston in *From Ritual to Romance*, a book referred to in Eliot's notes to *The Waste Land*, the hero and his land are one. The king's impotence and the land's sterility are inseparable phenomena. And his healing is the healing of the land. The healing comes about through a questing knight, Perceval, who has to survive a series of ordeals and come to the impotent king in his barren land and ask him a series of questions. The questions, which are extremely simple, present no problem for the king, and the answers reaffirm his unity with his land. In several versions of the myth, the questions and answers are these: "Who are you? I am the king. Who is the king? The king is the land. What is the land? The land is the king." The catechism reaffirms the king's competence, reaffirms the rule of metonymy as a fact, not a trope, and in the process reestablishes the unity of subject and object. After answering the questions, the king literally returns to his land by dying, a return which removes the curse from the land. It should be noted that before his wound the king and his land were one, but he was not conscious of it. After his wound, the king could no longer experience unity with his land but could not escape the conscious knowledge that he and his land were related. After his answers to the catechism, the king knows both the relation and a restoration of unity, and he knows both at the same time. These three phases are somewhat comparable to phases of awareness in any serious accident. Before the accident, mind and body are one, but the mind is not conscious of it. After the accident and while suffering the agony of a wound, the mind is acutely aware of both the relation of mind and body and their disjunction. After health has been restored, the mind and body move beyond the dualism of illness, but the mind retains both the dualistic phase and the transcendence of it. The three phases of the king's life, thus understood, correspond pre-

cisely to Bradley's three phases of knowledge—immediate, relational, and transcendent experience.

In the passage under discussion, the son of man is caught, like
Marie and like the wounded king, in relational experience. The
unity of immediate experience, of childhood, of youthful vigor, has
obviously passed, and the unity on a higher plane, which comes
with transcendent experience, with mythic imagination, or with
restored health, has not been achieved. The wound has been in-
flicted, and the curse is everywhere evident in this waste land of
stony rubbish, broken images, dead trees, dry stones, this land of
unrelieved heat and merciless light. The term "son of man" is a
conventional designation of Christ, used throughout the Bible. In
fact, Christ refers to himself some eighty times in the Gospels as the
son of man. In the context of Eliot's reliance upon Frazer's *Golden
Bough* and other anthropological studies in the history of religion,
it should also be noted that Christ, like the Fisher King, Osiris,
Adonis, Attis, and countless others, is a manifestation of the same
mythic impulse toward insuring the fertility of the earth by ritu-
alistically killing heroes and kings. The Christ of this intermediate
state of awareness (awareness of disjunction between himself and
his people), the Christ of the waste land of stony rubbish, would be
the smitten pre-Resurrection Christ. The speaker who addresses
Christ is not named, but as one who appears in a waste land and
asks questions of a wounded god-king, he is a formal equivalent of
Perceval, the questing knight who presents questions, the answers
to which can lift the curse. Or he may be thought of as a formal
opposite, for Perceval asks questions he knows can be answered,
whereas this speaker asks questions he knows cannot be answered.
A figure from one myth, Perceval, asks questions of a figure from
another myth, Christ, and the insistence that no direct answer can
be conceived is an indication that mythic solutions are no longer
possible. The prison of relational (intellectual, dualistic) experience
has snapped shut, with consequences that are powerfully suggested in this verse paragraph.

Consider, further, that Christ is the "son of man" only in one of
his manifestations. He is also the son of God. In Hegelian terms, he
is not an analytic either/or figure but a synthetic both/and figure.

This means that the central person in Christian culture is a hypostatic union of finite man in time and infinite god out of time. A consideration of Christ must lead to this simultaneity of time and timelessness, and thus, if faith is achieved (more precisely, if the incarnation is accepted), it will be an achievement of the transcendence of paradox in which a both/and arrangement of contraries will be as obvious and clear as it is, in relational terms, absurd. For these reasons, it follows that the address to the son of man by the anti-Perceval is a result of having separated his human and divine natures, of having isolated his finitude and earthly identity from his infinite nature. The address by the anti-Perceval suggests, in fact, that Christ has no divine nature. He who was thought a god is only a man trapped in a system of relations.

The episode can now be read (one of several possible readings at this point) as a comment on the effect of relational consciousness on religious (for the West, Christian) experience. The opposite of Perceval asks all gods, who within the relational modern consciousness are only anthropological curiosities, questions he knows they cannot answer. Their realms are heaps of broken images, contingent bundles of mere qualities, where light, a conventional sign of (paradoxically) both secular and divine knowledge, prevents knowledge of any metaphysical substance within those bundles of qualities. The hope of drawing water from the rock, substance from matter, as Moses did, is explicitly denied. One hope, however, remains: the red rock. The rock is a biblical and Christian symbol of the church; the red rock is a Frazerian symbol of the place of bloody sacrifice. Eliot's red rock, pulling in these associations, provides a shadow, a conventional sign of illusion, from which the one truth that is not illusion can be understood, fear in a handful of dust. Most important, the shadow is known to be a shadow, the illusions offered by the church are known to be illusions, but they nevertheless provide a point from which a special certitude can be experienced, the certitude of dread. The final point on the episode, however, must be a reminder that it consists of internal interpretations that we must experience as only the questing questioner's ideas, and those ideas, like those stated by Marie and the speaker addressing Stetson, are reflexively interpretative of the speakers themselves. They display the consequences of making interpretations from a limited perspective within relational knowledge.

The third section of "The Burial of the Dead" provides another variation on the relation between knowledge and the failure of transcendence, in this case, the transcendence provided by romantic love. The central episode, the drama of the hyacinth girl and her lover, is enclosed by two passages from Richard Wagner's romantic opera *Tristan und Isolde*. Eliot's *parergon* or framing device consists, on one side, of a passage from the first act of *Tristan und Isolde* and, on the other side, a line from the last act.

> *Frisch weht der Wind*
> *Der Heimat zu*
> *Mein Irisch Kind,*
> *Wo weilest du?*
> "You gave me hyacinths first a year ago;
> "They called me the hyacinth girl."
> —Yet when we came back, late, from the Hyacinth garden,
> Your arms full, and your hair wet, I could not
> Speak, and my eyes failed, I was neither
> Living nor dead, and I knew nothing,
> Looking into the heart of light, the silence.
> *Oed' und leer das Meer.*

Eliot's typescript draft simply juxtaposed the four lines from act 1 and the hyacinth girl passage. The last line, added by hand in revision, is clearly a deliberate change in the structure of the section. The radically altered structure (frame instead of juxtaposition) requires the reader to contrive a mode of interpretation that will mediate between the lovers from Wagner's opera and the lovers framed by their story. Both frame and internal story reveal the stress of love. Superficially, it appears that the mythic lovers fail in a glorious burst of tragic passion in their titanic love-death, whereas the contemporary lovers merely sputter into paralysis and silence. This interpretation is suggestive, but it does not take adequate account of the structure of frame and picture.

Using a frame is a way of directing focus. In the passage at hand, it peripheralizes myth and centralizes contemporaneity, or, in other words, it reveals myth as a frame for temporal life. This arrangement makes the hyacinth girl and her lover more vividly present and more emphatically themselves than Wagner's lovers. Using a frame also tends to stabilize whatever is framed, to define it and keep it from moving about. In fact, *parergon* and *ergon*, frame and picture, must of necessity mutually exclude each other and mutually define each other. But though Eliot's mode of presentation leads to a stabilization of the picture of the hyacinth girl and her lover, the fact that the frame is more powerful than the picture has a destabilizing effect. The historical and artistic potency of the Tristan story resists its designation as a frame, and with or without the reader's consent, the mythic lovers tend to usurp the center of the picture. The result is that parergon and ergon, frame and picture, change places in rapid succession, back and forth, like the stairs in a picture by Escher. (A better analogue is the way a shaded circle in a piece of optical illusion art will seem to change rapidly back and forth between concave and convex. It will never resolve itself permanently into one image or the other, and the two can never be seen simultaneously.) What many critics, following Joseph Frank's seminal essay "Spatial Form in Modern Literature," have seen as spatialization in the linear medium of language is actually a subversion of spatiality. Spatiality is undermined because the pattern is designed in such a way as to deny the conventional distinction between frame and picture. This pattern allows neither a reversal nor a standard relation but rather produces a situation in which opposite perceptions oscillate, a design which moves in its stillness and remains still in its movement. Eliot's technique in this passage produces an experience of radical uncertainty about what belongs where and when; it leads to a displacement of ambiguity from meaning to form.

It may be imagined that we have arbitrarily imported such concepts as the instability of forms and the oscillation of parergon and ergon in order to make sense of *The Waste Land*. But, in fact, we took these concepts from Bradley's *Appearance and Reality* and *Essays on Truth and Reality*, on which Eliot wrote his doctoral dissertation, and from the dissertation itself. Eliot was deeply preoccupied with such concepts at the very moment that the poem was taking shape in his mind. We now turn to a brief consideration of a few points from Bradley which will help clarify what is happening in Eliot's poem.

In the second chapter of this study, we discussed in some detail Bradley's three levels of knowing/being—immediate, relational, and transcendent experience. Our interpretation of *The Waste Land*, it will be remembered, is rooted in a conviction that, consciously or unconsciously, Eliot carried to the poem some of the Bradleian materials he had very recently outlined in technical terms in his dissertation. Bradley explains the three levels of knowing/being in *Appearance and Reality*, but he does not take them up in order. Because most philosophers of the last several centuries (for example, Locke, Hume, Hobbes, Mill) had followed Descartes and Newton in thinking dualistically, in terms of subjects and objects and the relations between them, Bradley begins *Appearance and Reality* with an all-out assault on dualistic thinking. He argues that dualistic and relational modes of thought are contradictory and unreal and always lead to "appearance" in contrast to "reality." Later, he will reinstate "appearances" by showing that, although they are not real in themselves, they are aspects of experience and therefore part of reality. Thus he redefines subject and object (unreal in themselves or in relation to each other) as subjective and objective aspects of experience. The Absolute, his all-inclusive many-in-one diversity-in-unity, consists finally of all appearances. He locates "reality" in an envelope of unity that encloses the relational world of common sense, an envelope consisting of immediate experience in the beginning and transcendent experience (finally the Absolute) in the end. (The words "beginning" and "end" introduce contradictions if taken strictly; they are metaphors for us.) In his dissertation, as we have pointed out, Eliot endorses this concept of an all-inclusive experience that begins in unity, falls apart, and returns to unity. And as we have also pointed out, Eliot shares Bradley's view that relational experience is a trap. Many of his early personae, such as Prufrock and Gerontion, are caught in this trap. We have also pointed out that most of the characters in *The Waste Land*—the Sibyl, Marie, Stetson, the son of man, and many others—are trapped in systems of relations.

We now come to our present point: the perspective of persons caught in relational experience. In the analysis of dualistic thinking in the first half of *Appearance and Reality*, Bradley concludes that relational knowing, that is, knowing that proceeds by the machinery of terms and relations, is a makeshift involving "perpetual oscillation and a shifting of the ground, so as to turn our back upon the aspect we desire to ignore."[3] In disposing of conventional ways of understanding what is real, he examines the division of the world's contents into things and their qualities, in grammatical terms, into nouns and adjectives. A lump of sugar, to use his example, is a thing, and sweetness, hardness, and whiteness are its qualities. He shows that there is no such thing as a lump of sugar apart from its qualities but that the lump of sugar is clearly not its qualities. He then moves to the argument that the lump of sugar is its qualities in relation; that is, a lump of sugar is not sweetness, hardness, and whiteness but all three existing in a precise relation which makes them into a lump of sugar. He shows, however, that a relation cannot constitute a thing. "Before" or "after" or "between," for example, are nonexistent in themselves; they exist only in the things they relate. But the things they relate, when subjected to analysis, fall apart into bundles of qualities which have no existence apart from being related in a certain way.

The question of how anything exists, on any posited level, is not capable of a logical answer; it is a matter of perceptual focus. We can look at cubes of sugar in a silver bowl on a cherry table as a pattern, or we can look at any one of them by adjusting visual focus. If we focus on the bowl, we perceive its shape, color, texture, weight, and so on, as qualities in relation. If we focus on the quality of color, we see it in the relation of contrast to adjacent colors and to all other known colors. We also see it in relation to all other levels of analysis which serve as its frame. The process of perceiving, whether we are philosophizing or not, is a process in which we relate qualities and subgroups of qualities and in so doing frame them. But our frame, as Bradley shows, will not stay still; its tendency is to alter from moment to moment, to dissolve, re-form, change places with the object it frames, and so on. In his dissertation and in his graduate school papers, Eliot defines an object in terms consistent with these ideas. An object, he says, is a point of attention from a limited point of view. What gives it objectivity is simply the moment of attention.[4]

Attending to anything, including attending to a relation, then, turns it into an object, an object no less for being located in the mind. And now we can see the disastrous way of thinking involved in terms and relations. Let A and B stand for qualities (sweetness and hardness) which have the relation R. A and B have no reality in themselves. To understand them, it is necessary to focus on them in relation, that is, on R. But if we focus on R, it becomes an object and assumes an immediate and necessary relation to both A and B. Bradley's conclusion is that we are forced by relations into an endless cycle which ends in utter abstraction and total nonsense. "[W]e are forced to go on finding new relations without end. The links are united by a link, and this bond of union is a link which also has two ends; and these require each a fresh link to connect them with the old."[5] As Bradley says, "this problem is insoluble."[6] A is related to B, but A is related to its relation, and its relation-to-its-relation is related in all directions, et cetera, to infinity. The matter ends with logic and common sense exploded into fractured atoms.

It is beyond question that Eliot at the time of writing *The Waste Land* had issues such as the above on his mind and, moreover, that he was alert to the problematic nature of structures and to the way in which they displayed a radical instability. He believed with Bradley that no object (point of attention under one aspect) can last for long even if (impossible, in any case) the subject and his environment remain still. Mental focus is always moving, causing foregrounds and backgrounds, edges and centers, causes and effects, nows and thens, movements and stillnesses, to change places with each other as rapidly as concave and convex alternate in an optical illusion. With Bradley's help, Eliot had arrived at a vision of a kaleidoscopic world that is always ready to break, re-form, and burst in the violet atmosphere of his mind.

Consider, as a way back to *The Waste Land*, that Eliot's concentration on these ideas was most intense during the years between 1914 and 1917 when he was learning the harrowing consequences of marriage to a woman with severe emotional problems, feeling the stress of abandoning his career, his family, and his native country. These stresses, the "lived experiences" of the poem, were magnified and validated by his awareness of the daily catastrophes of the war. At some point, we can be sure, the philosophic exercises ceased to be mere concepts and became keys for understanding both his personal sets of broken relations and the ruptures that seemed to be destroying Europe. From this viewpoint, Tristan, Isolde, the hyacinth lovers, and all of the pained figures in *The Waste Land* can be seen as manifestations of himself. His choice of German figures at the beginning and of the Wagnerian references in counterpoint with English settings may also have been suggested by the war. At any rate, this "relief of a personal and wholly insignificant grouse against life," as he called *The Waste Land*,[7] was, without contradiction of any kind, a picture of a world that seemed to be acting out in history a series of technical arguments on the incertitude of relations.

We can now consider the episode of the lovers in detail. There are seven figures involved, five of them major and two of them secondary. The major figures are Tristan, Isolde, King Mark, the hyacinth girl, and her lover. The secondary figures are the singer of the quoted song to Isolde and the messenger who tells Tristan that the sea is waste and empty. Looking at the episode in this detailed way reveals that no direct communication between any of the lovers is rendered. A sailor sings to Isolde, a messenger speaks to Tristan, the hyacinth girl commemorates the anniversary of an experience in the garden, and her lover recalls an experience that shut her out of his awareness along with all other phenomena, "Looking into the heart of light, the silence." In both frame and its content, a lack of communication between major figures is placed into the foreground. They are foregrounded in a way, however, that reveals through the given surfaces a background in which passionate communication has occurred. Between *"Frisch weht der Wind"* and *"Oed' und leer das Meer,"* Tristan and Isolde consummate an ecstatic and disastrous love, and King Mark and Isolde consummate an arranged marriage. In addition, the contemporary lovers remember a passionate encounter of a year earlier, an experience which led to a profound alteration of consciousness. In formal terms, those observations suggest that however much ergon and parergon continue to oscillate, they stand collectively as a compound frame or parergon for an ergon of background passions suffered by all five of the central figures. On this level of analysis, the same instability as previously noted makes problematic the relations between frames and contents. Isolation of lovers is presented as central, but this isolation in turn frames a known background which shows not isolation but intense and ecstatic union.

In the Tristan story, the love affair and the tragedy are precipitated by a love potion. The drug substitutes a contrived set of feelings for those that would normally prevail. This folk convention (the love potion and its consequences) is an important aspect of the Tristan story. In this passage, it serves as a counterbalance to the modern lover's report of an experience of an altered state of consciousness. As in "A Game of Chess" and "Portrait of a Lady," the woman's words are in quotation marks and supposedly direct speech, whereas the man's words are without quotation marks and presumably represent his thoughts.

> "You gave me hyacinths first a year ago;
> "They called me the hyacinth girl."
> —Yet when we came back, late, from the Hyacinth garden,
> Your arms full, and your hair wet, I could not
> Speak, and my eyes failed, I was neither
> Living nor dead, and I knew nothing
> Looking into the heart of light, the silence.

This passage is reminiscent of a moment of stasis which Eliot presents in his unpublished poem "Silence" (1910),[8] and it also recalls Gerontion's statement that he has lost all five of his senses. At any rate, it seems to be an experience that Eliot felt strongly about on a personal level. The phrase "heart of light," which was to reappear years later in "Burnt Norton," is particularly interesting. It is the kind of phrase found frequently in the literature of mysticism to describe moments of ineffable transcendence. It is also an obvious inversion of Conrad's heart of darkness, in which light, suggesting knowledge as it did a few lines earlier among "stony rubbish" and "broken images," is presented as perhaps more terrifying than darkness. The Conrad passage, as we have pointed out, had been Eliot's first choice for an epigraph for The Waste Land, discarded with reluctance when Pound didn't think it was right.

The preceding observations, taken together, form an interpretative environment which must be seen as surrounding the passage. They do not, however, yield a precise reading. To put it as directly as possible, the lover reports on an experience of having been unable to interpret his condition. But the experience happened to him a year before he reports on it, and his report consists of a contradictory interpretation of the condition of not being able to make any interpretations while, at the same time, being able to look directly into the inner essence of light. He says that his eyes failed and speaks of looking into a synaesthetic light and silence. The more we consider his report, the more curious it becomes. Synaesthesia is the blending of two or more of the five senses—"smooth, sweet, music," for example—and the speaker has an experience of the loss of his senses as a prelude to a synaesthetic fusion of sight and hearing, light and silence. Like the blind Tiresias, he "sees." If "heart" means center, then light, the medium of vision, is a frame for silence, the medium of isolation from knowledge. From a Hegelian perspective, the moment reveals the inseparability of Being and Nothingness if the first is suggested by the nonvisual vision of light and the second is suggested by the contained condition of silence. The most likely conclusion on the experience, however, is that it represents a moment of immediate experience in the Bradleian sense. Immediate experience, as we have pointed out, comes before consciousness of knowing. It involves infinitesimal moments, before perceptions have been organized into subjective and objective polarities. Further, as Eliot argues near the end of the first chapter of his dissertation, immediate experience does not happen anywhere to anyone. Only by the failure of experience to be immediate—by its having broken down into relational experience—do we have time, space, and selves. It is, he concludes, "annihilation and utter night." Eliot appears to have provided his character with an opening onto this timeless and selfless ground upon which time and selfhood are built. For the character, it is a reversion to a primal state, the place where he started, here known for the first time. We must remember, however, that Eliot's concern is the failure of love, but the memory after the consummation in the garden is ultimately a far more spectacular experience than anything Wagner provides. If love has failed, it has failed in an awesome way.

The fourth episode of "The Burial of the Dead" repeats, in a less obvious way, the formal ambiguity of frame and content. The first three and a half lines introduce Madame Sosostris in a tone of casual flippancy, and the last three lines conclude her speech with a return to a similar tone. In the center, she plays her role as a modern sibyl, dealing out cards, giving oracular warnings, and reporting on visions in a contrasting tone of seriousness.

> Madame Sosostris, famous clairvoyante,
> Had a bad cold, nevertheless
> Is known to be the wisest woman in Europe,
> With a wicked pack of cards. Here, said she,
> Is your card, the drowned Phoenician Sailor,
> (Those are pearls that were his eyes. Look!)
> Here is Belladonna, the Lady of the Rocks,
> The lady of situations.
> Here is the man with three staves, and here the Wheel,
> And here is the one-eyed merchant, and this card,
> Which is blank, is something he carries on his back,
> Which I am forbidden to see. I do not find
> The Hanged Man. Fear death by water.
> I see crowds of people, walking round in a ring.
> Thank you. If you see dear Mrs. Equitone,
> Tell her I bring the horoscope myself:
> One must be so careful these days.

Most commentaries on Madame Sosostris say that she is a contemporary debasement of the seers and oracles of myth, of which the Sibyl of Cumae and Tiresias are the most immediate examples. Such commentaries, of course, are responses to the tonalities at the beginning and end of the episode. These comments are somewhat helpful, but they are limited in that they are focused primarily on the trivial frame rather than the more serious contents; that is, they are the result of the reversal of parergon and ergon, frame and picture. The modern seer is framed by a tone of fashionable silliness, but what she sees in the central part of the episode is in a sense the whole poem. What Eliot said of Tiresias, that what he sees is the substance of the poem, is true in a fragmentary way of Madame Sosostris. In the early typescript, her speech was even more portentous, for it included a line from one of the greatest of all seers, Saint John the Divine: "I John saw these things, and heard them" (Rev. 22:8),[9] which means that, however fantastic "these things" may seem to be, they are actually true. Interestingly, in spite of the frivolous frame, in spite of seeing Madame Sosostris as a preposterous personage symbolizing modern decadence and the decay of religion, virtually all commentaries take seriously the need to interpret the cards she mentions and the tarot pack itself. The insufficiency of such readings lies partially in the failure to note the oscillation of frivolous frame and serious center.

Several helpful points emerge from attention to Eliot's structure in this passage. The first lines, the first half of the frame, are spoken by a person who introduces Madame Sosostris and who establishes a tone she herself adopts at the end of the episode. Though quotation marks are not used, everything beginning with "Here, said she," with the possible exception of the line from *The Tempest*, is presented as the seer's directly rendered speech. In the second half of the frame, then, the blending of the narrator's tone and the seer's words merges the two speakers. Taking note of this formal arrangement places the reader in a perspective to transcend the figures represented. This is accomplished as follows: The reader sees that narrator and the narrated voice of Madame Sosostris are, at the end, one; he sees, moreover, that the figures the seer speaks of reside within that compound of seer, narrator, and himself as reader. From the reader's perspective, all of these entities become adjectives (bundles of qualities) modifying themselves. The figures and the seer have no stable relation; neither do the seer and the narrator. There is a unifying perspective from outside the frame, deriving from the consciousness of the reader. But this unifying perspective cannot last, because focus of attention invariably moves back and forth from level to level of concern and back and forth between perception of center as frame and frame as center.

Another point can be made regarding the opening and closing lines, the framing element of the passage. The opening reflects incoherence, and the closing reflects paranoia. The narrator begins by announcing that Madame Sosostris is known to be the wisest woman in Europe, in spite of the fact that she has a bad cold. This is equivalent to hearing the news solemnly reported that Einstein is known to have been a great physicist in spite of the discovery that he sometimes had indigestion. The double voice of the last lines reveals that Madame Sosostris is an unduly cautious woman who fears that unknown persons may intercept the horoscope on its way to "dear Mrs. Equitone." Like most oracles, she fears an area of

events that she knows she cannot foresee. Both knowledge and the
pretense of knowledge, along with a gray area between them, lead
to an intensification of concern with what cannot be known. It could
be said, of course, that the paranoia is simply a pretense to inflate
the apparent value of the horoscope, but that is to say that where
paranoia does not exist it has to be invented. In either case, the
framing passages direct attention to the relation between incoherence and paranoia. The relation seems to be that paranoia
provides a counterbalance to incoherence. It does so by conferring
an imagined structure, an illusory coherence upon the world that
lies outside of what one actually knows. This point can be developed and clarified only after we consider the material inside the
frame: the process of divination through card reading.

The cards are dealt out specifically for the person who speaks the
episode's opening lines, the person who needs either coherence or
the knowledge that it is lacking. His or her card is the drowned
Phoenician Sailor, and even though the other cards are apparently
dealt in the same process for the same person, Madame Sosostris
ignores them and concludes with a warning to fear death by water.
Following the principle of internal interpretation which we have
discussed, the passage is noteworthy for its use of selective reading.
Madame Sosostris deals out six cards (eight if the "Lady of the
Rocks" and the "lady of situations" are taken as representing individual cards) but chooses to interpret only one. By some method,
Madame Sosostris knows which cards to ignore. (Perhaps she
chooses the drowned sailor because it is the only card that signifies
any specific fate.) Within the passage, incoherence is dominant.
Various cards, as Eliot says in his note, point to figures and episodes
elsewhere in the poem, but these cards and the directions of meaning they introduce do not fix a clear set of relations between the
cards. The Lady of the Rocks, for example, may be Marie, because
Marie feels free in the mountains; the Wheel may suggest the cycles
of nature or the helm of the ship in "Death by Water." This process
of inventing connections, however, does not lead to reliable messages or to an understanding of why Madame Sosostris does not
regard those cards as worthy of interpretative activity. One card (or
the absence of one) seems designed for the reader. Eliot notes that
he associates the Hanged Man (the missing card) with the sacrificial

hero in Frazer and with the hooded, hallucinatory figure in "What the Thunder Said." His absence suggests the irrelevance of salvation through the death of a savior type. Both presences and absences, however, remain as random reminders of both incoherence and uninterpretability. And since Eliot is candid in noting that his interpretations are both private and arbitrary, it is more than usually hubristic for critics to claim an ability to discover definitive meanings in the cards.

The one clear aspect of the passage is its presentation of randomness. Divination through card dealing is a form of the ancient oracular practice of sortilege, that is, of looking for knowledge in the results of a set of chance events. Soothsayers, for example, find messages in the spots or the entrails of animals ("presaging sausages," as Juvenal put it) or draw conclusions from the pattern made when a handful of bones is cast on the ground. In fact, they take any pattern perceived to be beyond human intentionality as an occasion for sortilege. Without an organized concept of chance, they see randomness as a window on the world of the gods who control the universe, a window through which a trained eye can read divine messages. In *The Roots of Coincidence*, Arthur Koestler notes that actuaries now can predict how many people in New York will be bitten by dogs each year. How, he asks, do the dogs know how often they are supposed to bite people?[10] The question, of course, is mistaken, but only in recent centuries has that realization become evident. The assumption for thousands of years has been that chance events are the interventions of a teleological intelligence into the world and that they are worthy of the seriousness attached to the words of the gods and their transcendent messengers. Contemporaneity, then, is stressed in the framing tonality of the episode, and antiquity is simulated in its central passage. From the first perspective, sortilege is meaningless; from the second, it is so charged with meaning that very little of it can be understood. The reader is left with two coexisting problems of knowledge: too little of it and too much. A binary perception yields two kinds of defeated perception, but a level that joins them yields an aesthetically fascinating blend of significant meaninglessness and meaningful insignificance.

80

Eliot's interest in chance (indeterminancy) and its relation to truth is paralleled by the interest of many scientists and artists in the early twentieth century. *The Waste Land*, in fact, was born in the context of the modern tradition articulated by Mallarmé's "A Throw of the Dice Never Will Abolish Chance," dadaism, Heisenberg's indeterminancy theory in physics, and Lautréamont's definition of a poem as the chance encounter between an umbrella and a sewing machine on a dissecting table. This modernist focus on chance includes, in philosophy, Bradley's critique of relations, which seems to abolish both chance and design, and also Nietzsche's casual attacks on what now are called transcendental signifiers. The notion that an idea can exist apart from the words that signify it is the foundation of both the Platonic and the Aristotelian tradition of thought. The assumed metaphysical sequence is, first, the concept that forms language; second, the words so formed in a mind; and third, the expression of those words to transfer the concept into other minds which can receive them only because they are already furnished with the same but not yet verbalized concept. In *Ulysses*, Stephen thinks derisively of "the Father, Word, and Holy Breath."[11] In Eliot's youth, the process was reversed by most philosophers. Words (conventional signs) came first, and only then could they be structured into concepts. The logos came at the end, not at the beginning. Truth, then, cannot be derived from a technique of divination like self-imbued trances, sortilege, or any of the other activities of oracles.

To return to the counterbalance of incoherence and paranoia: the first, as noted above, motivates the second. And as noted in our first chapter, in modern art and science chance has replaced causality, indeterminancy has replaced determinancy; in other words, incoherence and discontinuity have usurped the place of causality and continuity in both our physics and our metaphysics. "One must be so careful these days" because the contingencies of the world are now regarded as merely contingent. Things are only there. They are not there for a transcendent purpose, and they are not arranged in any knowable way. They cannot even be trusted to be entirely random. Some events are intended, some are not, and it is usually hard to tell the difference. This emphasis on chance can be related to the modern motif of paranoia. The word "paranoia" comes from Greek roots meaning "other mind." When one senses the presence "out there" of some design-making intelligence, that sense becomes profoundly important as an intuition of meaning in the universe. This intuition is comforting even when the other mind is suspected of insidious intentions. In this context, randomness can be seen as a way of bypassing meaninglessness, of bypassing one's own mind, and going directly to the intuited other mind. Incoherence in the first mind, of course, is still a sign of error, but that special form of incoherence called randomness can be a sign of perfect knowledge if it seems to come from the second or other mind. It should be noted that the monuments of modernism, such as *The Waste Land*, *Ulysses*, the *Cantos*, atonal music, and cubist art, all share the coexistence of an appearance of randomness with a readily discernible theory of design. We will have more to say on this mixture of transitionless form and careful structuring in our final chapter.

We have already considered an important aspect of the fifth and final episode in "The Burial of the Dead," the speech to Stetson as an illustration of certain consequences of relational knowledge. Unlike the preceding two segments, on the lovers and the oracle, this one does not begin and end with specifically given framing material, though as we shall note later, a frame is generated by associations and allusions.

> Unreal City,
> Under the brown fog of a winter dawn,
> A crowd flowed over London Bridge, so many,
> I had not thought death had undone so many.
> Sighs, short and infrequent, were exhaled,
> And each man fixed his eyes before his feet.
> Flowed up the hill and down King William Street,
> To where Saint Mary Woolnoth kept the hours
> With a dead sound on the final stroke of nine.
> There I saw one I knew, and stopped him, crying "Stetson!
> "You who were with me in the ships at Mylae!
> "That corpse you planted last year in your garden,
> "Has it begun to sprout? Will it bloom this year?
> "Or has the sudden frost disturbed its bed?

82

> "Oh keep the Dog far hence, that's friend to men,
> "Or with his nails he'll dig it up again!
> "You! hypocrite lecteur!—mon semblable,—mon frère!"

The opening lines of this section establish an ontologically unstable setting which oscillates between the images of real and mythic city. In formal terms, this means that the relations are already deliquescing and reconstituting themselves in rapid succession. The crowd is "flowing," and the speaker quotes Dante's reaction to the Vestibule of Hell with the line, "I had not thought death had undone so many." The scene is usually described as "death-in-life," an interpretative term which in our view distorts the passage. The relation of the scene to Ante-Hell is sometimes conveyed by quoting a formula such as Shelley's "Hell is a city much like London—/A populous and smoky city."[12] These and virtually all unitive descriptions falsify the scene by not recognizing that the city is at once both real and unreal, both London in 1922 and Ante-Hell as Dante presented it. In a photograph, this scene would be a double exposure, two cities that have the overlapping and faceted arrangement of cubism, both of them controlled as images by the term "unreal." As with the case of the concave convex alternation in optical illusions, the two scenes cannot be perceived simultaneously and their oscillation cannot be stopped. Here there is no question of ergon parergon reversal because neither city image is established as central.

The real/unreal city scene may be thought of in terms of cursive and recursive images. A familiar example of cursive and recursive images is the picture that at one moment shows two faces in profile looking at each other and at another moment a vase or urn. There is no way to tell which image is cursive and which recursive, but the viewer will tend to regard the first one seen as cursive and the other as recursive. He may try to fix the profiled faces and the urn into a single image, but he will be unable to unify and stabilize the doubleness without destroying the picture's most important characteristics. The same observation can be extended to Eliot's real/unreal city. Imposing illusions of unitive or stabilizing interpretations distorts and blurs the beauty of the entire passage.

These observations about the impropriety of merging cursive and recursive images into stable and unitive structures undercut the notion that modern literature is characterized by simultaneity. Joseph Frank, in his valuable theory of spatial form, argues quite persuasively that simultaneity is the goal of much modern literature. Such devices as ambiguity, irony, and self-referential structures, he maintains, are designed to subvert the work's verbal linearity and gather its parts together into a simultaneous complex. Thus he argues that Eliot's poem refers mainly to itself (instead of to anything outside of itself) and cannot be understood until it is reread and held all at once in memory. Pound's famous definition of a poetic image as an intellectual and emotional complex perceived in a single moment of time is excellent support for Frank's argument, and so, in another way, is Eliot's passage in part 5 of "Burnt Norton":

> Words move, music moves
> Only in time; but that which is only living
> Can only die. Words, after speech, reach
> Into the silence. Only by the form, the pattern,
> Can words or music reach
> The stillness, as a Chinese jar still
> Moves perpetually in its stillness.
> Not the stillness of the violin, while the note lasts,
> Not that only, but the co-existence,
> Or say that the end precedes the beginning,
> And the end and the beginning were always there
> Before the beginning and after the end.
> And all is always now.

The difficulty, however, is that neither reading nor seeing permits simultaneity of perceptions. And Eliot, as the rest of the verse paragraph from "Burnt Norton" clearly shows, was aware of the problem. "Words strain, . . ./Decay with imprecision, will not stay in place,/Will not stay still." Cursive and recursive must alternate in time, and semantic ambiguities must be understood in a sequence of ideas. Take, for example, "After the frosty silence in the gardens," the second line in "What the Thunder Said." It refers, in part and in any sequence, to Gethsemane, Stetson's garden, the hyacinth garden, Marie's Hofgarten, the Garden of Eden's "sylvan scene" (line 98), the antigarden of branches in stony rubbish, the

84

rose garden in "Burnt Norton," and on and on to no definite limit. Regardless of the order in which a mind takes note of these gardens, and regardless of how arduously that mind works to make them coexist in a single moment, they will always remain a sequence in time. It is a different kind of time from that experienced in moving from word to word as read in sequence, but it is not a spatial simultaneity. It is paralinguistic time, a succession that moves at a different rate from the rate at which the language that generates it moves.

To return to the "Unreal City" episode: situated in this fluctuating scene (and thus cursive and recursive himself), the speaker reports what he sees, thinks, and says. Like Dante in Ante-Hell (who as a tourist is not there in the same way as the figures he sees) and like any Londoner on the street at the morning rush hour, he sees an acquaintance and addresses him. As noted earlier, his speech illustrates the codes of nonmythic or relational consciousness. His speech can now be understood to illustrate oscillation between different time frames. When he speaks of being with Stetson in the ships at Mylae, he is in the kind of long time frame that can exist in the afterlife. In the next three lines, by contrast, he asks questions about "last year" and "this year." He follows his references to recent past and present with a warning about the immediate future and, therefore, is back in secular time. At this point, he addresses Stetson as "hypocrite lecteur!—mon semblable,—mon frère!" This line, the last one in "The Burial of the Dead," shatters all the cursive and recursive patterns noted so far. This sudden change demands careful consideration.

In his note on "Unreal City," Eliot directs attention to the opening lines of Baudelaire's "Seven Old Men," a poem included in *Les Fleurs du Mal*:

> *Fourmillante cité, cité pleine de rêves*
> *Où le spectre en plein jour raccroche le passant.*[13]

> [Swarming city, city full of dreams,
> Where the phantom accosts the passer-by in plain daylight.]

This note adds Paris to the complex of cities presented. If taken in a straightforward way, it makes the speaker a phantom or ghost who accosts a living person in broad daylight in the secular city. This reading is the symmetrical opposite of the Dantean perspective, where the speaker is a living person who accosts a specter in the unreal city of Ante-Hell. The "Fourmillante cité" line, like the "hypocrite lecteur" line that concludes the section, is also from *Les Fleurs du Mal*, and thus Baudelaire's volume suddenly emerges as a frame for the section. Flowers growing out of evil or corruption, beauty from decay, repeat the image of a garden that may bloom if the rotting corpse is kept buried. The Baudelairean frame, thus, adds several layers to the episode and energizes the feeling that it makes no difference whether the speaker is alive in contemporaneity or dead in a mythic city.

The last line of the "Unreal City" paragraph addresses the reader directly, but as continuation of an address to Stetson it also identifies him as a hypocrite lecteur, an identification which provides a fascinating twist.[14] In both technique and content, the last line focuses on problematic relations and on the grotesque reductionism resulting from the scientific explanation of the victim of vegetation rites as a kind of fertilizer. Calling Stetson a hypocrite points to his participation in this narrowly relational way of thinking. The speaker realizes that he himself exists on several planes in perpetual oscillation, and he reminds Stetson that contrary to his pretense, whether he is in London or the vestibule of hell or Paris, he is also trapped in unstable relations. Calling Stetson a reader is far more interesting than calling him a hypocrite. The Stetson passage was introduced with the words, "There I saw one I knew, and stopped him, crying 'Stetson!' " Beyond all possibility of misunderstanding, Stetson is a hearer not a reader, and the following passage is *cried*, not written. Nevertheless, Stetson is a reader. We might say that he is the listener to a speech that comes from a cursive-recursive source and that he is also Baudelaire's reader. It is much more to the point, however, to realize that the last line of the passage draws our attention to the "crying" speech as something that is written down on paper and only through the conventions of reading is mistaken for something spoken aloud.

Baudelaire's poem "Au lecteur" (from which Eliot's last line was taken) clearly functions as a comment on the conventions of reading. It is composed as a poem to be spoken and heard, but it insists on the fictive quality of that transaction. The fact is that the poem is written and read. It is hypocrisy to pretend that one is a listener where one is only a decoder of visual signs. Most important, the issue draws attention to the fundamental synaesthesia of written language. The reader sees words and as a result hears them. In the passage at hand, Eliot uses Baudelaire to bring the fact of synaesthesia into conscious (in Bradleian terms, "relational") focus. By bringing the conventional synaesthesia of reading into relational consciousness, he deconstructs it by forcing the reader to note that it is a convention. In other words, he is writing a poem which shows the most deeply rooted convention in poetry falling into pieces; that is, he reveals the dualistic underpinning of the conventions of reading.

In the "Unreal City" passage, then, Eliot takes Baudelaire as a model for self-reflexive shifts from writing as speech to speech as writing. He had other models as well. Mallarmé's "Throw of the Dice" uses several type sizes and arrangements of words on facing pages, in part to call attention to the conventions of reading; and Joyce's *Ulysses* plays at every opportunity with the conventions of his art. In this regard, it should be noted that the beginning of *The Waste Land* is prefaced by an elaborate arrangement of title, dedication, epigraph in two languages, and subtitle, all calling attention to themselves as written, not spoken, items. These items are not only written; they are printed, as the variety of type sizes and quotations in italics make plain. Almost as much as Swift's *Tale of a Tub*, the poem presents itself as a book, a manufactured object. The title page of *The Waste Land* can now be seen with the "hypocrite lecteur" line as still another kind of framing device and still another collapse of a supposed unity into a problematic relation.

What we have observed so far about "The Burial of the Dead" is that its internal relations, on any level of intentional focus, are unstable and variable. We have also observed that such relations as past and present, statement and interpretation, frame and center, narrator and subject of narrative, speech and writing, have become problematic because they have been rendered in the poem as issues to deal with consciously. As deconstructionist critics have illustrated, a reader can decide to read any text in such a way as to show its underlying instability of relations. Eliot, however, has presented a text that is already, in many ways, deconstructed. It is not necessary to go into the details of deconstruction theory to make this point. It is sufficient to observe that some of the most commonly held assumptions about how things are related are shown in the poem to be mere conventional constructs, habitual fictions.

The synaesthesia of writing as speech is the simplest example. Readers are so accustomed to the convention of reading words as though they are hearing voices that they are not conscious, usually, of the complex set of mental transformations they are performing. It is particularly illuminating, on this issue, to note what Egyptologists have discovered about the earliest translatable writings. Almost all surviving texts from the first thousand years of writing in Egypt are inventories and records of commercial transactions. Only a few inscriptions of a religious or quasi-literary kind are known. Those texts say that with the help of the gods they will be able to speak. "Please help these marks to cry aloud their song," they say, to use a loose paraphrase. In the beginning of writing, it is highly likely that the transformation of visual signs into spoken words was a magical event that did not always occur and that depended on divine intervention. These inscriptions were also self-reflexive; their subject matter was themselves. With modernism, even if the term is stretched to include such attacks on modernity as those of Swift, the long history of learning to hear seen shapes takes a swerve backward, toward its origins.

In our view, then, the many attempts to demonstrate that *The Waste Land* is unified are mistaken. The argument that the poem is unified by the presence of a single voice or persona is, again in our view, doubly misguided. It is misguided, first, because the poem makes so many shifts in scene, tonality, and language that the effort to defend the notion of a single voice forces the critic into unseemly mental gymnastics. Some of Eliot's oldest and best critics (Grover Smith, for example)[15] argue that a single narrator, such as Tiresias or Perceval or Marie, narrates the entire poem; some of Eliot's more recent critics (Calvin Bedient, for example)[16] argue that a single eccentric projects all the voices in the text, that he or she does "the police in different voices." These critics appear to be working from an assumption that a poem cannot be a good work of art if it is not unified in this way. In our view, that assumption is one of the conventional expectations Eliot is most at pains to root out, make conscious, and destroy. From a perspective within the poem, and from a perspective within any contemporaneous reading process, *The Waste Land* consists of many messages from a variety of sources. From an imagined mythic perspective that synthesizes the straight time line of subjectivity and the cyclical time line of objective nature, the characters and their interpretations melt into each other. A reading from either perspective is mistaken; only a process of taking note of their rapid oscillation allows a reading experience of the text as it stands. That experience is a notation of the difficult and yet necessary awareness of the interpenetrations of relational and transcendent experience.

Another reason why the argument that *The Waste Land* is unified by the presence of a single narrator must be abandoned is that it is based on the unexamined supposition that poems are a form of speech rather than writing. "Phonocentrism" is the habit of seeing printed words as frames or as media that convey the sound of a speaking voice and, with it, the presence of a person resonating his words. This habit of generating a present person from an imagined voice runs counter to a text like *The Waste Land* that, to use the terms of Worringer discussed in our first chapter, is characterized far more by abstraction than by empathy. Empathy, as Worringer uses it, involves the generation of presence and a movement toward merger with that present figure. For example, when Marie reports on her fear on the sled and quotes her cousin saying "Marie, Marie, hold on tight," the reader experiences the muscularity of that fear, the kinesthesia of the descent. "Hold on tight" creates empathy and a space that includes the reader along with the speaker. Phonocentrism, generated presence, and empathy are appropriate to that moment in the poem and to many other isolated moments, most memorably the physically arduous journey through the mountains in "What the Thunder Said." But the sudden shifts without transition, the intrusions of unforeseeable material, the oscillations of perspectives, the presentation of characters drawn in minimalist style—the "one-eyed merchant," for example, who has only one eye because he is only an image in profile on a card—all push the experience of the poem away from the kinesthesia, or evocations of muscular tension, away from empathy toward the remoteness from spatial presence that we call abstraction. Empathy and abstraction are dialectic polarities in the poem, and perhaps the two are conceivably unified from the binary perspective discussed in our previous chapter. Any imaginable unity, however, must allow for the variability of voice tonalities and the insistence of printed words to be seen first and heard later.

We conclude our reading of "The Burial of the Dead" with the observation that its five distinct episodes are not directly related to each other. Marie, the son of man, the lovers, the oracle, and the unreal city occupy separate modules like an arrangement of framed pictures in a gallery. Their existence under one subtitle is of course a principal way in which they are related. It is possible to see reasons for the order in which they appear, but these reasons are not conclusive. Of course, anyone can invent reasons why they must remain as they are and reasons why they should be seen as directly related, but most of those reasons will depend on extensive mental excursions into the contexts of background works. For example, as G. L. K. Morris pointed out in the 1950s and as Valerie Eliot substantiates in *The Waste Land Facsimile*,[17] Marie probably derives from the Countess Marie Larisch as she appears in her autobiography *My Past*. A whole system of relations and connections can be organized around the details in her autobiography. In fact, a journey into the deep background of this one allusion can enable a reader to merge all of the different modules, connect all of the broken images, and impose unity on the poem. But such sleuthing habits create more problems than they solve. The principal problem facing the sleuthhound is that the poem tends to expand to the size of the full context of each of its allusions and, further, to the size of each allusion in those works. The text thereby shrinks to an infinitesimal datum in contrast to the referential material required to impose an order on it. Any process of discovering relevance in the deep backgrounds of allusions mandates decisions about how to select and how far to go, and more often than not, these decisions cannot survive critical scrutiny. The autobiography of the Countess Marie Larisch, to return to our example, does form an interpretative environment for the poem, but it also forms in most readers a temptation to force the parts into a connectedness they simply do not possess.

It is most in accord with the text as it stands to hold that the episodes of "The Burial of the Dead" are not directly related to each

other. Their allusive relation comes not from their outside references but from references to later parts of the poem. Tristan and
Isolde, for example, form a motif that is repeated and varied with
references to Antony and Cleopatra (line 77), Dido and Aeneas (line
92), Adam and Eve (line 98), Philomela and Tereus (lines 99–100,
203–6), Elizabeth and Leicester (line 279), and Siegfried and Brun-
hilde (lines 277–78, 290–91). A parallel series of variations is initiated by the hyacinth lovers: the nervous woman and her consort in
"A Game of Chess," Lil and Albert, "nymphs" and city directors,
Sweeney and Mrs. Porter, Mr. Eugenides and the speaker who is
propositioned at line 212, the typist and clerk, the three Thames
daughters (lines 292 ff.), and the pair involved in the passage "your
heart would have responded/Gaily, when invited, beating obe-
dient/To controlling hands" (lines 421–23). Structurally similar sets
of variations emerge from each of the other episodes of "The Burial
of the Dead." Beyond the obvious examples, we can cite the mountains where Marie feels free, which return as ominous shapes in
"What the Thunder Said." The attempt to find and interpret transcendent signifiers, which is the purpose driving Madame Sosostris, returns in the story of the Buddhist priests trying to discover
the messages hidden in the voice of Prajapati, lord of thunder. The
bells of Saint Mary Woolnoth return in part V with the inverted
towers "Tolling reminiscent bells, that kept the hours" (line 384).
These citations could go on for several more pages, but that hardly
seems necessary. We should note, however, that one of the more
memorable passages from part V is another variation on the episode
of Marie.

> My friend, blood shaking my heart
> The awful daring of a moment's surrender
> Which an age of prudence can never retract
> By this, and this only, we have existed
> Which is not to be found in our obituaries
> Or in memories draped by the beneficent spider
> Or under seals broken by the lean solicitor
> In our empty rooms

These lines seem to have been prefigured by Marie's childhood
decision to "hold on tight" and surrender to fear by saying yes to a
perilous and irreversible descent.

These patterns, it should be noted, refer backward as well as forward. From the perspective of the poem's last section, the separate modules of "The Burial of the Dead" possess a unity that they could not possibly have had when initially encountered. From a reversed perspective, Marie's interpretations and memories, the son of man's "agony in stony places" (line 324), his walking shadow (lines 360–66), the seer's cards, the unreal cities, the desire to put Stetson's lands in order, all seem like aspects of a single narrative. When the multitude of other motif variations are cataloged, with the critical eye limited to material either literally present in the poem or directly adjacent to it in the foregrounds of allusions, the whole poem becomes a series of separated modules with no necessary causal or temporal or spatial relations to each other but held together by interlocking variations.

To put it another way, the poem requires a transcendent reading process. In this context, we use the term "transcendent" to mean only the transition from a narrow focus to a wider one. For example, the reader might at one moment concentrate on one word, "*Datta.*" Movement to a concentration on its immediate context—"what have we given?" and so on—is a transcendence to a larger group of signs. Moving from one level to the next is a movement through a series of transcendences toward a point of focusing on the poem as a whole. This description of transcendent reading could fit any text, from *Hamlet* to a shopping list, but it fits *The Waste Land* in a distinctive way. This distinctiveness results from the way it forces us to become aware of consciously making these transcendences. Here Bradley's analysis of knowledge and our reconstruction of the analogies Eliot might have made between that analysis and mythic consciousness are helpful as a description of what the poem is doing to us and what we are doing to the poem. Bradley, as we have discussed in some detail, analyzed knowledge into the three sequential phases of immediate, relational, and transcendent experience. The first is unified and unconscious, the second is disunified and conscious, and the third transcends the first two in a complex in which the paradox of their union, along with all other paradoxes, vanishes from the cognitive setting altogether. The kind of consciousness that transcends contraries enough to see no obstruction to belief in gods and their doctrines, or to accept a field of mere juxtapositions as a unity, is both mythic consciousness and the kind of consciousness *The Waste Land* asks its readers to achieve as the final phase of a series of transcendences in reading. Insofar as the reader is laboring to form the connections of backward and forward references upon which transcendent reading depends, he or she is in Bradley's relational phase. But the reader who has at once surrendered to the text and who perseveres in reading it will find that the conscious labor of reading is a stage leading toward a transcendence where relations are no longer a problem and the absurdity of feeling the poem as a unitive whole is no longer an absurdity but a simple fact. Careful readers can feel the approach toward such a perspective in every shift to a larger level. In the more comprehensive and more unified perspectives, they will experience (and this is a crucial point) both the actual disunity and the potential unity of the poem at the same time. These contraries occupy the fields seen from the binary perspective which the process of reading *The Waste Land* requires.

4 / Amalgamating Disparate Experience

Myth and Gender in "A Game of Chess"

> When a poet's mind is perfectly equipped for its work, it is constantly amalgamating disparate experience; the ordinary man's experience is chaotic, irregular, fragmentary. The latter falls in love, or reads Spinoza, and these two experiences have nothing to do with each other, or with the noise of the typewriter or the smell of cooking; in the mind of the poet these experiences are always forming new wholes.—Eliot, "The Metaphysical Poets" (1921)

Eliot's understanding of poetic epistemology is a version of Bradley's theory, outlined in our second chapter, that knowing involves immediate, relational, and transcendent stages or levels. The poetic mind, like the ordinary mind, has at least two types of experience: The first consists largely of feeling (falling in love, smelling the cooking, hearing the noise of the typewriter), the second largely of thought (reading Spinoza). The first type of experience is sensuous, and it is also to a great extent monistic or immediate, for it does not require mediation through the mind; it exists before intellectual analysis, before the falling apart of experience into experiencer and experienced. The second type of experience, in contrast, is intellectual (to be known at all, it must be mediated through the mind) and sharply dualistic, in that it involves a breaking down of experience into subject and object. In the mind of the ordinary person, these two types of experience are and remain disparate. In the mind of the poet, these disparate experiences are somehow transcended and amalgamated into a new whole, a whole beyond and yet including subject and object, mind and matter. Eliot illustrates his explanation of poetic epistemology by saying that John Donne did not simply feel his feelings and think his thoughts; he felt his thoughts and thought his feelings. He was able to "feel his thought as immediately as the odour of a rose."[1] "Immediately" in this famous simile is a technical term in philosophy, used with precision; it means unmediated through mind, unshattered into subject and object.

Falling in love and reading Spinoza typify Eliot's own experiences

94

in the years in which he was writing *The Waste Land*. These were the exciting and exhausting years in which he met Vivien Haigh-Wood and consummated a disastrous marriage, the years in which he was deeply involved in reading F. H. Bradley, the years in which he was torn between the professions of philosophy and poetry and in which he was in close and frequent contact with such brilliant and stimulating figures as Bertrand Russell and Ezra Pound, the years of the break from his family and homeland, the years in which in every area of his life he seemed to be between broken worlds. The experiences of these years constitute the material of *The Waste Land*. The relevant biographical details need not be reviewed here, for they are presented in the introduction to *The Waste Land Facsimile*. For our purposes, it is only necessary to acknowledge what Eliot himself acknowledged: the material of art is always actual life.[2] At the same time, it should also be noted that material in itself is not art. As Eliot argued in his review of *Ulysses*, "in creation you are responsible for what you can do with material which you must simply accept."[3] For Eliot, the given material included relations with and observations of women, in particular, of his bright but seemingly incurably ill wife Vivien(ne).

In the second part of *The Waste Land*, we have an example of how one poet transformed his material into art. The focus in "A Game of Chess" is primarily on women. Taking doomed female characters from art, history, myth, and contemporary life, Eliot creates a cubistic woman, a multiperspectival portrait of women in waste lands, of wasted women in history and nature. He structures this part of the poem by using the frame and picture arrangement illustrated in "The Burial of the Dead." As in an elaborately framed photograph of a mundane scene, the frame here is decorative, taken from the world of high art, and the picture is photographic, focused on the everyday world of failed marriages. Certain details are recognizable from Eliot's first marriage, but the picture here is a fiction, an aesthetic construction by a highly conscious artist.

The frame in "A Game of Chess" features two Shakespearean women, and the picture, a diptych, features two contemporary women. In the first lines, Eliot evokes the splendid but wily Cleopatra on her barge in the river Nile, and in the last lines, he first echoes and then quotes the simple but mad Ophelia on her way to

95

death by water. Within the frame of these two tragic figures, he suggests through allusion the presence of many offstage women, such as Dido, Eve, and Queen Gertrude. Like Philomela, who is mentioned in the first part of this section, most of these women have been violated or betrayed or exploited by men; most have suffered irreversible ruin.

The original title of this section was "In the Cage," an image which Valerie Eliot suggests in her notes to *The Waste Land Facsimile* refers to the Sibyl in the poem's epigraph.[4] The word "cage" was used in some Victorian translations of the *Satyricon*, although "bottle" is a more accurate translation.[5] But whether cage or bottle, the women in this part of *The Waste Land* are all entrapped; like the Sibyl, they are isolated and withered in their ability to know, to be, and to bear. Like her, these women are enclosed and dangled as decorations or amusements for men. The contemporary women in "A Game of Chess" brush their hair, complain of nervous ennui, drink and gossip in a tavern, and perform other mundane acts; they are more vividly present than their counterparts in myth and art. This section of *The Waste Land*, interestingly, is the only one that takes place exclusively on the inside of rooms; the other sections are set primarily in nature. The first half is set in a boudoir, the second in a pub.

"A Game of Chess" continues and develops Eliot's exploration of different ways of "knowing," in particular, of what could be called "female epistemology" and of the necessity that it be complemented by "male epistemology" and, further, of the necessity that both be transcended. The wasting of human beings of both sexes can be seen as one of the consequences of separating female and male modes of knowing/being, that is, of separating perception from reason, experience from faith. These matters are a variant of the idea that isolation and consequent barrenness result from perceiving reality in terms of subjects, objects, and relations; unity and consequent fruitfulness result from going beyond relations, from transcendent knowing. It should not be thought that Eliot's attention to women is restricted to "A Game of Chess." The title, as we shall point out, is feminine, the epigraph deals with a female knower (the Sibyl), the first lines focus on Marie, and the first section has Madame Sosostris and her tarot cards at its center. This focus on women, as we shall see, is also a major element in "The Fire Sermon."

Eliot's focus on women cannot be understood apart from some attention to myth. In the myths that form the background of *The Waste Land*, those taken from Frazer and Weston, the land is the feminine counterpart of a king or lord. The importance of women in the poem becomes strikingly clear when it is realized that a waste land is in mythic terms equivalent to a barren or unhealthy woman. Although some myths show the impotence of kings and gods to be caused by a failure of the feminine earth, most myths, and certainly the ones Eliot refers to centrally, put it in the opposite way. The king falls first into incapacity or guilt, and his land follows him into barrenness and disease. He is responsible for the catastrophe that befalls both himself and his land, and he suffers both physical pain and the anguish of separation from his land. The maternal figures (the land and all of its female occupants) suffer, but without the added anguish of being responsible for setting things right. If they are saved, it will have to be done for them. This mythic pattern assigns all blame to the male figures, divides suffering between male and female, and makes the rejuvenation of the female contingent on the death of the male. In philosophical terms, the male is a subject and the female is an object. Health and fruitfulness require the unity of male and female, of subject and object, either before time in immediate experience or after time in transcendent experience. The irresolvable dualism of subject and object (and of man and woman) in the center is inseparable from the triumph of the relational consciousness that locks both into closed systems and prevents communion.

The main epistemological analogues of mythic male and mythic female are, respectively, reason and perception. Reason (also, under some conditions, faith or revelation) provides knowledge of what cannot be directly perceived. Mythic fathers, it will be remembered, are remote. They live in the sky and send down their messages from a distance. When they visit the earth to engender heroes and kings in the wombs of mortal women, they come in disguise. Their presence is usually unknown until it is announced by an oracle after their departure. Their children know these sky fathers, if at all, by inference, faith, or revelation. And their hero sons know them the same way. On the contrary, earth mothers and the mortal mothers of half-gods are known empirically; they are present in the flesh to be directly experienced. These distinctions in myth are equivalent to the obvious distinctions drawn from common experience. Mothers are known empirically, in the womb and at the breast, but fathers are known, if at all, by believing the reports of others. The same must be said, with even more emphasis, about the knowledge mothers and fathers have of their children. Mothers know their children because they bear them; fathers know them as a matter of faith. *"Amor matris,"* says Stephen Dedalus in *Ulysses,* "subjective and objective genitive, is the only true thing in life. Paternity may be a legal fiction."[6]

If it is granted that the mythic male is an equivalent of reason and faith as a way of knowing and that the mythic female is an equivalent of empirical certainty, it follows that myths on the subject of the failure of male and female to merge in a satisfactory way are symbolic renderings of the insufficiency of either epistemological mode when separated from the other. The fundamental assumption in most epistemological thought, during the entire history of such thought, is that reliable knowledge can be achieved only when rational conclusions can be verified by observations or when observations fit into a rationally derived pattern. Though both modes are mental, reason is experienced as a subjective process and observation is experienced as objective. This is one of many variations on the need for a harmonious and complementary coexistence of the polarities of self and other, male and female. In simpler terms, deserts can bloom and metaphorical waste lands can be transformed only through the harmony of the sexes. The connections between myth and epistemology could not have been missed by Eliot. He was a student of Cornford and the Cambridge anthropologists, and Cornford's *From Religion to Philosophy: A Study in the Origins of Western Speculation* was published in 1912, shortly before Eliot began his seminar on myth and interpretation with Professor Royce. Cornford's thesis, as indicated by his title, is that Greek philosophy had its beginning in primitive myth and religion.

With these speculations in mind, consider the function of Tiresias in both *Oedipus Rex* and *The Waste Land.* In the first, he is a reliable source of knowledge that others must gain only through an arduous process of collecting evidence. In the second, he is exactly the same kind of source, but what he knows is trivial. In *Oedipus Rex*, his androgyny is not relevant; in *The Waste Land*, it is emphasized for, having been both male and female, he can fuse reason and perception into perfect knowledge.

For modern students of myth, such as Cornford, Weston, and Eliot himself, the fact that Tiresias is the only figure in Sophocles' play who is qualified to interpret its action is related to his sexual history. Similarly, the circumstances surrounding Oedipus can also be related to gender in myth. The crimes Oedipus is guilty of are inseparable from the incompleteness of his knowledge. His crime is ignorance, and his punishment is knowledge. In epistemological terms, the acts of parricide and maternal incest are the crimes of murdering mind and marrying matter (no pun intended). Oedipus is ignorant *because* he has split reason from observation and, conversely, he split them *because* he was ignorant. In mythic terms, by embracing his mother he embraced the earth, and by killing his father he cut himself off from his transcendent origin.

The gods referred to in *Oedipus Rex* are transcendent, speaking only through oracles. They convey another standard implication of myth: The important gods are remote and masculine. To worship mothers, the land, or any earthly female is to commit the heresy and plain redundancy of worshiping the obvious. The same issue occupies the center of *Hamlet*. The prince receives information from his father as transcendent messenger, but in the process of seeking verification by observing his mother he moves through a series of misperceptions into a fatal series of delays. In the closet scene in *Hamlet*, the son sees his father's spirit, but his mother sees nothing. Eliot echoes this scene in the pseudodialogue of "A Game of Chess." This is a matter of importance to which, in due course, we will return.

Consider, as the final item in this review of mythic associations, that the men of myth move on a rectilinear time line between birth and death. Like Oedipus, they may make temporary curving paths backward toward origins. Such a return is an outrage, and its ultimate failure and punishment confirm the necessity of going beyond each moment of existence in a sequence of irreversible movements.

My friend, blood shaking my heart
The awful daring of a moment's surrender
Which an age of prudence can never retract
By this, and this only, we have existed   (lines 403–6)

Those who interpret Eliot's lines as related primarily to Kierkegaard or Sartre are missing the fundamental mythic significance. Individual, unique selfhood is a function of that process of emerging from the cycles of nature and taking steps into terrains which an age of prudence can never reverse. The final price of this emergence from the seasonal and other cycles of nature is mortality, a final fact which closes the frame around the life and individualizes it with a last irreversible event. The paradox of this mythic biography, however, is that it both represents and makes possible the curvilinear immortality of the earth. Without individuality, there are no heroes or kings, and without heroes or kings, there is no one to unify the land through metonymic mergers and no one whose death can rejuvenate it when it is barren. When mythic women become individuals, they do so, like Jocasta and Queen Gertrude, by the same process of transcending nature and paying the price of mortality. Their tragedies, however, place their humanness at the center of focus without placing them in a position to unify and rejuvenate the land. They merely suffer and merely die. The catastrophes of mythic women are not last events that move the gods to take away famine, plague, and political disorder. Their condition is for this reason more painful than that of the heroes. They cannot become significant sufferers, and they are also isolated from the primal female condition of being the oscillating earth itself. The way is now prepared for an understanding of *The Waste Land*'s gallery of unhappy women. Following our description of Eliot's method of presenting the women in "A Game of Chess," we will return to these mythic analogues and to their relations to his philosophical studies and his dissertation on F. H. Bradley.

"A Game of Chess" begins with thirty-three lines of description, the longest descriptive passage in the entire poem. The scene consists of a woman seated before a mirror at her dressing table, evidently brushing her hair. The woman herself is not described, but selected aspects of the room, its walls, its fireplace and mantel, its contents, and its atmosphere are described in detail. The most

100

remarkable thing about the passage is the way it creates a powerful awareness of the woman without describing any part of her. The single reference to her, at the end of the passage, "her hair/Spread out in fiery points/Glowed into words, then would be savagely still," is so surrealistically transformed that it cannot be experienced as a descriptive detail. Nevertheless, she is a clear presence at the center of her environment. The most noteworthy aspect of that environment, beyond its designations of ornate affluence and its resemblance to a painting by Fragonard, is that it consists mainly of signifiers pointing away from its occupant toward literary and mythic figures.

> The Chair she sat in, like a burnished throne,
> Glowed on the marble, where the glass
> Held up by standards wrought with fruited vines
> From which a golden Cupidon peeped out
> (Another hid his eyes behind his wing)
> Doubled the flames of sevenbranched candelabra
> Reflecting light upon the table as
> The glitter of her jewels rose to meet it,
> From satin cases poured in rich profusion;
> In vials of ivory and coloured glass
> Unstoppered, lurked her strange synthetic perfumes,
> Unguent, powdered, or liquid—troubled, confused
> And drowned the sense in odours; stirred by the air
> That freshened from the window, these ascended
> In fattening the prolonged candle-flames,
> Flung their smoke into the laquearia,
> Stirring the pattern on the coffered ceiling.
> Huge sea-wood fed with copper
> Burned green and orange, framed by the coloured stone,
> In which sad light a carvèd dolphin swam.
> Above the antique mantel was displayed
> As though a window gave upon the sylvan scene
> The change of Philomel, by the barbarous king
> So rudely forced; yet there the nightingale
> Filled all the desert with inviolable voice
> And still she cried, and still the world pursues,
> "Jug Jug" to dirty ears.
> And other withered stumps of time

101

> Were told upon the walls; staring forms
> Leaned out, leaning, hushing the room enclosed.
> Footsteps shuffled on the stair.
> Under the firelight, under the brush, her hair
> Spread out in fiery points
> Glowed into words, then would be savagely still.

The passage describes a room full of fragments of objects of art; interestingly, it is written in such a way that the passage seems to be a replica of the room in that it too is full of bits and pieces of art. It begins with a near-quote from Shakespeare—Enobarbus's description of Cleopatra on her barge. The notes connect "laquearia" to the *Aeneid* and "sylvan scene" to *Paradise Lost*, bringing Dido and Eve in as vague parallels to Cleopatra. The effect of such quotations and notes is to join the actual language of the poem to the objects it describes. The room contains framed pictures of "the change of Philomel" above the mantel and of other sad tales—"withered stumps of time"—decorating other parts of the wall; the stanza that describes them is decorated with similar signifiers. In this particular passage, the poem tends to be close in kind to the event it describes. Eliot's technique here is to have the language that describes the room describe itself at the same time. His words and the objects they describe point at each other like facing mirrors. Eliot's consciousness of this self-referentiality may account for the bizarre image in which the woman's hair glows into words. They appear, from this perspective, to be the words of the poem itself.

One of the many fascinating aspects of this passage is that the language points both to itself and beyond itself in all directions except toward the woman at the center of the picture, she whose room is described. She is located within a system of differences, and that system is "hushing the room enclosed." Though surrounded by significance, she signifies nothing herself and no signifier refers to her. Her room is cursive—directly drawn—but she is recursive. Several points about the woman are noteworthy. First, she may be young, middle-aged, or old. The passage gives no clue. Second, she may be beautiful or homely. Again, the language keeps her appearance a secret. This would normally not arise as an issue. Marie, Madame Sosostris, and the rest have no appearances at all, but the woman at her dressing table is surrounded with so many vividly described things that her invisibility becomes a major datum arising from the reading process. Third, she exists in an ambiguous time period. Her setting suggests the eighteenth century, especially her use of candlelight in ornate seven-branched candelabra. But the fragment of the "Shakespeherian Rag" and the reference to a "closed car" which appear in the lines to follow place her in the exact period in which the poem was written, the early 1920s. Fourth, she may or may not be presented as a real person. She could as easily be a recursive area in a painting. If she is not to be regarded as real, then the voice that speaks at line 111 could be someone else who has been looking at the picture or imagining it. The passage obliges us to hold these possibilities together as coexisting realities.

The detail about the woman's hair glowing into words is particularly suggestive. Whether or not it is read as a reminder of the poem's self-reflexivity, it draws attention to the problematic relations between language and images. The world encloses words, but words can be media enclosing worlds. Whenever the distinction is subverted, as in the image of the woman's hair, the dualism of signs and things signified coalesces, for brief moments, into a unity. Calling attention to that unity, however, reduces it to a merely conceptual unity rather than a felt one.

The dressing room description contains a mixture of tangible and intangible objects. "Chair," "marble," "candelabra," and the like are tangible, whereas "Reflecting light," "glitter," "odours," and "smoke" are intangible. In this particular passage, the intangibles permeate and transform the tangibles. The glow on the marble is more vivid than the marble itself, and the odors of perfumes cause the light to fling smoke against the "laquearia," thus creating a "sad light" in which "a carved dolphin swam." Solids, free-floating qualities, and figures in art works adjust themselves into a relation in which the free-floating qualities dominate.

The single most important experience emerging from this analysis is the experience of objects in the process of disappearing into the qualities that modify them. The hierarchical relation of nouns to adjectives is reversed. Nouns or things are normally thought of as essential, their qualities as peripheral and accidental. Here the qualities appear to take over the central position, calling attention to the idea that objects are only bundles of adjectives, heaps of broken images. It is not only that the woman's room becomes a parergon that displaces its central figure, the woman herself; it is also that each item within the environment undergoes the equivalent displacement. The passage begins with the observation that "The Chair . . . /Glowed on the marble," and "the glass/ . . . Doubled the flames of sevenbranched candelabra/Reflecting light upon the table as/The glitter of her jewels rose to meet it." The chair vanishes into the glow, the candelabra into its light and flames, the table into the light; the jewels disappear into their glitter; and all of this light meets and is reflected in the mirror which would normally reflect the woman's face. Light, whether as glow or glitter, is a variegated set of qualities surrounding, framing, and even making visible the objects in the room, but here light swallows the objects it is supposed to reveal. In this passage ergon and parergon do not change places in an oscillation. In fact, they cannot do so, for the centers within the sets of framing qualities vanish as soon as one tries to form images of them by stripping away the surface glitter in search of the solid thing within it.

These effects suggest that the passage is a verbal variation on impressionism, luminism, or any other kind of painting that emphasizes light at the expense of the objects from which light is reflected. Such painting, whether done with colors or words, energizes a dialectic of abstraction and empathy. The viewer (reader) notes the absence of objects, or their removal into a vague distance, and then compensates for their abstraction by making a conscious effort to see them clearly and thus bring them back into a space like his own. The effort, when it succeeds, does so only partially and for brief moments. Things and their analyzed qualities alternate as points of focus, producing the experience of alternating abstraction and empathy, distance and closeness.

In *Heart of Darkness*, a work which was in Eliot's mind during the composition of *The Waste Land*, Conrad provides both vivid examples of the luministic technique and a commentary on its implications.

> In the offing the sea and the sky were welded together without a joint, and in the luminous space the tanned sails of the barges drifting up with the tide seemed to stand still in red clusters of canvas sharply peaked, with gleams of varnished spirits. A haze

> rested on the low shores that ran out to sea in vanishing flatness.
> The air was dark above Gravesend, and farther back still seemed
> condensed into a mournful gloom, brooding motionless over
> the biggest, and the greatest, town on earth.[7]

Two pages later, after several more descriptive passages of a similar
kind, Conrad introduces his narrator, Marlow. Conrad's explanation of the way Marlow tells a story is a commentary on the way
Conrad is writing this novella, a set of instructions to the reader of
Heart of Darkness.

> The yarns of seamen have a direct simplicity, the whole meaning
> of which lies within the shell of a cracked nut. But Marlow was
> not typical . . . and to him the meaning of an episode was not
> inside like a kernel but outside, enveloping the tale which
> brought it out only as a glow brings out a haze, in the likeness of
> one of those misty halos that sometimes are made visible by the
> spectral illumination of moonshine.[8]

By alerting his reader to the issues of surface qualities and central
essences, Conrad presents him with an interpretative key. By the
time Marlow interprets Kurtz as "hollow to the core," the reader has
been immersed in a world where everything is either a shell without
content or a cloud of free-floating adjectives.

Eliot's woman in the first half of "A Game of Chess" is, like
Conrad's Kurtz, the hollowness at the center of a field of hollow
surfaces. In a specific philosophical sense, she is a metaphysical
substance, that which is left over after every perceivable quality is
removed. Like the invisible man in films, she is known only when
she is covered up. When naked, the invisible man cannot be known
except as a voice. The woman in the poem is an absence manifested
by her enclosing surfaces and by her voice. It thus is not at all
unlikely, at this stage of analysis, that Eliot is suggesting that she be
imagined as a ghost, an impalpable and intangible essence.

The long description of the woman's dressing room is ended by a
reference to footsteps shuffling on the stairs. The caller is male,
presumably her husband. A quasi-dramatic scene follows in which
the woman, a person who has been presented as an absence,
speaks to a man who remains silent but who ceaselessly thinks and
responds mentally. Her words, indicated by quotation marks, are

juxtaposed throughout the scene with his thoughts. Eliot uses the same technique in a much earlier poem, "Portrait of a Lady," where it also conveys the isolation of a woman and her gentleman caller.

"My nerves are bad to-night. Yes, bad. Stay with me.
"Speak to me. Why do you never speak. Speak.
"What are you thinking of? What thinking? What?
"I never know what you are thinking. Think."

I think we are in rats' alley
Where the dead men lost their bones.

"What is that noise?"
                              The wind under the door.
"What is that noise now? What is the wind doing?"
                              Nothing again nothing.
                                                        "Do
"You know nothing? Do you see nothing? Do you remember
"Nothing?"

        I remember
Those are pearls that were his eyes.
"Are you alive, or not? Is there nothing in your head?"

                                                        But
O O O O that Shakespeherian Rag—
It's so elegant
So intelligent
"What shall I do now? What shall I do?"
"I shall rush out as I am, and walk the street
"With my hair down, so. What shall we do to-morrow?
"What shall we ever do?"
                              The hot water at ten.
And if it rains, a closed car at four.
And we shall play a game of chess,
Pressing lidless eyes and waiting for a knock upon the door.

The man and woman in this scene provide textbook examples of what Bradley means by relational experience. They cannot experience communion or transcendence of any kind because they are isolated, imprisoned in their own heads. Every sensation, every feeling, is filtered through the mind, through memories and desires and desperate needs and fears. This situation is particularly noteworthy because, as Calvin Bedient has pointed out and as is evident in the *Facsimile*,[9] this man and woman are linked to the hyacinth girl and her lover in "The Burial of the Dead," and thus should be associated with one of the most poignant evocations of lost immediacy in the entire poem. The questions the woman addresses to her present visitor are patterned exactly upon the confession of the hyacinth lover. "I could not/Speak, and my eyes failed, I was neither/Living nor dead, and I knew nothing." In the passage at hand, the woman asks

> "Do
> "You know nothing? Do you see nothing? Do you remember
> "Nothing?"
> . . . . .
> "Are you alive, or not? Is there nothing in your head?"

Actually, locked into relational experience, he is paralyzed by knowing, by remembering, by thinking, by interpreting. He remembers his previous experiences of unity and by thinking about them makes them a part of his present prison. In the original drafts of *The Waste Land*, the question "Do you remember nothing?" is followed by "I remember/The hyacinth garden."[10] The parallels between the two scenes include emphasis on the woman's hair, wet in the first passage, dry and spread out in fiery points in the second. Hair is also mentioned in connection with the woman's threat of running out onto the street as she is (presumably in her dressing gown) with her hair down. The parallels include, in addition, emphasis on a "heart of light." In the hyacinth garden passage, the term seems to refer to an immediate experience, in the Bradleian sense; in the boudoir scene, the all-obliterating light is associated with enclosure in the woman's room, with entrapment in a system of qualities—in other words, with relational experience in the Bradleian sense.

The association of this woman and her visitor with the hyacinth girl and her lover suggests that the background of this scene includes moments of high passion. In the present situation, the male interprets that background in highly negative terms. His response to the woman's question about what he is thinking is "I think we are in rats' alley/Where the dead men lost their bones." In the *Facsimile* drafts, his response was "I think we met first in rats' alley."[11] Noticing the change from "we met first in" to "we are in" rats' alley reveals the fact that the male is interpreting the history of the relationship and that part of his interpretation involves the backward extension of their present isolation over the immediate experience of the hyacinth garden. He seems to say that they are in rats' alley and indeed have always been there, for that is where they met. This transforms the hyacinth garden itself into a rats' alley. Like Prufrock and Gerontion, the male here is always thinking, and as with them, the consequences include isolation, loss of senses, paralysis, death. He filters the present through art and religion, through Shakespeare and Madame Sosostris, for he remembers the line from *The Tempest* which appears in the middle of her reading of the tarot cards and is followed by "Here is Belladonna." Again like Prufrock, this man sings to himself. His Shakespearean rag picks up both the beautiful transformation line—"Those are pearls that were his eyes"—and, as Grover Smith has observed, the hollow howls ("O O O O") of Lear and Othello.[12] The startling backward superimposition of this diseased relationship upon the hyacinth garden lovers, of the quasi-hysterical neurasthenic upon the hyacinth girl with her arms full of flowers, of the intellectual and remote male upon the passionate lover, and of the room with the mirror upon the heart of light compels the reader from perspective to perspective without respite.

The conjecture that the woman in this scene may be a ghost assumes special relevance when it is remembered that *Hamlet* is a major subtext in the poem (particularly in this section), and when it is noted that her speech to her silent visitor echoes the closet scene in *Hamlet*. Startled by the spirit of his father, Hamlet asks his mother if she sees it. She, of course, sees nothing. Startled by wind, the woman in this scene asks her visitor what it is. He has heard all of this before, knows the mornings, evenings, afternoons, and does not bother to answer. But he does see her and take note of her comments. For the reader, however, she is invisible, a voice emanating from the empty space at the center of a long description of her environment. For the reader, the effect is that of a ghost speaking. The effect is a cursive-recursive oscillation of female essence and actual female. The woman is a cubistic overlapping of viewpoints, a ghost asking her visitor if he can see a ghost. The reader cannot see the woman, and her visitor cannot see the ghost.

The ghost motif in the scene is reduced to another level of irony within irony by the use of wind as its initial stimulus in the woman's mind. Eliot is using a familiar etymological pun. Most words for spirit, ghost, mind, and soul have evolved from words that once meant only wind or breath. The ambiguity is seen in such words as inspiration and respiration, *Geist*, gust, ghost, and aghast. In "Gerontion," Eliot uses wind not to mean spirit but to mean the absence of spirit; he strips wind of its religious and mythic values by forcing the reader to understand it as mere wind. The following lines, for example, conclude a section that describes an ambiguous communion service in "depraved May."

> Vacant shuttles
> Weave the wind. I have no ghosts,
> An old man in a draughty house
> Under a windy knob.

Similarly, in "What the Thunder Said," the chapel is empty, "only the wind's home" (line 388). A chapel is supposed to be the home of the spirit of God, and the Chapel Perilous in the grail story is haunted by evil spirits, but here the chapel is neither occupied by spirit nor haunted by ghosts. On the contrary, it contains only literal wind and is haunted by the absence of spirit. Eliot here reverses the history of words, taking meanings back to their origins. In other parts of the poem, he does the same with water; he demythologizes it, turning its power to cleanse and purify into the physical effect that it has upon a victim of drowning.

To return to the passage at hand, the woman is startled by wind. At first, she is afraid, thinking the noise might indicate danger. She wants to know what it is and what it is doing. Her first question causes the man to reflect that wind is only wind, but her second— "What is the wind doing?"—reminds him of a passage from Dante in which wind had a definite function and a definite meaning. He remembers Paolo and Francesca in the second circle of Hell being punished for lust. In the *Facsimile*, the question "What is the wind doing?" is followed by "Carrying/Away the little light dead people." As Valerie Eliot points out in the *Facsimile* notes, this line is an allusion to Dante's desire in *Inferno* 5 to speak to those two who go together carried lightly on the wind.[13] This means that the man in

"A Game of Chess" fluctuates between hearing wind that is only wind and, at the same time, wind that is both the spirit and the agent of God, punishing the spirits of humans for sins committed in the flesh. Wind is of course also speech. Words are wind woven by the shuttles of throat and mouth into systems of difference. And wind is not only divine spirit, the breath of God, but also human spirit, the breath of life. Insofar as the woman in this part of the poem is a ghost, she is wind producing wind (words) signifying fear of wind (ghosts). Insofar as she is an actual person, she is also wind producing wind.

The silent visitor acknowledges his linkage to the troubled woman by including himself as her partner in tomorrow's chess game: "And we shall play a game of chess." He also includes himself as her companion in the predictable trivialities of a typical day. The chess game is a way of superimposing an order of an artificial kind on the already clearly ordered day. It is sometimes suggested that a game, like art, has order whereas life has none, but that is a mistaken assumption. The passage specifically refers to the order of a hot-water bottle at ten and a closed car at four. By doing so, the passage reveals a rigid and utterly boring order, an invariable structure of days and nights that is repeated endlessly. What is called for is unpredictability as an evasion of the diurnal cycle's pattern. In *Man's Rage for Chaos*, Morse Peckham advances the fascinating thesis that art is often a means of introducing anarchy into the painful order of life. He reverses all the clichés in this area of discourse and makes a fine, though overstated, case.[14] *The Waste Land* as a whole might be seen as such art, as Eliot's contribution to the universal effort to subvert the tedium of natural cycles and conventional narrative structures.

In the passage under discussion, the game must be seen as an alternative way of structuring time. Within the game, there are unambiguous rules and definite purposes, but outcomes are usually unpredictable. Outside the game, there are no clear rules and no final purposes, but everything is completely predictable. There is an occlusion of two orders in the images of their lives and their game. The difficulty with Peckham's thesis is the same as the difficulty with the opposing cliché. Order and chaos are not polar opposites; they are results of judgments made from different perspectives. Within one closed system, any other system appears ordered in a different way. A worker, for example, may long for his vacation and, halfway through his vacation, long for a return to work. What seems to be a satisfactory structure is a sequence of changing or overlapping structures.

These observations bring us back to the concepts of transcendent experience and binary perspectives. Disorder is related to seeing anything from within a single system, from a single point of view; order is related to seeing one or more systems from a position outside those systems, a position which enables the viewer to perceive them as a unity. The mode of consciousness implied by the judgment that contraries are part of more comprehensive wholes is suggestive of what Bradley and Eliot called transcendent knowledge and what we have called mythic consciousness. This does not mean that the figures in the scene will achieve a unitive cognition. They will continue to experience the orders of day and game as parallel patterns while waiting for something unexpected, "a knock upon the door." From the reader's perspective, however, the lovers and the chess players, their mornings and afternoons, their time patterns inside and outside the game, along with the eventual knock upon the door that balances the earlier footsteps that shuffled on the stair, along with the ambiguities of ghostliness and tangibility, cursive antiquity and recursive lives within it, move in the direction of a transcendent unity. This unity contains rather than resolves paradoxes. The fragments move toward unity because they can be perceived from perspectives outside all of their enclosures. The demand for transcendence of paradox is addressed to the reader, not to the characters in the poem. They have no way of imagining its possibility. Their "lidless eyes" cannot evade the persistent glow and glitter of their irresolvable world. These observations have nothing to do with metaphysics. They assert only that a figure in an impressionistic painting has no choice but to remain as an arrangement of jagged and disconnected spots of color, whereas a viewer of the painting is free to look for a perspective that resolves the fragments into something he can identify.

"A Game of Chess," as we have pointed out, is a diptych with a Shakespearean frame. As is true in all diptychs, the panels are both similar and dissimilar. In this case, each panel portrays an unfruitful sexual relationship. Within this similarity, however, the panels can instantly be seen as contrasts. The setting of the first is a dressing room, and both general scene and props suggest affluence. The characters are nameless and faceless, but they pose and speak and think in such a way that there can be no doubt that they belong to the upper middle classes. The setting of the second part of this diptych is a pub. The main character, who is absent, is named Lil, a truncated form of Lily, the flower of Easter, the flower of the "cruellest month" in the waste land. Her husband, like many boys born in Queen Victoria's reign, bears the name of Albert, the royal consort. And one of the sons, like many boys born to English soldiers fighting in the First World War, is named for King George V. The speaker in this scene, a friend of Lil and Albert, speaks and behaves in a manner that leaves no doubt that she and her friends are poor and belong to the lower social classes.

When Lil's husband got demobbed, I said—
I didn't mince my words, I said to her myself,
HURRY UP PLEASE ITS TIME
Now Albert's coming back, make yourself a bit smart.
He'll want to know what you done with that money he gave you
To get yourself some teeth. He did, I was there.
You have them all out, Lil, and get a nice set,
He said, I swear, I can't bear to look at you.
And no more can't I, I said, and think of poor Albert,
He's been in the army four years, he wants a good time,
And if you don't give it him, there's others will, I said.
Oh is there, she said. Something o' that, I said.
Then I'll know who to thank, she said, and give me a straight look.
HURRY UP PLEASE ITS TIME
If you don't like it you can get on with it, I said.
Others can pick and choose if you can't.
But if Albert makes off, it won't be for lack of telling.
You ought to be ashamed, I said, to look so antique.
(And her only thirty-one.)
I can't help it, she said, pulling a long face,
It's them pills I took, to bring it off, she said.
(She's had five already, and nearly died of young George.)
The chemist said it would be alright, but I've never been the same.
You are a proper fool, I said.

Well, if Albert won't leave you alone, there it is, I said,
What you get married for if you don't want children?
HURRY UP PLEASE ITS TIME
Well, that Sunday Albert was home, they had a hot gammon,
And they asked me in to dinner, to get the beauty of it hot—
HURRY UP PLEASE ITS TIME
HURRY UP PLEASE ITS TIME
Goonight Bill. Goonight Lou. Goonight May. Goonight
Ta ta. Goonight. Goonight.
Good night, ladies, good night sweet ladies, good night, good night.

The characters in the boudoir scene exist in a private room in a private world and long for change, for some significant catastrophe that would impose structure and interject meaning into their daily round. The characters in the pub scene exist in a public place; they anticipate major changes in their lives, "if Albert makes off," and recall past events that have profound consequences. The first scene is characterized by light and in part by silence, the second by shadows and rapid speech, with the narrator contending with the barman for attention. The woman in the first part is present but invisible; on the other hand, Lil, the focal figure of the second part, is absent but visible, vividly and empathetically evoked. The first woman's age, appearance, and health are not revealed; indeed, her very existence is called into question. But Lil is clearly presented. She is thirty-one years of age, looks much older, has bad teeth, has borne five children; she has misspent her allowance and ruined her health with an abortion; she is married to Albert who has just completed four years of service in the army, who is disgusted with her appearance and threatens to leave her for someone who is still able to give him a good time. Lil serves hot gammon for Sunday dinner, invites her friend over when Albert is home, and tells the friend all their troubles. The reader is as overwhelmed with personal data here as he or she was with information about decor in the earlier scene. What do these contrasting methods imply, and what happens when they are brought together as a single framed portrait?

The answers emerge when the female figures in the two panels are superimposed. The first is a recursive area within a picture, a presence out of which a voice emanates. The second is a cursive picture with a past, a probable future of abandonment, and no voice at all. The first, to put it another way, has no body. She exists beneath the seeable qualities of light and shade. The second has a body that is a severe burden to her and a husband who exists only to exploit it on the rare occasions when he is present. The first feels the stress of not knowing how to impose a straight line structure upon her repetitious days and nights, whereas the second is trapped in an ongoing process of events that makes her both a victim of biology and a victim of mistaken attempts to alter its processes. Lil is being destroyed by both fertility and an effort to avoid it, and the whole situation is likely to cause the loss of her only source of security, Albert, who is also the source of her suffering. Too little sense of structure in the first woman is matched with too much in the second. The result of the superimposition of the two is a cubistic portrait of a woman. Eliot's technique here does not allow this portrait to be viewed as one figure; it forces the reader to see an overlapping, faceted, and layered structure. This compound structure is Eliot's portrait of a lady, his suggestion of the female presence which suffers at the center of and which in myth is identical with a waste land. The realization that Eliot in "A Game of Chess" has created a framed diptych of a woman causes the earlier females—the Sibyl, Marie, the hyacinth girl, Isolde, Madame Sosostris—to return as facets of the picture, and later in the poem the typist, Thames daughters, and others will also add facets.

Allusions also contribute facets to this emerging portrait. Cleopatra is a reference to the use of sexuality to gain political power, Dido to the use of political power to hold the wandering warrior Aeneas. The first is destroyed by Rome after she had captivated with feminine charm two of its leaders, whereas the second is destroyed by the future founder of Rome when she fails to captivate him. Eve is the mythic source of fertility and the victim of Satan's seduction; Philomela is a mythic figure who was raped and mutilated by the barbarous king and then transformed into an "inviolable voice," the nightingale. Ophelia is a reference to innocence driven to madness and death as a result of tangled events which have only a tangential relation to her. And as Grover Smith has recently pointed out, Shakespeare's Imogen, also victimized by men, is undoubtedly present. Most of the descriptive details in the boudoir scene come from Iachimo's description of his wife's bedroom, details he is memorizing in order to humiliate her. Smith notes that the tapestry in Imogen's room depicts Cleopatra on her barge and that Imogen has fallen asleep reading "The tale of Tereus," the page "turn'd down/Where Philomel gave up."[15] Cleopatra, Eve, Dido, Philomela, Ophelia, Imogen—all of these doomed women exist as adjuncts to male power and as victims of it. Aspects of all of them are distributed throughout the composite portrait of a lady presented by "A Game of Chess."

Many critics take one or more of these figures—Cleopatra, Dido, Philomela, Eve, Ophelia—as the perspective from which to interpret the contemporary figures. Specific literary and mythic figures, however, cannot form a point from which to interpret contemporary women, for the literary and mythic women are also part of Eliot's picture, variations on the contemporary figures. A perspective can be discovered by returning to the myths undergirding Eliot's poem. As we pointed out early in this chapter, a waste land in myth is a barren or unhealthy woman. Lil is unhealthy and now perhaps barren from the effects of the abortifacient. The first woman is mentally distressed and virtually paralyzed. Both are depleted physically, intellectually, spiritually. In myth, the land is rendered barren by the failures and sins of males. Lil has become sick and perhaps barren by being treated as an adjunct of Albert's lust. The first woman, in a more subtle way, has also been paralyzed by a male, whom she now begs to give her a structure she cannot imagine providing for herself. Further, women in myth represent the condition of the circularity of the seasons and generations. The first woman is trapped in empty revolutions of repetitious days. She longs for anything (even catastrophe) that will enable her to escape the tormenting cycles of her life. Her "Stay with me" doubles Lil's fear that Albert will leave her and, along with the earth mothers of myth, defines her existence and health as contingent on male potency and continence. The feeling established by the allusions makes it certain that he will not stay with her and that, in due course, Albert too will vanish. Like Prufrock, who thought of himself as a secondary character, only "an attendant lord," in the story of his own life, women are supporting players in the dramas of their personal existence. From the perspective supplied by myth, it is clear that perceiving women as secondary characters or supporting players in the game of life leads to a waste land.

Finally, myth associates females with direct experience and males with reason, faith, or some other method of gaining knowledge of what cannot be observed. In myth, female closeness and male remoteness form the complementary conditions for both health and knowledge. In *The Waste Land*, such complementarity does not exist, and as in myth, this absence of connection is associated with disease and waste. Eliot's women exhibit reversals of the standard mythic modes of knowing. The first woman sees what is not there (reflections of reflections of reflections), and she misinterprets what she hears, the wind under the door. Also, she loses her sense of smell, which is drowned in strange synthetic perfumes. Further, she herself cannot be seen by the reader, just as the absent Lil cannot be seen by the characters in the tavern. The point is that, in this poem, the empirical mode associated in myth with women is defeated or distorted. This defeat of the empirical is conveyed both by their words and actions in the poem and by Eliot's mode of presenting them in verbal colors and sounds. The world associated with experience and observation is presented as an unclassifiable array of unstable relations or broken images.

The failure of men to cohere with women is, from the perspective of myth, the failure of rational processes to cohere with observations. The objects of reason and faith are abstract, like Eliot's first woman, and the objects of perception are empathetic, like his second woman, Lil. But here both kinds of objects, abstract and empathetic, are feminine; no complement of opposites occurs, and thus no certainty or health exists. An obvious implication is that androgyny is a mythic analogue of knowledge. Tiresias, therefore, sees all because he is a complete, self-contained structure of opposites. In the absence of androgyny, collaboration between male and female is the necessary condition of both health and knowledge. At this point in the analysis, it should be clear that categories normally compartmentalized into isolated mental cells should be thought of together. The categories are, first, erotic life and, second, intellectual life. In "The Metaphysical Poets," Eliot located the dissociation of these categories in the English poetic tradition, but he was deeply aware that the divorce of erotic from intellectual, plea-

116

sure from knowledge, feeling from thought, was a recurring catastrophe in history and before it. It was, in fact, the basis for both religion and art. The challenge is to remarry the two modes. In *The Waste Land*, the unlikelihood of that reconciliation is presented, but presented in a way that obliges those who wish to read it to search for modes of transcendent perception. A poem of despair can be known only through a reading method that implies absurd hope.

Our reading of *The Waste Land* is based on Eliot's own ideas about the interpretation of interpretations, as stated in his graduate school papers and in his dissertation. Before pursuing our reading into later parts of the poem, we would like to call attention to a few specific points he made in regard to the interpretation of myth and in regard to the difference between facts and interpretation. Some of Eliot's most interesting remarks on these subjects occur in a graduate school paper on the interpretation of primitive ritual. [16] In this paper and in other discussions of myth, it is clear that Eliot had mixed feelings about Frazer's work in *The Golden Bough*. As a collector and classifier of folklore, Frazer was superb. But as an interpreter of his material, he was not to be trusted. The major problem was Frazer's lack of attention to the nature of interpretation. Frazer collected myths and fragments of myths and then tried to reconstruct their original meaning. But as Eliot points out, his facts (myths) are themselves interpretations. Furthermore, they are his own interpretations, not the interpretations of the people who in the distant past grounded their religion in them. [17] In the introduction to *Savonarola*, Eliot mentions some of the problems he had been wrestling with for well over a decade.

> Some years ago, in a paper on *The Interpretation of Primitive Ritual*, I made an humble attempt to show that in many cases *no* interpretation of a rite could explain its origin. For the meaning of the series of acts is to the performers themselves an interpretation; the same ritual remaining practically unchanged may assume different meanings for different generations of performers; and the rite may even have originated before "meaning" meant anything at all. [18]

The most important implication for our immediate purpose is that Eliot sees history as a sequence of varying interpretations of interpretations of interpretations, with subsequent interpretations blocking access to former ones. It is a situation in which original interpretations are absolutely irrecoverable. And as he remarks, the rite may have originated in what could be called the immediate experience of the race, before the conscious experience of meaning became a datum in human minds.

In reading "A Game of Chess," we have used a perspective from the traditional associations within myth, associations which relate females to observation and males to reason or faith. We regard these associations not as facts about the primitive mind but as facts about the tradition of interpreting myth. Both in his graduate school papers and in his dissertation, Eliot is clear about the difference between facts and interpretations. Following Bradley, he defines a fact as "a point of attention which has only one aspect, or which can be treated under one aspect. A fact, then, is an ideal construction, and has its existence within a more or less variable sphere of practical or scientific interest."[19] In this definition, a fact does not exist in and of itself; it is generated by paying attention to or noticing something. Two terms are needed for a fact: the one who attends and the point attended to and isolated thereby from everything else. But three terms are needed for an interpretation: the one who attends, the point attended, and the entity or class of entities signified by that point of attention. The interpretation is created (and the fact destroyed) by the attribution of significance. A signifier (such as a religious rite) can remain the same whereas its significance (its meaning) can change from generation to generation, from person to person within one generation, and even from person to person within a single family. Eliot argues in his seminar paper that what one generation calls fact the next will call interpretation, but actually, both generations are dealing with interpretations.

An important consequence of this way of thinking is that facts as such can, by definition, have no meanings at all. This is not an argument that the universe or life has no meaning. Such an entity as "life" cannot fit the definition of a fact as an isolated point of attention; and even if it could, the attribution of meaning would dissolve its status as a fact, would transform it into an interpretation. The definition also implies that facts can only exist in a brief instant of time, since points of attention have a tendency to point in other directions toward alternative facts; that is, points of attention

118

tend quickly to take on significance. After the phase of immediate experience, facts or signifieds move into a phase of relational experience in which they become signifiers—and so on in a sequence with no limit this side of a metaphysical absolute.

The relevance of these notions to the human conditions of lovelessness, confusion, and paralysis dramatized in *The Waste Land* becomes clearer when it is recalled that facts, whether they are defined technically as Eliot defined them, or assumed in common sense as most people define them, are normally associated with observation; interpretations, on the other hand, whether defined technically or not, are normally associated with reason or faith. In terms of the history of the interpretation of myth, facts are objective and feminine, whereas interpretation is subjective and masculine. Our reading of the poem is inseparable from the following point: Neither facts nor females, however one thinks of either term, can exist in isolation from a rationally or emotionally derived environment. Objects, whether they are persons or stones, cannot even be imagined except in relation to a framing subject. In his dissertation, Eliot put it this way:

> Facts are not merely found in the world and laid together like bricks, but every fact has in a sense its place prepared for it before it arrives, and without the implication of a system in which it belongs the fact is not a fact at all. The ideality essential to fact means a particular point of view, and means the exclusion of other aspects of the same point of attention. There is a sense, then, in which any science—natural or social—is *a priori*: in that it satisfies the needs of a particular point of view, a point of view which may be said to be more original than any of the facts that are referred to that science.[20]

Points of view are subjective fields in which points of attention occur. Subjectivity, whether it is in a rational or an emotional phase, whether it is reading Spinoza or falling in love, writing on Bradley or marrying Miss Haigh-Wood, is necessary to the existence of objectivity. Early in this chapter, in a review of conventional associations with myth, we noted that the terms "woman," "land," and "objective observation" are linked and that the terms "man," "remoteness" or "invisibility," and "reason" or "faith" are linked in a parallel way. We also noted the epistemological tradition that defined knowledge as either a direct perception in a context or a rational inference drawn from such perceptions. Certain knowledge occurs when both rational and empirical operations reach identical conclusions. When we put these associations and traditions together, both in their narrative forms in myth and in their abstract forms in logic, and then add Eliot's key arguments given first on the issue of interpreting primitive ritual and later on the implications of Bradley's ideas, we have constructed the context in which *The Waste Land* resides and in which it should be read. In "A Game of Chess," the focus is upon the disconnection of men from women and upon all that such a rupture implies. In "The Fire Sermon," as we shall show, the focus is upon the consequences of a loss of desire. That loss has awesome implications as, soon, we shall see.

5 / Transcending the Moral Point of View

"The Fire Sermon"

The way up and the way down are one and the same.—Heraclitus

The controlling allusion in "The Fire Sermon," by force of Eliot's title, is to the Fire Sermon of the Buddha, which Eliot says in a note to line 308 "corresponds in importance to the Sermon on the Mount." The Buddha's sermon, delivered to a thousand priests, consists of three questions and three answers. The first question asks what is on fire. Naming the senses one by one, the Buddha explains that the senses and any knowledge received by the senses are on fire. His comments on the eye come first and are illustrative of his comments on the ear, the nose, the tongue, the body.

> The eye, O priests, is on fire; forms are on fire; eye-conscious-
> ness is on fire; impressions received by the eye are on fire; and
> whatever sensation, pleasant, unpleasant, or indifferent, origi-
> nates in dependence on impressions received by the eye, that
> also is on fire.[1]

He adds that the mind is also on fire and that all impressions dependent on the mind are on fire. The second question is: "And with what are these on fire?" The answer is: "With the fire of passion, say I, with the fire of hatred, with the fire of infatuation; with birth, old age, death, sorrow, lamentation, misery, grief, and despair are they on fire."[2] The third quesiton is implied: How can these fires be extinguished? The Buddha answers that the process of perceiving that the senses and the mind are on fire will of itself generate an aversion for pleasure and knowledge and that the aversion will put out the fire. The thousand listening priests perceive that they are on fire, a perception which leads to their libera-tion. The overwhelming image in the Buddha's sermon is fire; it is used in almost every sentence. It refers not only to the raging and uncontrolled fire of passion but also to the willed and controlled fire of purification. Fire is also used to indicate the instability and unre-

121

liability of any knowledge received through the senses or through the mind.[3]

Fire is also important in a second major allusion, that to Augustine's *Confessions*. Eliot's note to line 309 says that "the collocation of these two representatives of eastern and western asceticism, as the culmination of this part of the poem, is not an accident." In the passage Eliot alludes to, Augustine confesses his lustfulness, admitting that he had immersed himself in the filthy cauldron of the city of Carthage, that he had wallowed in the pleasures of the flesh. The opening sentence of chapter 3 of the *Confessions* is: "To Carthage then I came, where there sang all around me in my ears a cauldron of unholy loves."[4] Eliot concludes "The Fire Sermon":

> To Carthage then I came
>
> Burning burning burning burning
> O Lord Thou pluckest me out
> O Lord Thou pluckest
>
> burning.

The Buddha and Saint Augustine and the powerful background texts they bring to this part of the poem are central in most interpretations of *The Waste Land*. Most critics focus on the fact that "The Fire Sermon" contains several sordid sexual episodes and conclude that like the Buddha and Augustine, Eliot is condemning the fires of sexual passion. Grover Smith, for example, calls this section a "dramatization of lust" and also discusses the importance of the symbolism of fire.[5]

The common interpretations of "The Fire Sermon" fail to take into account a number of paradoxes. First, this section of the poem does not even remotely resemble a sermon. Its language can be called descriptive and mimetic, but by no means can it be called hortatory or any other term appropriate to a sermon. Second, its dominant image is not fire but water. It begins with a river description which includes a refrain from Spenser: "Sweet Thames, run softly, till I end my Song." It concludes with the songs of the Thames maidens, women whose sexual episodes are associated with the river Thames. The rivers in this section of the poem are city rivers and heavily polluted. Third, its sexual episodes are not characterized by passion or hatred

or remorse or by any emotion that could be compared to fire. In our
second chapter, we quoted the longest episode, that of the typist
and the clerk who make love on her divan after dinner. This episode
is introduced with the lines:

> At the violet hour, when the eyes and back
> Turn upward from the desk, when the human engine waits
> Like a taxi throbbing waiting,

and concludes with the lines:

> She turns and looks a moment in the glass,
> Hardly aware of her departed lover;
> Her brain allows one half-formed thought to pass:
> "Well now that's done: and I'm glad it's over."
> When lovely woman stoops to folly and
> Paces about her room again, alone,
> She smoothes her hair with automatic hand,
> And puts a record on the gramophone.

The typist is framed by images (human engine as taxi, human arm
as arm of gramophone) that indicate she is an automaton, and the
clerk is presented as an animal who occasionally has an itch that
requires scratching. This section is a dramatization not of lust but of
the absence of lust. Lust is sinful desire, desire which is so violent as
to exclude self-control; or, as in Augustine, lust is the orientation of
intense desire toward forbidden objects instead of toward God.[6]
The Buddha's admonitions and Augustine's confessions—their
"Burning burning burning burning"—would be unintelligible to
the typist and the clerk and to all of the lovers described in this part
of *The Waste Land*. And yet, Eliot says that bringing the Buddha,
Saint Augustine, and the lovers together is not accidental. This
intentional collocation, of course, is Eliot's, and it requires us to try
to understand what the figures have in common.

The Buddha and Saint Augustine preach a similar message: Salvation involves overcoming the lusts of the flesh. They evoke cities
throbbing with superheated sexuality where the life of spirit is impossible. Graduation to Nirvana or union with God can be achieved
only after such passions are overcome. Asceticism of this kind is
related to the fact that erotic life creates temporary states of transcendence in which a sense of unity is achieved through an anni-

hilation of quotidian consciousness. One of the poems alluded to in this section of *The Waste Land*, Marvell's "To His Coy Mistress," ends with the recognition that sex alters time: "Thus, though we cannot make our sun/Stand still, yet we will make him run." Time does not exist for lovers in the throes of physical passion. Sometimes the dualities of self and other also vanish, leaving the lovers in a state of immediate experience, a downward transcendence into the body.

Most preachers against physical passion, including the Buddha and Augustine, are mindful of the fact that sex and religion constitute rival modes of achieving unity. Ascetics commonly note that transcendent states originating in sex are brief; and, of course, they try to motivate their listeners to strive for the opposite and upward transcendence into spirituality. But for all the genuine differences between physical and spiritual transcendence, they share one result: an abolition of quotidian or relational consciousness. Eliot's secular city is a place where people cannot imagine transcendence of any kind. They are incapable of spiritual transcendence, but also they are incapable of physical transcendence. They are bound upon the wheel of relational consciousness, as incapable of lust as of mystical experience.

It should also be noted that both the Buddha and Augustine associate the knowledge of good with the knowledge of evil. The lovers in "The Fire Sermon" are creatures for whom good and evil would be unintelligible concepts. In *The Waste Land*, these lovers point to the ideas of Charles Baudelaire, whose work provides much of the moral underpinning of the poem and whose "cité pleine de rêves" and "hypocrite lecteur!—mon semblable,—mon frère!" we discussed in our chapter on "The Burial of the Dead." In one of his journals, called *Fusées* (Rockets), Baudelaire recounts being involved in a discussion about the greatest pleasure of making love. One of his companions, a hedonist, suggests that the greatest pleasure is in giving pleasure; another, a patriot, that the greatest pleasure is in generating future citizens. The third, a moralist, maintains that "the supreme and singular joy of making love resides in the certainty of doing *evil*."[7] Being human means knowing good and evil and being able to choose between them. Baudelaire suggests that sanitizing sex removes one of the glorious occasions for knowing and choosing evil and thus greatly impoverishes

124

the human spirit. In a 1930 essay, Eliot discusses Baudelaire's satanism and his preoccupation with evil and damnation. He quotes Baudelaire's aphorism "la volupté unique et suprême de l'amour git dans la certitude de faire le mal" and adds:

> This means, I think, that Baudelaire has perceived that what distinguishes the relations of man and woman from the copulation of beasts is the knowledge of Good and Evil. . . . he was at least able to understand that the sexual act as evil is more dignified, less boring, than as the natural, "life-giving," cheery automatism of the modern world. For Baudelaire, sexual operation is at least something not analogous to Kruschen Salts.
>
> So far as we are human, what we do must be either evil or good; so far as we do evil or good, we are human; and it is better, in a paradoxical way, to do evil than to do nothing: at least, we exist. It is true to say that the glory of man is his capacity for salvation; it is also true to say that his glory is his capacity for damnation.[8]

This passage is the best possible commentary on the sexual episodes in "The Fire Sermon."

Baudelaire held to a nineteenth-century variant of antinomianism, the theological concept that through God's gift of grace in Christ, people are freed not only from Old Testament laws but from all laws. It derives from Saint Paul's opposition to legalism in morals and ethics but throughout the centuries has been extended to justify total lawlessness. It also often means, as in Baudelaire, that knowing good presupposes knowing evil. The great philosopher, he says, must first be a great debauchee. Baudelaire's position is parallel to the basic structural idea underlying the *Divine Comedy*, the view that the downward road into hell must be taken en route to purgation and paradise. The similarity of the two is underscored in "The Burial of the Dead" by Eliot's superimposition of Baudelaire's city of dreams on Dante's Hell. Philosophical antinomianism, of course, is much older than Dante or Saint Paul; it goes back at least to Heraclitus, whose "The way up and the way down are one and the same" Eliot used as the epigraph to "Burnt Norton." And it continues into the present. Visual approximations of this idea are the trademark of the modern artist M. C. Escher.[9]

The paradox of downward and upward transcendence, the idea

that the way down and the way up are the same, has rough equivalents both in Bradley's philosophy and in myth. In Bradley, the road to the Absolute begins in the ideal unity of immediate experience, which Eliot calls "annihilation and utter night."[10] Consideration of that void, however, leads to "an all-inclusive experience outside of which nothing shall fall."[11] Eliot makes it plain that both the beginning in a precognitive condition and the hypothetical end, in the Absolute—in Bradley's words, a "positive non-distinguished non-relational whole"[12]—are conceptualizations of nothingness as a reality bordering consciousness. Up and down, back and forth— all transcendences lead in the same direction. Without a religious leap of some kind, one cannot ascribe evil to one pole and good to the other. Each is annihilation and utter night. Later in this chapter, we shall turn to the variation on upward and downward transcendence found in Bradley's reflections on ethics, reflections which are particularly helpful in understanding the moral landscape of "The Fire Sermon."

In the vegetation myths Eliot drew on for *The Waste Land*, the way down is also the way up, for death is a necessary step toward immortality. The antinomianism of life through death, good through evil, is vividly clear in the waste land myths, for both the general health and the king's transcendence require his death. Because the king and his land are one, and because this metonymic identity of king and land, central subject and peripheral object, is felt without question, antinomianism is all-pervasive. It is part of the structure undergirding the mental state or point of view shared by members of the community. Unless members of a community share this sort of unconscious antinomianism, in fact, a myth cannot function as a unifying point of attention; in Yeats's great image, "Things fall apart; the centre cannot hold."

One irony here is that Eliot has reached a position in which he understands myth with such clarity that he can also understand why it cannot function at all. "After such knowledge, what forgiveness?" The answer to Gerontion's question is that after a technical scientific knowledge of myth and religion there can be no forgiveness because such knowledge strips value from all of the imaginable directions of transcendence. Death and resurrection, evil and goodness, physical passion and spiritual ecstasy, and all such movements are equally meaningless. From this perspective, all that is left is the quotidian center where limited transcendences—shifts of focus from scene to scene or from pattern to detail—constitute the only remaining mental movements. "The Fire Sermon" is not only about the modern dilemma of automatons but also about the dilemma of philosophers and moralists whose knowledge locks them into a relational realm, whose consciousness blocks not only forgiveness but transcendence of any significant kind. On several levels, then, "The Fire Sermon" is concerned with the absence of fire and the irrelevance of sermons. It evokes a desire for something to desire. The second Thames daughter perhaps illustrates best the condition of entrapment within a narrow range of values with her answer to her lover's weeping and promise of "a new start": "What should I resent?" With nothing that matters at stake, both apologies and resentments are beside the point.

Seen this way, "The Fire Sermon" reveals a clear thematic continuity in *The Waste Land*. The five episodes of "The Burial of the Dead" focus on issues their characters regard as intensely important. Marie appears to lead a vague life devoted to evading the cycles of nature, but she cannot remove from the center of her consciousness the fear in her childhood experience on the sled. The questioner and the son of man directly encounter "the agony of stony places" and "fear in a handful of dust." The lovers have transcendent experiences, and Madame Sosostris emerges from a tonality of casual crankishness to make interpretations that assume the seriousness and validity of existence. Even the compound of Stetson and his questioner and accuser evokes a painful sense of lost chances for transcendence. The characters in "A Game of Chess" also have strong feelings of distress, though their distress is to themselves a matter of some vagueness. Lil and the affluent woman are desperate for a structure they cannot provide for themselves. Unlike the hyacinth lovers, they can see no point of passionate transcendence against which to measure their present relational condition. "The Fire Sermon" moves beyond these situations into a realm where figures have no sense of what is lost or denied them. Memory and desire are not mixed in their minds because nothing is important enough to occupy either mental category. Here at the center of *The Waste Land*, we encounter the ultimate deprivation: the inability to feel and the absence of suffering. There remains only the final extinction offered in "Death by Water" to complete the thematic continuity. From this perspective, the renewal of anguish in "What the Thunder Said" comes across as an exhilarating affirmation, but that is a matter for later discussion.

"The Fire Sermon" opens with a description of the coming of winter to the river Thames. The scene includes images of desolation, desertion, death. The mythic creatures who once frequented riverbanks have long since departed, and their successors, future bureaucrats and their ladyfriends, have been gone long enough for their litter to have washed away. The single person left in this demythologized landscape is a poet, a highly conscious one who is in a hurry to finish his song and leave. The wind still blows, but it is demythologized wind and, as in the abandoned chapel of part V, it passes by unheard.

The river's tent is broken: the last fingers of leaf
Clutch and sink into the wet bank. The wind
Crosses the brown land, unheard. The nymphs are departed.
Sweet Thames, run softly, till I end my song.
The river bears no empty bottles, sandwich papers,
Silk handkerchiefs, cardboard boxes, cigarette ends
Or other testimony of summer nights. The nymphs are departed.
And their friends, the loitering heirs of city directors;
Departed, have left no addresses.
By the waters of Leman I sat down and wept . . .
Sweet Thames, run softly till I end my song,
Sweet Thames, run softly, for I speak not loud or long.
But at my back in a cold blast I hear
The rattle of the bones, and chuckle spread from ear to ear.

The scene shows some movement, but within the narrowed area of relations we have identified as the location of "The Fire Sermon," shifts from scene to scene and from pattern to detail take on a gratuitous quality. They are not movements in the direction of a transcendence to a realm of value but apparently random montage effects. Take, for example, the two metaphoric transformations with which the description begins. The foliage overhanging the river is a tent, and the fallen leaves on the bank are clutching fingers. The movement from summer to winter is figured as the transformation of a canopy into dying hands. The fingers prefigure "White bodies naked on the low damp ground," but the tent metaphor initiates nothing. From a mythic perspective, the two metaphors call attention to the way vegetation and human life were once unified as aspects of a single force of fertility, but that perspective only serves to dramatize their disconnection from each other into completely separate classes. It is reasonable to suppose that the metaphors of tent and fingers are deliberately designed to illustrate a tropological incoherence at the beginning of this part of the poem. The incoherence of the two tropes is coherent with the mental incoherence resulting from the breakdown of the mythic unity of vegetative and human life.

Other dubiously coherent shifts follow. For example, the line from Spenser's "Prothalamion"—"Sweet Thames, run softly, till I end my song"—initiates a rich sequence of transformations. First, it generates a recursive image of the sixteenth century, both as a real scene on the river and as a fragment of a past tonality in poetry. Second, in a passage designed to read like flat speech, it calls attention to the speaker as a poet and to itself as a song and thus transforms the style and genre of the passage. The speaker's consciousness of tradition and its loss is emphasized, and the self-referential aspect of the quotation is underscored when the line returns.

> Sweet Thames, run softly till I end my song,
> Sweet Thames, run softly, for I speak not loud or long.

The felt distinction between song and speech is blurred like the conventional distinctions between reading and writing, seeing and hearing. Third, as a quotation from a song addressed to a bride going down the river to her wedding, the line points to the sailor's song on shipboard to Isolde in part I, to Elizabeth and Leicester in an ironic way, to Cleopatra on her barge, to the Thames daughters having sexual experiences in boats, and to the fusion of boat and woman near the end of part V:

> The boat responded
> Gaily, to the hand expert with sail and oar
> The sea was calm, your heart would have responded
> Gaily, when invited, beating obedient
> To controlling hands

Also, the bridal party in Spenser's ship is linked backward to mythic wood nymphs and forward to contemporary nymphs who have departed along with the heirs of city directors.

The most important observation here is that these shifts in scene and in direction of reference do not move in any direction suggesting a possible unitive perspective. In earlier parts of the poem, references motivate sequences of transcendences from one level to another. For example, Madame Sosostris suggests shifts in focus to the Cumaean Sibyl and Tiresias. Each phase in the process of noting the changes in focus takes the reader to more remote and thus more inclusive perspectives. Madame Sosostris knows practically nothing and is paranoid; the Sibyl knows all but wants to die; Tiresias knows all, does not consider dying, and tells what he sees. Though these shifts in focus do not lead to a final perspective from which the reader can see the whole poem as a substantial unity, they constitute a clear direction of mental movement toward such a merger of viewpoints in a final place from which all events coalesce into a whole. That kind of hermeneutic sequence is precisely what is eliminated from "The Fire Sermon." Tent and fingers, bridesmaids, nymphs, the littered river, city directors, and even the collapse of song into speech are shown merely to flicker in and out of the reader's gratuitous points of attention. This technique is an abandonment of past procedures in the poem and must be perceived as an attempt to show antitranscendent patterns. Where no directions of movement into either erotic passion or spiritual unity are imaginable, movement will take on the quality of movement for its own sake, montage for the purpose merely of establishing random fluctuation as the modus operandi of a consciousness that is not only relational but unaware that anything else can be imagined.

The montages that follow continue the pattern of blocking transcendent movement or at least of making it seem far-fetched. "By the waters of Leman I sat down and wept" is the most abrupt shift so far in "The Fire Sermon." The line clearly echoes the Old Testament. In Psalm 137:1, the lament "By the rivers of Babylon, there we sat down, yea, we wept, when we remembered Zion" is spoken by Jews who have been taken as slaves by Babylonians. Annotators sometimes associate the line with Eliot's situation while writing the poem. He had been sent to Switzerland to recover from physical and mental exhaustion and wrote part of the poem on the shores of Lake Geneva. Other annotators relate the line to the grief of Marie Larisch and other figures of exile in the poem. None of these interpretations, however, reveals any direction of transcendence. The line stands finally as a voice from another country, perhaps another time, and even perhaps a cursive-recursive alternation of places and times, entering the text to widen its field of fluctuations. That field, ranging in space from England to Switzerland and in time from the sixteenth century to the twentieth, is the poem's scene at this point.

The second verse paragraph returns to the general urban landscape of the opening lines. It is still winter, but the river has become a dull canal behind the gashouse, with rats creeping through the vegetation and naked white bodies on the damp ground. The speaker is revealed as a fisherman, an extraordinarily literary one who knows the works of Marvell, Shakespeare, Verlaine, and, as Grover Smith has pointed out, James Joyce.[13]

> A rat crept softly through the vegetation
> Dragging its slimy belly on the bank
> While I was fishing in the dull canal
> On a winter evening round behind the gashouse
> Musing upon the king my brother's wreck
> And on the king my father's death before him.
> White bodies naked on the low damp ground
> And bones cast in a little low dry garret,
> Rattled by the rat's foot only, year to year.
> But at my back from time to time I hear
> The sound of horns and motors, which shall bring
> Sweeney to Mrs. Porter in the spring.
> O the moon shone bright on Mrs. Porter
> And on her daughter
> They wash their feet in soda water
> *Et O ces voix d'enfants, chantant dans la coupole!*

The first stanza, it will be recalled, ended with an allusion to Marvell's "To His Coy Mistress."

> But at my back in a cold blast I hear
> The rattle of the bones, and chuckle spread from ear to ear.

In the middle of the second stanza, the allusion returns, with a variation:

131

> But at my back from time to time I hear
> The sound of horns and motors . . .

"To His Coy Mistress" is a seventeenth-century *carpe diem* poem which takes the form of a conditional syllogism. The first paragraph informs the lady that if they had all the time in the world her coyness would be no crime. The second reminds her, through a series of images of death, that they are quickly running out of time. And the third concludes with "therefore" they should make sport while the sun shines, so to speak. The second part of Marvell's syllogism begins with:

> But at my back I alwaies hear
> Time's winged Chariot hurrying near:
> And yonder all before us lye
> Desarts of vast eternity.

Eliot follows Marvell by multiplying images of death—bones, rats, naked bodies on the wet ground. And he reduces Marvell's marble vault to "a little low dry garret." Eliot departs from Marvell, however, in two conspicuous ways. First, he includes a synaesthetic mixture of hearing and seeing. Marvell's second line tells what he hears behind his back, the sound of time's chariot gaining on him, and his fourth line reports what he sees ahead, eternity as a vast unrelieved waste land. Eliot's second line also tells what he hears in the cold wind at his back: "The rattle of the bones, and chuckle spread from ear to ear." But Eliot's line includes a detail that can only be seen, the spreading of the chuckle from ear to ear. Something heard conjures up something seen, thus splitting the experience into a binary datum that places the chuckle in one mental location and its source in a death's head in another location. Second, Marvell's lover is contemplating his own death in the future, but Eliot's speaker is considering the deaths of others—brother and father—in the past. The shifts to the Fisher King and Prince Ferdinand in *The Tempest* are shifts to more inclusive contexts and continue a pattern of variations initiated by Madame Sosostris in part I. But there is a crucial difference between what Marvell is doing and what Eliot is doing. The musings upon death in "To His Coy Mistress" are offered as part of an argument, as part of a pattern with a purpose. Marvell's threats of death have the precise and immediate

132

end of convincing a woman to make love. In contrast, Eliot's musings upon death are gratuitous; there is no purpose and can be no argument. Replacing clear arguments with gratuitous shifts of scene is a technique indicating confinement in a realm where arguments are pointless, where purposes and convictions do not exist.

Eliot's first variation on Marvell, as we have remarked, follows its model in accumulating serious images of death. His second variation, however, seems to deny the seriousness of death altogether.

> But at my back from time to time I hear
> The sound of horns and motors, which shall bring
> Sweeney to Mrs. Porter in the spring.
> O the moon shone bright on Mrs. Porter
> And on her daughter
> They wash their feet in soda water
> *Et O ces voix d'enfants, chantant dans la coupole!*

The shift from time's chariot to a modern traffic jam and then to gossip of prostitutes can be read as an attempt to escape from the preceding *memento mori* details or as a simple process of cutting from one subject to another; many critics read it as an equation of modern life and death. The important point, however, is that it is a transition from the last traces of transcendence into a realm of random montage. However meaningless and disconnected they may be, musings upon death provide some contrast between the conditions of being and not being. But now the only contrasts are within quotidian life.

A closer look at what happens in the reading of these lines may be helpful at this point. Marvell's poem provides "Time's winged Chariot" as the sound to be heard, Eliot's first variation provides "The rattle of the bones, and chuckle spread from ear to ear" as the synaesthetic construct to be experienced, and his second variation on Marvell produces "The sound of horns and motors," which will somehow motivate Sweeney to visit Mrs. Porter. At this point in the recognition process, four unrelated scenes are locked together: a chariot, a rattle chuckle, a traffic jam, and a visit, presumably to a prostitute. Consider, further, that Eliot's note associates "The sound of horns and motors" with the following lines from John Day's "Parliament of the Bees."

When of the sudden, listening, you shall hear,
A noise of horns and hunting, which shall bring
Actaeon to Diana in the spring,
Where all shall see her naked skin

The scenes multiply in many directions. The modern traffic jam, the seventeenth-century scene of English fox hunters, the ancient mythic forest where gods and goddesses reside, and the contemporary residence where Sweeney, Mrs. Porter, and her daughter play games with soda water all flicker in and out of focus. Certain kinds of analogies between the pictures call attention to themselves: chariots, motorcars, and horses as ways of riding; the death's head chuckle, the sound of traffic, and the laughter and singing at Mrs. Porter's party; Diana's bath and foot washing; the death of Actaeon and the insouciance of Sweeney in earlier poems. These analogies, however, neither unify the scenes nor expand by contrast the mental spaces between them. They merely constitute a medium of changing relations in which they exist.

A closer look at the Actaeon story mentioned in John Day's poem reveals a mythic perspective on these pictures, a perspective from which they form a coherent pattern among themselves and in relation to the preceding lines emphasizing death. Diana is the goddess of both hunting and chastity. This will seem like a strange combination until it is remembered that hunting is a primitive food-gathering method that does not depend on sexual fertilization of the earth. Her chastity is matched by her modesty, so when the mortal hunter Actaeon sees her naked in the bath, she cannot permit him to survive such a vision. He is transformed into a stag, his dogs dismember him, and the privacy of the goddess is preserved. The story conveys a commonplace message: Mortals cannot survive certain kinds of knowledge; they cannot survive looking directly at naked divinity. Safe knowledge is knowledge of disguising surfaces, enclosing bundles of qualities. In the deep background of the montage pattern, thus, a perspective resides. It is another variation on the theme of knowledge and its consequences. Unlike Actaeon, Sweeney is safe. He will see nothing. And the reader who does not discover the perspective provided by the Actaeon myth will see only the random flickerings of discrete phenomena; but once he acquires that perspective, he is in a transcendent position from which meaningless shifts coexist with interpretations of meaning within them.

This verse paragraph ends with a variation of a bawdy ballad and a quotation from a poem about the Holy Grail. Eliot says in a note that the ballad was reported to him from Australia. In several versions, Mrs. Porter and her daughter are prostitutes who wash themselves after visits from customers.[14] The poem, Paul Verlaine's "Parsifal," tells of the knight's mastery of the fires of lust (including lust for young boys with small breasts), his conquest of a beautiful woman, and his healing of the wounded king. The poem ends with Parsifal worshiping the chalice while the boys' choir sings in the dome. "*Et O ces voix d'enfants, chantant dans la coupole!*" In Wagner's *Parzival*, which Verlaine has in mind, the choir sings at the ceremony preceding the restoration of the wounded king and the lifting of the curse from the waste land.

It is customary to read the line about Mrs. Porter washing her feet in soda water and the quotation from Verlaine as perversions of religious rituals and experiences. Certainly the reference to prostitutes seems to debase to triviality both the foot washing of Christ and the purification of the Fisher King after he has answered the knight's questions and is ready to heal the land by sacrificing himself. The purification ceremony can be seen as further debased when it is noted that the speaker in Verlaine's poem who is so interested in the boys' choir has just complimented himself for having overcome a perverse sexual attraction toward young boys. These readings, however, miss a necessary point. If Verlaine's speaker expresses profane and abominable lust, he nevertheless is burning with something; he at least expresses something strongly felt. If the horseplay with soda water and feet is part of an intense drunken revelry, it is also something strongly felt which may take its participants out of their relational, quotidian selves, at least for a few moments. The point here is the Baudelairean idea that feeling something is better than feeling nothing. We are closer to Eliot's habitual mode of ironic dialectics if we realize that from one point of view a parody of foot washing and a sacred rite of foot washing have equal value insofar as they both constitute a transcendence. The same must be said of whatever pederastic motives underlie the reaction to the children's voices. "Be drunk," writes Baudelaire, "on wine, poetry, religion, as you please. But be drunk."[15] In other words, transcend the relational.

The montage is ended by the sounds of birds:

> Twit twit twit
> Jug jug jug jug jug jug
> So rudely forc'd.
> Tereu

This brief stanza is an allusion to the myth of Philomela and her sister Procne, daughters of the king of Athens, and of Procne's husband King Tereus of Thrace. It is alluded to in parts II, III, and V of *The Waste Land* and in almost all interpretations is of special importance. The story, reported by Ovid in *Metamorphoses*, is one of transformation through cruelty and death. Like other marriages in *The Waste Land*, that of Procne and Tereus was loveless, wrong from the beginning because not blessed by the bridal goddess. After five unhappy years with Tereus, Procne convinces him to fetch Philomela from Athens for a visit. As he returns with Philomela, he takes her into the woods and rapes her. When she threatens to tell Procne, he cuts out her tongue and rapes her again before abandoning her, and then tells Procne she has been slain. Philomela manages to weave a tapestry telling the story and sends it to Queen Procne, who brings her back to the palace. Procne avenges her sister's rape and mutilation by murdering her own son and serving him in a stew to his father, Tereus. When Tereus discovers what he has eaten, he is horror-struck and pursues Procne and Philomela. The cycle of revenge is interrupted at this point, for before he can kill them the three are changed into birds. Tereus becomes a hawk, Procne a swallow, and Philomela a nightingale.

In "The Fire Sermon," Eliot evokes this horror tale by using the syllables associated with the birds and by referring to the rape—"So rudely forc'd." Of the many implications, one is related to the emphasis in this part of the poem on moving beyond the closed, flickering world of relational experience. Foot washing with soda water is one distortion of a sacred ceremony, and listening to a boys' choir with sodomistic intent is a stronger distortion of a sacred moment. The rape and mutilation of Philomela and the subsequent murder of the child involve multiple distortions of sacred moments.

136

But both King Tereus and Philomela achieve transformation and release when the gods turn them into birds. This story is dreadful, but at least it involves a radical transformation, a transcendence through crime and agony into the peace of an alternate point of view.

The words suggesting the voices of birds who were once human beings locked in a spectacular contest of cruelty not only function as allusions to a mythic transcendence and as an oblique prefiguration of the bloodiness of Hieronymo near the end of the poem; they also function as a simultaneous reduction and expansion of language. "Twit," "jug," and "Tereu" are words that mean nothing. They are pure nonsignifiers. But that purity of meaninglessness exists only in the minds of those who speak those words—swallow, nightingale, and hawk. When encountered by the reader, they signify the presence of birds as illusions created by human speakers who wish to convey that presence without naming it. No bird ever made a sound like "jug," just as no cock says "co co rico" and no thunder ever sounds like the syllable "DA."

At the climax of the sequence of montages opening "The Fire Sermon," this coalescence of significances and insignificances serves as a summation. We are alerted to take every item in a multiple way, ranging from the pole of maximum transcendence to the pole of no transcendence at all. If birds mean nothing when they sing, poets mean a variety of messages when they contrive words to quote them. If "twit," "jug," and "Tereu" are mere quotations of birds, they nevertheless point to the catastrophes in the myth. If "Tereu" quotes the hawk who was once the wretched king, the nonsense syllable comes within a phoneme of pronouncing his name, Tereus. That closeness, however, is presented as a pointless coincidence, a witless pun, just as the coincidence later of the conventional Sanskrit *Da* and three words beginning with those letters is a contrivance of interpreters attempting to explicate what they regard as transcendent signifiers. The poem has moved through Spenser, Shakespeare, Marvell, Day, a popular song, Verlaine, and miscellaneous lyrics about birds to a moment when words are made to stand alone as mere sounds that call attention to their status as both meaningless syllables and conveyers of unlimited significance. If there was a time, as Eliot speculates, "before 'meaning' meant anything at all," then perhaps there is a time after meaning when the primal purity of insignificance will return. Such a speculation is identical in form to Bradley's phases of cognition that are before and after time.

When "The Fire Sermon" is seen as a whole structure, the opening variations ending with bird sounds and the closing fragments mixing Saint Augustine and the Buddha form a setting for two contrasting kinds of central episodes. The first consists of love stories in fragmentary form, and the second of a brief evocation of the communal life of "fishmen" in a public bar near the church of Magnus Martyr. The pub scene, with its mandolin music, is brief and easy to overlook, but its apparent irrelevance to the erotic episodes surrounding it suggests that Eliot had a reason for placing it at just this point in the very middle of the poem. The point of centering this communion scene will become clearer following an examination of the sexual anecdotes that frame it. The structure of "The Fire Sermon," then, is concentric—involving frames within frames. The opening variations and the sermons against lust frame a set of variations on sex with minimum lust which in turn frame a short episode on the communion of workers in a bar and the splendor of a contiguous place of communion, the church of Magnus Martyr.

The love stories—Queen Elizabeth and Robert Leicester along with five contemporary couples—combine to create different versions of the motif of mechanical sex, of copulation without passion and without an awareness of the knowledge of good or evil. Mr. Eugenides makes his proposition, the typist and clerk couple with the zeal of automatons, and three women recall events on the river. In addition, Tiresias narrates his voyeurism as a contrast to his history of more active and consequential erotic misadventures. In contrast to the lovers in the first two parts of *The Waste Land*, these lovers feel nothing, expect nothing, and resent nothing. These human relations are minimal precisely because they occupy the Bradleian center of pure relation itself. That center is bordered by immediate and transcendent cognitions which provide directions of conceptualized value. But these borders are, as we have noted, no longer imaginable, for where relations alone exist, relations themselves fade into the most mutable and problematic condition. If, as

Bradley argues in *Appearance and Reality*, *A* is related to *B* in a certain way, then that relationship is itself related to both *A* and *B*, generating a limitless array of contingent modes of relation.[16] It is only where all these relations are themselves related to a cognitive mode involving no relations at all that the experiences of relational clarity and stability can be conceived. Put simply, our reading of the "love stories" is based on the guess that Eliot is writing about human relations in approximately the same way that he had thought about philosophical concepts of relation. The information necessary to prove this guess correct is not available and probably does not exist. But the value of the idea for reading *The Waste Land* is both incalculable and unique.

Eliot's techniques in presenting the fragments of love stories raise a number of interesting questions. The first fragment presents Mr. Eugenides, evidently the merchant foretold by Madame Sosostris.

> Unreal City
> Under the brown fog of a winter noon
> Mr. Eugenides, the Smyrna merchant
> Unshaven, with a pocket full of currants
> C.i.f. London: documents at sight,
> Asked me in demotic French
> To luncheon at the Cannon Street Hotel
> Followed by a weekend at the Metropole.

Does Mr. Eugenides have one eye only, as shown earlier on the tarot card? If so, is his lost eye a sort of halfway point in the movement toward the no-eyed Tiresias? Or is his eye missing because, like his image on the card, he is frozen into profile? These questions have no answers in any conventional sense. The text generates uncertainties that exfoliate in many directions. These uncertainties generate a sense of the potential of both abstraction and empathy. The heraldic imagery of the one-eyed figure in profile is static and two-dimensional, but the Levantine unshaven traveler who has lost an eye in unknown adventures is empathetic, three-dimensional, present. Abstraction and empathy continue to oscillate between cursive and recursive versions, with no substantial clues for the reader who desires a definitive interpretation.

Other questions branch out from the previous ones. Does the

name Eugenides mean anything worth noting? Probably not, but one cannot ignore the eugenic possibilities of meaning. Does he have only one pocket full of currants because, forever in profile, he has only one pocket? His commercial documents, Eliot remarks in a note, are "sight drafts." Is the reference to sight related to the questions about his ability to see? Madame Sosostris deals out a blank card which she says is something the one-eyed merchant carries on his back, "Which I am forbidden to see." Is that deep mystery revealed as a mere sight draft? Or is Mr. Eugenides carrying something else on his back, or is there something on the back side of the card that he must inhabit? These questions seem trivial until it is noted where they lead. Who is the only figure available in this vicinity of the poem who can be trusted to see all about the figure? Tiresias is the clear answer. The suggestion that Tiresias is narrating the poem eleven lines before he names himself does not reveal the answers to these questions, but it does remind the reader that a point of view exists from which answers are clear and unproblematic. The reader cannot see from that perspective, but a mythic blind androgyne can. This awareness is another suggestion of the transcendent reading process we discussed earlier. Clarity as such does not emerge, but at least there is a motion toward an inclusive perspective.

The branching of questions now accelerates. If Tiresias is the narrator, then is it necessary to suppose that Mr. Eugenides invites him to lunch and a weekend at the Metropole? If so, does this suggest that Tiresias is just as multiform, abstract and empathetic, remote and close, as the merchant? Does it suggest that Tiresias has received a concrete homosexual invitation? Tiresias is a man, though in the dim past he has been a woman, and he is still preoccupied with the vestiges of that transsexual episode. On the other hand, it is possible that past and present—linear time—is irrelevant to the condition Tiresias inhabits. After all, as a figure from myth, Tiresias is not in time at all, even though he can interact with those who are time-bound. He can receive the merchant's proposition, watch the typist and clerk, accuse Oedipus, visit Hades, and live as man and woman all at once in a dimension where time does not exist, the transcendent dimension of mythic fiction. It would be as improper to say that he rejects the proposition to go to a homosexual haunt as to say that he accepts it. Similarly, it is impossible to say that the proposition was homosexual, for Tiresias, in and out of time, is "throbbing between two lives," male and female, real and ideal, fact and fiction.

The purpose of raising all of these questions is to clarify the radical lack of clarity in the experience of reading this poem. It is a special kind of limited uncertainty, however, for it suggests that somewhere, outside of the text, there is a perspective from which questions would vanish and all would be plain. Even without Eliot's note to the effect that what Tiresias sees is the substance of the poem, the reader should be able to see that Tiresias's perspective is more comprehensive and should thereby be challenged to achieve that mythic perspective. The reader is inside the text attempting to get out of the closed system so he can see it as a substance and discover its essence. His position and its movements are key dramatic components of the structure of the poem.

We have argued earlier that Eliot's note on what Tiresias sees suggests that *The Waste Land* has no substance from any perspective that is actually available to the reader. No reader can see as Tiresias sees, and most readers will not grant Tiresias existence in the same way that they will grant it to, say, the typist, the clerk, Marie, Madame Sosostris, and some others. Conventions of reading converge to trap the reader into supposing that fabulous figures in a narrative are less real than commonplace figures, even though it is well known that both types are imaginary. The ghost is a contrivance, but so is Hamlet. Don Quixote is imaginary and so is his windmill, but he seems to be a fact within a fiction, whereas his monstrous adversary seems to be a mere fiction. The examples are obvious and endlessly numerous. The point, though, must be considered carefully. Eliot's technique obliges the reader of *The Waste Land* to dismantle these reading conventions by making them overt, by foregrounding what is normally not considered at all. Tiresias, clerk, and typist share a common condition: They are fictions, referential illusions in a sequence of words. The hierarchy of realism, here, ceases to function.

Eliot's ways of particularizing these personages corroborates the idea that he is dismantling the conventions of reading. Tiresias, he says in a note, is "a mere spectator and not indeed a 'character,' " but he is described in greater physical detail than are any of the others. Mr. Eugenides is described with a single word, "unshaven." He may be one-eyed, and he speaks "demotic French," but he remains, even on a narrow realistic level, a vague minimalistic image. The clerk is slightly more visible, but even here the figure remains vague. He is young, carbuncular, has a bold stare and a look of assurance. But these details do not permit the reader to visualize him. "Carbuncular," the one term that specifically describes him, is a facial variation on "unshaven," the one pictorial detail for Mr. Eugenides. That these terms suggest unattractive images is less important than their minimalism and their limitation to faces. The typist is even more vague as a presence. Not one descriptive term applies to her. Like the woman at her dressing table in "A Game of Chess," she is invisible. Her environment and cast-off clothing—"Stockings, slippers, camisoles, and stays"—are presented, but as is the case with the woman in the dressing room, her person emerges only in a reference to her hair—"She smoothes her hair with automatic hand."

In contrast, Tiresias, the mere spectator, gives several descriptive details about himself. He is blind and old, a man with "wrinkled female breasts," "wrinkled dugs." Further, he reminds the reader of his history and abilities. Though blind, he can see, and further, he can foresee the future. Specifically, he can foresee the clerk's arrival and the drama to be enacted upon the "divan or bed." He has "foresuffered all," because he has experienced sexuality as both male and female. He seems to complain about the triviality of his current experiences in contrast to his past situation in Thebes and in the realm of the heroic dead. The main effect of this self-presentation is that Tiresias emerges as a solid figure, a body with vivid anomalies, to dominate the scene. Focus on the bodies of the lovers would have been more predictable, because even the most casual sex produces a dominating focus on the particularities of bodies. Here, however, sex occurs without any reference to bodies at all and with almost none to physical appearance. Only the spectator/speaker has a body, and he is viewing from a dimension beyond all particularities. What Tiresias sees, to put it another way, is not reported in detail, but what he feels about his own body is substituted for the bodies before him.

142

Such techniques of presentation work against the convention of narrative. A figure from myth is supposed to be shadowy and not quite real, a speaking trope. But merchants, typists, and clerks are understood to be real and ubiquitous. When such conventional expectations are reversed, the effect is to call into question such polarities as ends and means, message and medium, narrative and narrator. Normally messages and narratives have the position of ergon, central essence, whereas media and narrators are framing methods, parerga, peripheral, and accidental positions. As in the episode of Tristan and Isolde and the hyacinth lovers, ergon and parergon switch positions. Tiresias is the parergon, who takes over the central position, forcing a scattering of merchant, typist, and clerk, along with all human sexuality, into positions on the fringe of perception and concern.

Nevertheless, conventions of granting presence and factuality to objects of narrative, especially when they are familiar types in familiar actions, draw attention back to the vaguely drawn typist and clerk and away from the vivid solidity and kinesthetic body of Tiresias. The effect is an unstoppable oscillation. Eliot argued in his dissertation that, wherever a subject and an object stand in a state of dualism, the subject perceiving them becomes a third term uniting the first two as adjectives modifying each other. Tiresias is a subject, the lovers are objects, and the third term, which resolves the subject–object dualism into a unity, is the reader's mind. The difficulty with this argument is that the reader is obliged by the narrative technique to experience the continual oscillation of subject and object, Tiresias and the lovers. If the reader's mind is not the place where a unity can be achieved, then such a place is not available except as a hypothetical subjectivity occupying a perspective beyond all known positions.

A contrary effect is created by the voices from the river. Like Tiresias, Wagner's Rhine maidens are mythic creatures, but they do not emerge in physical detail. Their lament is prefaced by lyric stanzas describing the urban river sweating oil and tar.

> The river sweats
> Oil and tar
> The barges drift
> With the turning tide

143

Red sails
Wide
To leeward, swing on the heavy spar.
The barges wash
Drifting logs
Down Greenwich reach
Past the Isle of Dogs.
            Weialala leia
            Wallala leilala

        Elizabeth and Leicester
Beating oars
The stern was formed
A gilded shell
Red and gold
The brisk swell
Rippled both shores
Southwest wind
Carried down stream
The peal of bells
White towers
            Weialala leia
            Wallala leialala

The cry of the Rhine daughters comes from *Gotterdämmerung*. The women tell Siegfried, who is soon to be killed, the story of how the dwarf Alberich took the gold from them by the stratagem of swearing to reject all love forever. Their song of woe—"Weialala"—is sung to a quietly lyrical, resigned music. They are accustomed to their bereft condition and do not seriously hope that Siegfried will give them back what they have lost. The Thames daughters, similarly, speak in tones of unconcern about events that happened while afloat on the river.

        "Trams and dusty trees.
    Highbury bore me. Richmond and Kew
    Undid me. By Richmond I raised my knees
    Supine on the floor of a narrow canoe."

        "My feet are at Moorgate, and my heart
    Under my feet. After the event
    He wept. He promised 'a new start.'
    I made no comment. What should I resent?"

144

"The Fire Sermon"

> "On Margate Sands.
> I can connect
> Nothing with nothing.
> The broken fingernails of dirty hands.
> My people humble people who expect
> Nothing."
>   la la

The Rhine maidens, like Tiresias, provide a mythic perspective on the contemporary scene, but, unlike him, they do not show any concern about anything; in fact, they do not in any psychological way differ from the women on the Thames. A mood of valueless detachment prevails on both sides of the mythic realistic division. The oscillation of focus does not occur. There is a mere juxtaposition. If there is a framing structure, it is made up only of the object, color and movements that impressionistically represent the river itself and its urban environment. "The Fire Sermon" has exhausted its repertoire of improvisations on the technique of shifts from pattern to detail within a narrowing range of values. The final "la la" comes as a "Who cares?" at the moment when techniques of minimalization have reached the vanishing point.

The "la la" is the nadir of *The Waste Land*, and just at this point, when all value has disappeared, the voices of Saint Augustine and the Buddha provide fragments of intense concern.

> To Carthage then I came

> Burning burning burning burning
> O Lord Thou pluckest me out
> O Lord Thou pluckest

> burning

The old desperation about cooling the fires of lust falls as a sequence of aftershocks on a city already cooled to the point where not only lust but feeling itself has departed. The sermons are spectacularly irrelevant. Eliot's figures feel no desire, resent nothing, and expect nothing. No directions of significant motion are imaginable now, not even the oscillation of focus imposed by earlier techniques of presentation. If the reader is to find any value here, it would have to be the value of value itself. If Augustine and the Buddha are projecting the burning of lust, they can only be lusting for lust itself—for

145

an idea or a sin or an adversary against which to define their sermons. *The Waste Land* has reached its lowest and most desperate moment—the extinction of desperation itself.

We can now return to the center of "The Fire Sermon," the moment of clear value which is situated in the heart of *The Waste Land*. The following stanza is placed between the sordid episode of the typist and the dismal music of the Thames maidens.

> "This music crept by me upon the waters"
> And along the Strand, up Queen Victoria Street.
> O City city, I can sometimes hear
> Beside a public bar in Lower Thames Street,
> The pleasant whining of a mandoline
> And a clatter and a chatter from within
> Where fishmen lounge at noon: where the walls
> Of Magnus Martyr hold
> Inexplicable splendour of Ionian white and gold.

The preceding verse paragraph ends with the mechanical music of the gramophone, and the present paragraph begins with a reference to the passing of "This music." "This music crept by me upon the waters" is a quotation from *The Tempest*, spoken by Prince Ferdinand as he remembers the music that calmed both the fury of the sea and his grief for his father. Eliot's draft, included in *The Waste Land Facsimile*, suggests that the speaker is fleeing through the night from the music of the gramophone, seeking sanctuary in Michael Paternoster Royal, one of the city churches.

> "This music crept by me upon the waters"
> And along the Strand, and up the ghastly hill of Cannon Street,
> Fading at last, behind by flying feet,
> There where the tower was traced against the night
> Of Michael Paternoster Royal, red and white. [17]

These five lines are condensed to two in the final version of the poem. And now, for the first and last time in the poem, the city is addressed as a place that is neither unreal nor depressing. The speaker (Tiresias or not; it does not matter here) can sometimes hear a pleasant music from the public bar, a music in direct contrast to the typist's gramophone, the Wagnerian lament, the "Shakespeherian Rag," and the poetry of the poem itself. The music is not only

146

the sound of a mandolin; it specifically includes the "clatter" and "chatter" from inside the pub where "fishmen lounge at noon." In an unpredictable and brilliant shift, Eliot places the splendor of Magnus Martyr's white and gold within the bar and within the music itself. The effect is a manifold affirmation. It is not simply that a community exists here or that the church is beautiful or even that an analogy is drawn between the communion of workers and the communion within the church. It is an affirmation created by a dazzling artistic technique.

The technique by which Eliot achieves this affirmation can be seen more clearly by considering the passage as a single trope with subsections. The city is metonymically reduced to one of its smallest rooms, the bar. In the process, the city's population is represented by the "fishmen." Their music is contained within the room, but the music contains the spectacular architecture of Wren's church. City, bar, music, the walls of Magnus Martyr, the series moves inward, through containers and things contained until the final term of the series is larger than all but the first term. Further, the last element is produced by a synaesthetic transformation. Music is heard, and one of the voices within the music is the array of colors, "Inexplicable splendour of Ionian white and gold."

Reading now becomes a truly creative activity. The reader may wish to understand only that an island of communal feeling still exists in the midst of epidemic isolation. Or he may wish to understand only that the church is an unused relic of a past community which can be evoked in special moments. He might even wish to accept this passage with a poignant sense of the speaker's position outside that communal music in the bar. These readings are helpful, to some extent, but they do not take sufficient account of the metonymic and synaesthetic structure of the passage.

To apprehend that structure as it stands is to include those partial readings within a much larger experience. It is an experience of a complex trope which can make no impact as either a cluster of experiences or a set of ideas and feelings. Specifically, the passage cannot be apprehended at all from any ready-made perspective. The key to the experience is the deceptively simple line: "Where fishmen lounge at noon: where the walls." The use of a colon and the repetition of "where" presents us with a set of relations that cannot exist in the world. The walls of Magnus Martyr cannot be in the bar and cannot be in the music—except in the alternative universe, the heterocosm,[18] which the poetry invents. To see this brief passage as it is written is to recognize that the reader must invent a universe from which to read and perceive if he is to experience the coherence in what he has read. The affirmation of community is an affirmation of both the artist's creativity and the reader's need to complete the creation of a heterocosmic point of view. We have noted the stimulus to transcendent reading elsewhere in the poem, but no other passage makes the demand more forcefully. All that is required to see this stimulus is a willingness to read the sentences exactly as they are written. The reader, existing outside the poem, has the burden of making sense and value. On the other hand, the figures in the poem are free of such burdens; they drift without desire.

The narrowing range of the poem's emotional reference and the widening field of its techniques can be profitably understood in the context of the moral concepts Eliot brought to bear on his work. The antinomianism which he brought from his study of both the religious and the literary traditions, discussed earlier in this chapter, has structural parallels to Bradley's analysis of experience and to the mythic materials from Frazer that undergird *The Waste Land*. In one way or another, Baudelaire, Frazer, and Bradley imply that opposites like good and evil or beginning and end are in a special sense identical conditions. In Eliot's phrase, the beginning and the end are "annihilation and utter night." And Baudelaire, Frazer, and Bradley imply that health is somehow contingent on transcendence of the relational realm, on moving either forward or backward to a unified world.

Bradley's ideas on ethics, more complex than those of Baudelaire or Frazer, are part of the background Eliot brought to *The Waste Land* and are particularly interesting in regard to "The Fire Sermon," the section of the poem most concerned with morals. Bradley's only sustained consideration of moral philosophy occurs in *Ethical Studies* (1876), his first book. His discussion is informed throughout by an awareness that all moral philosophy involves a focus on polar opposites such as bad and good, the is and the ought, and the individual and the state. He insists that these and all binary oppositions are relational illusions that cannot ground moral action. When the second edition of *Ethical Studies* was published in 1927, Eliot wrote the review for the *Times Literary Supplement*. *Ethical Studies*, as Eliot notes in his review, is primarily an attack on English utilitarianism.

> The *Ethical Studies* are not merely a demolition of the Utilitarian theory of conduct but an attack upon the whole Utilitarian mind. For Utilitarianism was, as every reader of Arnold knows, a great temple in Philistia. And of this temple Arnold hacked at the ornaments and cast down the images. . . . But Bradley, in his philosophical critique of Utilitarianism, undermined the foundations.[19]

Eliot goes on to claim that the attack on utilitarianism is the "social basis of Bradley's distinction, and the social basis is even more his claim to our gratitude than the logical basis."[20] That Eliot's own gratitude to Bradley is related to the critique of utilitarianism is a clue to understanding Eliot's moral position in "The Fire Sermon." The episode of the typist and the clerk, for example, is often read as the product of a prudish mind. Such a reading fails to take account of Eliot's philosophical sophistication and also ignores his continuing critique of utilitarianism.

Utilitarianism is based on a simple formula—the greatest happiness (or the greatest pleasure) for the greatest number. It is generally associated with progress, both moral and material. Most people, Bradley claims, tend to believe that "increase of progress means increase of pleasure," that "advance in goodness and knowledge" and "increase of pleasure" are inseparable.[21] Utilitarianism, extremely popular in the nineteenth century, was advocated chiefly by John Stuart Mill and his disciples. Bradley explains: "The end for modern Utilitarianism is not the pleasure of one, but the pleasure of all, the maximum of pleasurable, and the minimum of painful, feeling in all sentient organisms, and not in my sentient organism."[22] Utilitarianism's claim to be moral is based in part on this emphasis on collective rather than individual pleasure, and also in part on the designation of some pleasures as "preferred" or "higher." But Bradley argues that utilitarianism is neither moral nor logical. He clearly demonstrates, for example, that its defenders fail to clarify the meaning of happiness, the difference between happiness for the individual and for the group, and the difference between happiness within moments and happiness as an ultimate summation of a process. Bradley shows that the whole concept of "happiness" or "pleasure" is too subjective to serve as the foundation of a moral philosophy. Bradley also attacks the opposite tendency, the formalism of Kantian ethics. Pleasure for pleasure's sake is based on naive individualism, and duty for duty's sake leads to despotism.[23]

Bradley's attack on Mill and Kant, on pleasure and duty as moral principles, is immediately helpful in reading "The Fire Sermon." Eliot's presentation of the personages in this section of the poem— the nymphs and heirs of city directors, Sweeney and Mrs. Porter, Mr. Eugenides, the typist and clerk, the Thames daughters—suggests variations on the consequences of making either happiness or duty a moral guide. When her lover departs, the typist has only one half-formed thought: "Well now that's done: and I'm glad it's over." She is a product of a society which has institutionalized pleasure, which makes sex another duty, like working and preparing food. Mill's happiness, or what must pass for it, has replaced Kant's categorical imperative. The fact that sex fails to provide happiness is beside the point; the typist goes grimly about the prescribed routine of doing what is supposed to provide pleasure. She can be seen as Eliot's contribution to Bradley's ridicule of this "philistine" philosophy of institutionalized satisfaction.

In "My Station and Its Duties," the most positive chapter in *Ethical Studies*, Bradley anticipates some of the principles he was to use in his later and more famous works. He insists, as he was to do ever afterward, that nothing is real or meaningful in or of itself, that everything gains existence by being within a context or system. He uses this principle to support his attack on utilitarianism. What is an individual? he asks. And he replies that an individual is a mere figment of the imagination; there has never been nor can there ever be such a creature as J. S. Mill's "individual": "The 'individual' man, the man whose essence his community with others does not enter, who does not include relation to others in his very being, is, we say, a fiction."[24] From the argument that individuals are fictions, Bradley moves to his definition of the community as a "moral organism" of which each individual is a part. He avoids utilitarianism by

150

placing the focus on the community as an organic whole instead of supposing that it is a mere aggregate or "heap" of persons whose happiness can be quantified. If society is a whole system, a moral organism, each person has the obligation to act in a manner appropriate to his position within that organism, with the qualification that positions within society are more flexible than within physical bodies.

In strictly logical terms, these notions lead to Bradley's central paradox. First, moral choices cannot be made from positions within society as organism because those making the choices are, insofar as they are only components, incapable of individual choices. If, for example, a kidney "chooses" to be wicked by ceasing to perform the duties of its station, no one would regard it as wicked. It would only be defective. Second, moral choices cannot be made from a position outside such an organism because in that situation the individual is either isolated (a Robinson Crusoe) or afloat in a radically unstable system of relations. A wicked act would be virtuous from the perspective that would follow it almost immediately. In short, relativistic morals are not moral in any sense.

Where, then, do morals exist, if they exist at all? Bradley's answer is that they do not exist within moral philosophy, that they exist either before a person has begun to focus on moral philosophy or after he has managed to transcend (or ignore) all moral questions. Ethical questions cannot be settled within ethics. Bradley deconstructs ethics the same way that he deconstructs utilitarianism, arguing that all moral philosophy, including his own, must fail, that true morality is possible only outside of moral reflection.[25] This position anticipates his views on the levels of cognition, for here he is insisting that being moral comes either before (immediate experience) or after (transcendent experience) the conscious debate on moral issues (relational experience). Discursive reasoning with its essential generation of opposites and its necessary proliferation of referential illusions has little or nothing to do with making moral judgments.

One reason that casuistry, or reasoning about morals, has so little to do with morality is that any act, when considered from many sides, can be found to be good in some way. Moral reasoning neutralizes morality. Or, as Bradley remarks, "the vice of casuistry is that, attempting to decide the particulars of morality by the deductions of the reflective understanding, it at once degenerates into finding a good reason for what you want to do."[26] In other words, the effect of placing moral questions as such into the focus of everyday life has been to rob people of any clear notion of what is or is not moral. The only way to foster public morals is to contrive, somehow, to forget them altogether. Similarly, there is abundant evidence that the act of reflecting on happiness, of choosing it as a goal to be pursued, turns it into an infinitely receding condition, a "perishing series" like the tomorrows that are always by definition unreachable. Happiness, like morality, has to be a by-product of other pursuits.

The moral point of view, then, can never be final; it automatically generates polarities and contradictions that beg to be resolved and finally implies a higher point of view, one which is found only in religion. "Reflection on morality leads us beyond it. It leads us, in short, to see the necessity of a religious point of view."[27] As David Bell argues in "The Insufficiency of Ethics," an essay to which we are indebted, Bradley is much closer to Kierkegaard than to Hegel in advancing these ideas.[28] The Danish philosopher's existentialist version of the teleological suspension of the ethical is almost the same as Bradley's transcendence of moral perspectives. Both ideas require a position that is not to be found in the ordinary world.

"The Fire Sermon," then, is *The Waste Land*'s moral and spiritual nadir; at the same time, it contains the poem's most dazzling affirmation, the scene of the fishmen lounging at noon outside the pub and the church. In the context of Bradley's moral reflections, Tiresias, along with the whole mythic tradition, is both inside and outside the moral world described by the poem, both inside and outside the urban world of merchants, typists, and clerks. He oscillates between perspectives on others and on himself. He sees himself as a fiction within the organism of history, and he also sees himself alone, isolated from the community. If what he sees is indeed the substance of the poem, the substance of the poem is the moral ambiguity of these oscillating perspectives. If the poem has no substance from any other viewpoint, then it has no unitive substance at all but only a "throbbing between" that cannot stop. On the opposite end of the spectrum from Tiresias are the fishmen outside the pub. They seem to be part of a social organism in which morality is real because unfiltered through moral philosophy, in which moral action rises naturally and unconsciously. Within the surrounding incoherence, this episode provides a cell that is morally coherent. By reflecting upon it, the reader should be able at least to imagine the possibility of a point of view from which the broken fragments of the modern world would be morally coherent.

6 / Annihilation and Utter Night

The Hermeneutical Cycle in "Death by Water"

If anyone assert that immediate experience, at either the beginning or end of our journey, is annihilation and utter night, I cordially agree.—Eliot, *Knowledge and Experience*

In the introduction to his mother's poem *Savonarola*, referred to earlier in this study, Eliot offers a few passing remarks on the nature of interpretation. The date of these remarks is 1926, a dozen years after he had taken a course on interpretation from Josiah Royce at Harvard, ten years after he had completed his dissertation on Bradley, and four years after he had published *The Waste Land*. The comments on his mother's poem, brief though they are, indicate that his understanding of the nature of interpretation had remained fairly constant for a number of years after writing his dissertation, years encompassing the composition of *The Waste Land*.

> Some years ago [in 1913–14, in the Royce seminar], in a paper on *The Interpretation of Primitive Ritual*, I made an humble attempt to show that in many cases *no* interpretation of a rite could explain its origin. For the meaning of the series of acts is to the performers themselves an interpretation; the same ritual remaining practically unchanged may assume different meanings for different generations of performers; and the rite may even have originated before "meaning" meant anything at all.[1]

He indicates, as he had indicated years before, that a distinction must be drawn between acts and meanings assigned to them, that is, between acts and their interpretations. He also suggests that a distinction be made between internal and external interpretations, that is, between interpretations made by those within the time period and those made by future generations, a point insisted on in many of his essays, including "Tradition and the Individual Talent." And finally, he maintains in the 1926 passage that interpretations cannot recover facts or even explain the origins of facts; an interpretation is something added, something which "tells more . . . about the age in which it is written than about the past."[2] The *Savonarola* introduction points back to Eliot's most detailed discussion of interpretation (except, perhaps, for his dissertation), the seminar paper on the interpretation of primitive ritual. The notes taken by the class secretary in Royce's seminar survive, notes containing many observations on a conversation between Royce and Eliot on the subject of interpretation.[3] The seminar paper itself has not been published, but generous excerpts from it are included in Piers Gray's book on Eliot's intellectual development.[4]

"Death by Water" and "What the Thunder Said" call special attention to interpretation, and thus it is important at this point to offer a few observations on interpretation as Eliot seems to have understood it. Some philosophers would urge that perception is interpretation, that to perceive is to interpret, by definition. But Eliot in the Royce seminar paper and in his dissertation uses the word to refer to an activity that comes after and builds upon perception.[5] He distinguishes between a "fact" as "a point of attention which has only one aspect" and the "interpretation" of that fact as an assignment of meaning, a movement beyond the fact to something else.[6] Interpretation is a first-order process of transcendence, a mental movement beyond the object focused on in a given moment. Fact perception can be confined to a single instant or, conceptually, to a position outside time altogether; interpretation, on the other hand, implies a time sequence.

Put another way, perception involves two terms, the perceiver and the thing perceived. Interpretation adds a third term, the meaning assigned to the thing perceived. In the process of adding that third term, relations are multiplied. At one instant of time, only the mind with nothing to take note of exists. Call this instant an interval between perceptions, some state analogous to the blank moment between frames of a film. At another instant, the mind centers an object, isolates it from both other points of attention and the blank instants between them. The act of placing an object at the center of attention, to follow the definition Eliot gives in his dissertation, makes it a fact and thus requires a sense of that mind's relation to the centered object. The subsequent act of assigning significance to the object turns the fact into a means to an end (the interpretation), thus decentering it. For example, one can notice a pebble by stepping on it. In pausing to identify it, one need not assign significance to it. It is only a pebble, only a point centered in attention within a brief time period. The pebble is not stored in long-term memory, and it quickly ceases to exist; the mind moves on to other points of focus. In such an episode, surely common enough to make it perverse to deny it, no signifier–signified relations occur, unless one wishes to call neurological codes that carry sensations to the brain by such names. That kind of insistence, however, obscures any distinction between automatic processes and the movement of consciousness. In the sense that Eliot uses the word "interpretation," no interpretation occurs. The moment with the pebble was a moment outside of meaning.

If, to continue with the same example, one notices the pebble and then thinks of it as a member of the large class of objects, stones in general, interpretation thereby occurs. The single object stands for or points toward many other things. Those other things now become a collective fact, centered, a class granted an existence it did not hold before. Other shifts might occur. Stones in general may point to mineralogy, to Dr. Johnson's rock, to the philosopher's stone, to *The Waste Land*'s stony places, to rock 'n' roll, or to getting stoned as a biblical adulteress or as a drug user. An interpretative chain reaction can hurl meanings explosively in many directions, and assignments of meaning can be carried on in a limitless way. Signifiers point to signifieds, which in turn point to other signifieds and so on to no logical ending. Some of the elements in the field of shifting significance are verbal, but some are not. Moving from a stone to a mountain is not necessarily a verbal shift, whereas moving from a pebble to the Rock of Ages can only be a linguistic shift.

The distinction that Eliot makes between internal and external interpretations is an important one. In the *Savonarola* introduction, he is referring primarily to the difference made by being "inside" the time frame to which the interpretation refers and being "outside" of it. In the seminar paper, he takes up this question in regard to Durkheim's epistemology. Durkheim argues, correctly, that "that which we know from without differs from that which we know from within."[7] Eliot evaluates this principle in regard to generalizations about primitive societies and their religious beliefs. In thinking about primitive societies, we are limited in that there is no way for us to position ourselves "inside" their world. The primitives, however, were limited (as everyone is) in that they were confined within their time frame and could not see themselves as part of a whole.

The principle Eliot applies to societies can be extended to refer to texts, with internal and external interpretations referring to the distinction between interpretations occurring within the text and interpretations made by the reader of the text. We illustrated this point in our introduction by quoting the famous opening lines of "The Love Song of J. Alfred Prufrock." The principle is of the essence in reading *The Waste Land*, for the poem consists largely of "different voices" caught in the act of interpretation. "April is the cruellest month," for example, can be read as an assignment of meaning by a figure in the poem, possibly named Marie. The statement first isolates a time of year by naming it, then decenters it by shifting attention to its meaning, "cruellest month." This assignment of meaning by Marie is an internal interpretation. Once the reader has understood that Marie has conveyed an interpretation, he then goes on to interpret Marie's interpretation, to decide the significance of her assignment of meaning. This is external interpretation. Of course, the reader has the option of refusing to interpret the textual fact. He may do only the first-order interpreting involved in knowing what the words mean and how they form an utterance. Such detachment, however, is rare. Most readers will be curious about why the internal interpretation is made and then will move on through successive utterances to more and more interpretations. It is important to note that a proliferation of internal significations tends to defeat external attributions of significance. As internal significations increase in quantity and complexity, the likelihood of common external significations decreases. In other words, it becomes less likely that readers will agree on meanings to be assigned from outside to the aggregate of meanings stated inside the text by characters.

A point worthy of underscoring is that neither the internal nor the external interpretations should be equated with Eliot's interpretation. We cannot say that Eliot says "April is the cruellest month," only that he presents us with a heterocosm in which a character says this. Her interpretation does not give us access to the poet's interpretation but, on the contrary, complicates and blocks access to his. In interpreting her interpretation, we are not interpreting his, which is another thing altogether and irrecoverable. We cannot say that Eliot says "Consider Phlebas, who was once handsome and tall as you," only that he presents us with a narrator who moralizes in this way.

The final point in this brief survey of Eliot's ideas about interpretation derives from the fact that all interpretation is strictly limited in what it can achieve. Interpretation can never lead to absolute truth or definitive conclusions, and therefore, in a special sense, it is usually experienced as finally falling short in some way. Often, too, the more inventive and elaborate the interpretation, the more intense the sense of its inadequacy. Because of this shortfall, reading (external interpretation) often produces a circular experience which we call a "hermeneutical loop."[8] When a text is decentered through the assignment of meaning or, in other words, through the process of interpretation, the text is pushed aside by that meaning and then an external thought, the reader's thought, takes its place. After considering the thought, the reader often decides that it is insufficient or aesthetically less desirable than the initial textual fact. As a result, the interpretation dissolves, and the original item in the poem returns to the center of focus. The reader has moved outside the poem, found a meaning, considered it, and returned to the poem as such; in a sense, he has returned to the moment before interpretation. But it is a return with a difference, a difference made by the process of trying to interpret. The hermeneutical loop effect acknowledges that there is a posthermeneutical stage, a stage which is in a sense *after* meaning.

The hermeneutical loop effect is a way of referring to what happens when serious readers struggle with a complex text like *The Waste Land* (or with a simple text like a nursery rhyme). The stages of interpretation can also be thought of in terms of Bradley's stages of cognition. The move from immediate to relational to transcendent experience is similar in some ways to the movement away from the text through the hermeneutical process followed by the posthermeneutical loop back to the text.

These principles of interpretation are useful in reading "Death by

158

Water," a short lyric which insists on being interpreted and, at the same time, mocks any interpretation we can discover. Coming after "The Fire Sermon," it offers a release from tension, complexity, and anxiety. Its rhythm is seductively soothing, its syntax gentle, its tone elegiac, its diction simple and universal. Its references to immersion, forgetting, drowning, and dying produce in the reader a sense of a peaceful ending. The concluding move from narrative to moral, from third person to a direct address of Everyman, is a time-honored and widely recognized signal of closure.

> Phlebas the Phoenician, a fortnight dead,
> Forgot the cry of gulls, and the deep sea swell
> And the profit and loss.
>   A current under sea
> Picked his bones in whispers. As he rose and fell
> He passed the stages of his age and youth
> Entering the whirlpool.
>   Gentile or Jew
> O you who turn the wheel and look to windward,
> Consider Phlebas, who was once handsome and tall as you.

The closural effect of "Death by Water" is too striking for the reader to pass it without notice, and yet, the most important point is that the closural techniques turn out to mock themselves. By utilizing psychologically powerful techniques of closure in a section that is in a penultimate position, Eliot parodies the experience of closure in art and in thought. "Death by Water" closes itself, but it does not close the poem of which it is a part. The first three parts of the poem end with a denial of closure, and the fifth part ends with a merely formal benediction. The fourth part consists of a conventional closure in an interior position and thus subverts the concept of an ending. Eliot's practice here would be analogous to following Prufrock's classically closural "Till human voices wake us, and we drown" with a sequence of unanswerable and open-ended disturbances.

The position of "Death by Water," then, calls for interpretation. Perhaps even more than its position, the content of this section asks to be interpreted. The appearance of water in a poem called *The Waste Land* calls attention to the possibility of revival and rebirth. The myths behind the poem associate water with the lifting of the curse from the land. Jessie Weston follows her chapter on the waste land with a chapter on "The Freeing of the Waters." And here, following Eliot's guided tour of his own waste land, we find in "Death by Water" his lyrical variation on the mythic sequence. Death, in his sources, particularly in Frazer, Weston, and the Bible, is the prerequisite for life, and in all three, death by water is a central ritual in physical and spiritual rebirth. In all three, death is an end which is a beginning.

"Death by Water" also cries out for interpretation because it is a powerful and conspicuous instance of Eliot's habitual use of ambiguous water references, several specifically focused on submarine existence. "Death by Water" is bound to be a climactic moment for a reader of Eliot's early poetry and prose. Consider, for example, such references in "Prufrock" as "I should have been a pair of ragged claws/Scuttling across the floors of silent seas" or the asssociation of consciousness and drowning that ends the poem. Or consider the following description of the hero's laughter in "Mr. Apollinax."

> His laughter was submarine and profound
> Like the old man of the sea's
> Hidden under coral islands
> Where worried bodies of drowned men drift down in the
> green silence,
> Dropping from fingers of surf.

We need not recite the long list of Eliot's water references, but we should note that most readers of *The Waste Land* will recognize in this section a serious and formal treatment of one of his obsessive images, an image of disturbing ambivalence associated with overwhelming questions of the meaning of life and death. The poet's obsession with water is also evident in the discarded portions of the poem included in *The Waste Land Facsimile*. The original "Death by Water," almost ten times as long as the published version, is a narrative of a sea voyage and shipwreck, and two discarded fragments also focus on death by water.

"Death by Water," then, is a major moment in *The Waste Land*. The drowned man motif brings together many figures, episodes, and themes from Eliot's sources, from his early work, and from within the poem. And yet, when Pound objected to parts of this section,

Eliot considered cutting all of it. Pound rightly protested: "I DO advise keeping Phlebas. In fact, I more'n advise. Phlebas is an integral part of the poem; the card pack introduces him, the drowned phoen. sailor." Phlebas is "needed ABSOlootly where he is."[9] In the following analysis, we will indicate our own reasons for agreeing with Pound's protest.

"The Burial of the Dead," as virtually all commentators on the poem's water references note, contains a warning to "Fear death by water." This warning, part of Madame Sosostris's reading of her tarot cards, is addressed to someone inside the poem. "A Game of Chess" begins with an allusion to Cleopatra's life on the river and ends with a poignant allusion—"good night, sweet ladies, good night"—to Ophelia's death by water. And "The Fire Sermon" describes life on and beside various rivers in images that suggest that this life by water is in a figurative sense death by water and that a literal death by water would be preferable. By the time the reader reaches part IV, "Death by Water," he has encountered a complex sequence of references to water, rivers, boats, wetness, and dryness. In part V, "What the Thunder Said," which we shall discuss in our next chapter, the emphasis changes from death by water to desire for water. The reader discovers, in the so-called water-dripping song, this desire pushed to an extreme, and then the anticlimactic lines, "Then a damp gust/Bringing rain." Before the end of the poem, he will discover another river, another boat, and more fishing.

Attributing meaning to these (and many other) water references involves what we call external interpretation. The process takes one into many fields, some of them remote from the text. Because the waste land is the controlling or privileged term, and because Eliot instructs the reader to consider *The Golden Bough*, water must refer in some way to a rejuvenating element, and death by water must refer in some way to ritual. The reader may think of Christian baptism, Frazerian archetypes of death and rebirth, Freudian return to the womb, or even of fish as a traditional fertility symbol, to name only a few potential meanings. The "death" in "Death by Water" can mean the negation that must precede affirmation; or it can mean that old archetypes are themselves dead and thus suggest that water is only water for drinking or for drowning.

The unmistakable presence of all of the archetypes related to rebirth seems to be mocked by the absence of any indication of a sacramental and redemptive presence. Phlebas does not seem to be preparing for rebirth. On the contrary, he is described as quietly decomposing and entering the whirlpool. The water cleanses his bones, not symbolically but literally; the death by water is death by water; the "putting off of the filth of the flesh"[10] is literalized. At its end, this brief elegy turns to warn the reader to be mindful of Phlebas as one who died at sea. He was handsome and tall, and he could sail as well as Ulysses himself. But now he is merely dead.

Or is he? In the context of the Frazerian myths, Phlebas is related to Osiris, the god whose body was placed in a current which carried it from the place of his death to the place from which it would be taken from the water as a symbol of rebirth.[11] In "Dans le Restaurant," a current simply carries Phlebas far away, destination unspecified. In "Death by Water," the function of the current changes. Instead of carrying the body to the place of resurrection, "A current under sea/Picked his bones in whispers." This revision undermines any suggestion of resurrection; instead of floating downstream to be plucked out, the body decomposes en route and is pulled into a whirlpool. The most striking word in the new line, however, is "whispers"; the statement that the bones were picked in whispers whispers a line from Ezekiel 37 (a basic subtext of part I), "Son of man, can these bones live?" but does not whisper any answer.

In "L'Aquarium," a poem about death by water by Laforgue, one of the early Eliot's favorite poets, drowning is imagined as pleasant because it symbolizes existence without mind, pure vegetative happiness.[12] The tone of Eliot's elegy carries the same suggestion, a kind and easy exit into a "condition of complete simplicity" costing "not less than everything." Was Madame Sosostris simply a false prophet to warn her client to fear dying by water? "Annihilation and utter night" have seldom been so attractive. But again, the text whispers that Eliot's poetry and Eliot's mind do not permit such simple answers. One of the troublesome features of this section of the poem is the suggestion that consciousness survives death. This suggestion could be ironic or could be just part of linguistic entanglement, but it is clearly present. Phlebas is said to have "Forgot the cry of gulls, and the deep sea swell/And the profit and loss."

The odd detail here is that this "forgetting" takes place two weeks after his death. In "Dans le Restaurant," "Forgot" is in the imperfect (*oubliait*), emphasizing continuing rather than completed action. Recalling the drowned men's "worried bodies" in "Mr. Apollinax," the reader notes that Phlebas's descent to mindless nonexistence is complicated by a postmortem forgetting, by a suggestion that Phlebas is himself a witness to his descent through the stages of his life into the whirlpool; his descent is also complicated by an allusion to Ulysses' last voyage as narrated by Dante (clear in the first draft, subdued in the final one).[13] In "Dans le Restaurant," the narrator remarks that it was "painful" for Phlebas to have to pass through the stages of his former life, suggesting perhaps the physical pain of the death itself but also the psychological pain or spiritual anguish of witnessing a postmortem descent through the stages of his former life.

The realization that Phlebas's decomposition is complicated requires an acknowledgment that the narrator's warning is complicated. Is it merely a warning, for example, that all shall die? Or is it a statement that death is all? Do the classical allusions and the classical tone indicate that this address to the reader is an updating of Aristotle's exercise in logic ("All men are mortal. Socrates is a man. Therefore, Socrates is mortal"), a restatement using Phlebas instead of Socrates? And what of the context of this warning within the poem itself? Does the perception that the warning is an internal interpretation change its significance for the reader who is trying to assess external significance? It is, after all, a line in a poem about a waste land—in a special sense, a poem about the twentieth century, a demythologized age in which water is for most people no more than H_2O. What about the reader's awareness that Eliot is a master of irony, the awareness that irony, like water, is everywhere?

All of these readings prove unsatisfactory, forcing a return to the text as text and, in the process, illustrating our concept of the hermeneutical loop. Whatever may be said of this section cannot be said with any finality. The tale of Phlebas refuses allegorization, refuses to be caught in final statements of meaning. This intransigence is clear not only from a close reading of the text but also from attention to the form. Consider, for example, the function of water as metaphor coexisting with dry and barren land as metaphor. The latter is privileged because of the poem's title, but the former is far more frequent in its appearances. There is water everywhere, especially in the section called "The Fire Sermon." Despite the ubiquity of water, its opposite, the dead land, is dominant in the reader's picture of the whole poem. In a sense, land is a frame for water in the poem, but the dominance of the frame, the competition between the frame and the picture, generates an oscillation of the type described earlier in this book. The oscillation of ergon and parergon thus produced is a crucial aspect of the presentation—a movement more than a meaning. If the poem had permitted a conventional understanding of these two metaphors, the reader would have been unable to have evaded the sense that water is a signifier pointing in the direction of salvation for, after all, irrigation is an obvious way of making waste lands bloom again. The reader is returned to the text, but having looped through tortuous interpretative exercises, he now experiences the text in a new way.

If Eliot had omitted "Death by Water" altogether, the conventional expectations created by the use of water in a poem about a desert would have produced an entirely different work. The longing for water in "What the Thunder Said" would have signaled the possible presence of a healing, sacramental element in a spiritually dry realm. As the poem stands, however, it is difficult to attach any sacramental value to water. "Death by Water" desymbolizes it by treating it literally as an element in which to drown. There is a change but no "sea-change/Into something rich and strange"; his body rises and falls, falls and rises, but both rising and falling are literal, an effect of the tides; there is a descent but in the final analysis no ascent, a death but no rebirth, no archetypal womb that Phlebas can return to for maternal comfort. The world within the poem is one in which symbols fail, one in which mythologies collapse in a heap of broken images. This literalization of ancient symbols (from water as symbol to water as H_2O), this demythologizing and desacramentalizing, is a central aspect of Eliot's representation of the waste land.

"Death by Water," then, forces the reader to interpret but fails in the end to permit the reader to grasp any satisfactory meaning. This refusal to concede adequate meanings outside itself brings the reader back to the text, a movement which illustrates our idea of the hermeneutical loop. This movement beyond interpretation can best be characterized as posthermeneutical. The reader's experience beyond meaning includes the experience of interpretation, an experience which does not yield adequate meaning but which cannot fail to enrich subsequent experience with the text. The water pattern will not be the same when the reader recenters it after giving up on external interpretations. The reading process invents and reinvents borders, and this process makes a difference. For example, water imagery is bordered at first by contrasting imagery and by internal interpretations. Later it receives all the borders, containers, or frames that come with various interpretations. Finally, it is bordered by the interpretative activity itself when it returns to being only water imagery again. The hermeneutical loop effect involves a movement beyond hermeneutics which is a return to the starting place, the text, but in the posthermeneutical state the text is changed (or the reader is changed). Having come through the experience of the loop, the reader of *The Waste Land* will be in possession of the experience of the poem's existence before and after meaning. This is another manifestation of Bradley's movements from immediate through relational to transcendent experience.

In strictly literary terms, the hermeneutical loop can be accurately thought of as a defeat of symbolism, as a refusal of the text to become a means to an end. It is hard to imagine water in a context of dryness, lovelessness, anomie, and disorder failing to be a symbol of hope. Its defeat as a symbol, its status as antisymbol, is thus a special achievement. A nonsymbol is a nonsignifier, a centered fact defined as such by its refusal to be permanently cast into the supporting role of pointer toward something other than itself. The reader may be tempted to suppose that nonsymbols are symbols of the failure of symbols in the modern chaos the poem evokes. But that supposition leads to an infinite regression that is conspicuously unsatisfying. At some point, there must be a return to water as water, the beginning and the end of meaning.

One of the problems here—a cause of resistance to reading which acknowledges a hermeneutical loop—is the confusing ambiguity of the terms "meaning" and "significance" and the additional confusion between internal and external interpretations. If one uses meaning as a synonym for value, one will say that "life has no meaning" equals "life has no value." But if the words are confined to the act of finding what things signify, they are irrelevant to questions of value. To say that life has no significance is only to say that life is not a sign pointing beyond itself to something else. And to say that life has no significance in the world of the poem (internal interpretation) or in the reading it receives (external interpretation) is not to say that Eliot is declaring that life has no significance. We make no claims at all about how Eliot might interpret his poem. Thus the once negative statement is transvalued, making it possible to think of the "nonsignificance" that is a precondition of perceiving things simply and accepting them as they are. Some figures within *The Waste Land* tend to see everything as an occasion for attributing meaning, thereby multiplying relations. Some readers are addicted to the same practice. But readers have a distinct advantage over figures within the poem; they are free to experience the transcendent condition of unity that nonsignificance after meaning provides.

The original version of "Death by Water," as we have noted, is nearly ten times as long as the present one. The longer version is an account of a sea voyage and shipwreck, involving hallucinations, storms, and death. The setting of this voyage and shipwreck is the Atlantic Ocean, just off the New England coast where Eliot spent many happy days sailing in his youth. The lines describe a journey that begins at Cape Ann, passes the Dry Salvages, and moves north toward better fishing waters. In cutting this episode from *The Waste Land*, Eliot cut the only part of the poem that refers in any explicit way to his American experience. In dropping it, he also lost or muted one of his classical sources, the Ulysses story. Valerie Eliot's note to the *Facsimile* says that this narrative was "rather inspired" by the Ulysses Canto (xxvi) of the *Inferno*.[14] The Ulysses of Homer and the Ulysses of Tennyson are also present in the lines he chose to delete.

One of the many surprising aspects of this brief but tonally serious elegy is its tendency to entangle the reader in wordplay. The word "current," for example, associates Phlebas with Mr. Eugenides, the merchant with "currants" in his pocket. The drowned Phoenician Sailor and the one-eyed merchant appear on the tarot cards in "The Burial of the Dead." Madame Sosostris tells her client that his card is the drowned Phoenician Sailor, to which he reflects, "Those are pearls that were his eyes." The identical reflection recurs in "A Game of Chess," thus associating Madame Sosostris's client with the silent visitor in the dressing room. The way that wordplay produces patterns of identities that spread themselves throughout the poem can also be illustrated by noting the "profit–prophet" pun. Insofar as the drowned man is the Smyrna merchant, he has forgotten not only the profit and the loss but also the prophet he invited to the Metropole and the Cannon Street Hotel. The homophone connects Tiresias and the merchant by fusing the occupational concerns of each. Prophet and profit are one. At least in a linguistic sense, Mr. Eugenides' proposition has been accepted and consummated.

The wordplay, actually, is pervasive. The name Phlebas, which Eliot seems to have made up, is a pun on *flee-bas*, an English and French compound meaning "escape downward," and perhaps, as suggested by F. N. Lees, a respelling of the Latin *flebas*, meaning "you were weeping."[15] These are suggestive variations in an elegy for a victim of drowning. Grover Smith suggests that Phlebas was concocted from the Greek word *phleps* or *phlebos*, meaning "vein" and also, like the Latin *vena*, meaning "phallus." Smith interprets this as an association of Phlebas with Osiris, one of the phallic gods of *The Golden Bough*.[16] And what of "Phoenician"? Is "Phoenician" a reference to the phoenix reborn in fire and thus a whisper (ironic or not) of resurrection? Or, since Eliot was reading Joyce while *The Waste Land* was forming in his mind, could it suggest Joyce's favorite park in Dublin? Does "dead" announce the presence of Daedalus— and therefore of both Joyce and his longest story—who must in turn produce Icarus as the best-known drowned man in myth? These exercises could go on endlessly, but perhaps they can be concluded by noting that Phlebas forgot the "cry of gulls." "Gulls" are people who are easily fooled. They too are present, if only as academic critics who read in this way.

The fact that an ostensibly simple elegy about release from complexity should involve the reader in word games, however, is worth further consideration. One explanation of these apparently pointless and somewhat indecorous games is suggested by an awareness that the long sea narrative in the original "Death by Water" points to the character of Ulysses. The simultaneous use of the Ulysses myth and word games is an unmistakable trace of the fact that Eliot was reading Joyce's *Ulysses* in installments as *The Waste Land* was taking shape in his mind. In fact, "Dans le Restaurant" was published in the September 1918 *Little Review*, an issue which also printed the sixth installment of Joyce's novel.

In a number of ways, Joyce served as Eliot's contemporary inspiration. He illustrated for his fellow artists the importance of making words take on a life of their own. And it was Joyce who spread the self-serving message that Ulysses was, in Victor Bérard's analysis, a Phoenician and therefore a Semite.[17] The modern Ulysses, then, had to be a Jew, as Joyce's Leopold Bloom in some of his moods and in part of his heritage was. The words "Gentile or Jew" can refer with precision to Leopold Bloom, a man who does not know which term refers most accurately to himself; they also echo Joyce's "jew or gentile" in the "Nestor" episode. Joyce's character, however, does not go to sea and could not be the drowned sailor. But the prototypes of Joyce's Ulysses are possible drowned sailors. Dante's Ulysses—which seems to have been foremost in Eliot's mind—dies at sea. The deleted lines just prior to the present text of "Death by Water" are an allusion to Ulysses' last voyage as told in the *Inferno*, in which disaster blocks the aged hero from sailing to the mount of Purgatory.[18] The impossibility of achieving secular purification is Dante's message and is an aspect of Eliot's. In a sense, Dante's Ulysses is a Pelagian whereas Eliot's, like Joyce's, is a utilitarian.

None of these observations means that the drowned man here is Ulysses. The drowned man is Phlebas the Phoenician, and as the last lines suggest, the drowned man is Everyman. The whirlpool mentioned in the text suggests the vortex of Wyndham Lewis and Ezra Pound. Their notion was that a work of art should be like a whirlpool that pulls all meanings into it. The emptiness of "Death by Water" seduces the reader to desire to fill it. Vorticism is a rejection of the traditional notion that language necessarily involves closure. If a text specifies its meanings, explains its ideas, and reports on the nuances of its emotions, it is thereby closed. Insofar as it refuses to limit its implications, it is open-ended. It is only a superficial paradox, thus, to say that "Death by Water" gains in complexity and all-inclusiveness to the extent that it limits itself to noncommittal simplicity.

One fascinating instance of wordplay in *The Waste Land* can be associated with Eliot's and Bradley's critique of utilitarianism. In a suggestive essay on Eliot and the classics, William Arrowsmith argues that "Phlebas" is a variant of Philebos, the title of one of Plato's dialogues and its focal character.[19] Arrowsmith suggests that Eliot is providing a clue which the reader must follow up by considering its implications for the poem as a whole. This clue is especially important because it occurs, with slight differences, in two of Eliot's poems, "Dans le Restaurant" and *The Waste Land*.

Plato's *Philebos* concerns the fallacy involved in living for pleasure. Socrates leads the young man named Philebos through a series of questions to make him realize that pain and pleasure are inextricable from each other. The principal examples are drawn from the practice of comic artists who must use liberal admixtures of humiliation to enable the audience to experience pleasure. Socrates establishes the importance in comedy of the character types *eiron* and *alazon*. The first pretends to be ignorant in order to trap others into being pompous. The second, usually an official with great power and vanity, pretends to be wise and virtuous. His pretense is stripped from him repeatedly, thus providing the source of comedy's pleasure and moral importance. It is plain, Socrates argues, that the interdependence of pleasure and pain illustrated in comedy also exists in the world of social interactions outside art. The pursuit of pure pleasure is therefore a pursuit of something that does not exist outside an ideal realm.

The critique of utilitarianism that we noted in "The Fire Sermon" is thus repeated in "Death by Water." The life devoted to pleasure or happiness is doomed to failure because pleasure and pain form a self-destructing polar design. Such a life is constantly putting itself into a condition of irreconcilable relations where paradoxes prevent simplicity. These relations suggest the ever-receding simplicity sought by anyone, utilitarian or saint, who is in search of an unmixed and unchanging end. If Plato's view of comedy resides in the background of "Death by Water," it is appropriate for puns to dominate its foreground because of the way they illustrate irresolvable ambiguity. The original version of "Death by Water" presents a variation on this motif by having a sailor suffering from a "comic gonorrhea" emerge from a brothel.[20] Secular happiness is here given a familiar refutation.

In one of *The Waste Land* manuscripts, Eliot associates the experience of immersion in water with confusion. This suggests that death by water may have been for Eliot a literalization of such common metaphors as being "at sea" or "over one's head." Such terms as "swamped," "awash," and "adrift" are also generally used to suggest confusion. Since the unconscious tends to take metaphors literally, a state of confusion or disorientation may well produce at levels beneath the rational consciousness images of drowning. The connection is explicit in the following fragment.

> As a deaf mute swimming deep below the surface
> Knowing neither up nor down, swims down and down
> In the calm deep water where no stir nor surf is
> Swims down and down;
> And about his hair the seaweed purple and brown.
>
> So in our fixed confusions we persisted, out from town.[21]

The principal implication of this reading of drowning as motif and "Death by Water" as a section of *The Waste Land* is that in Eliot the image of drowning may mean precisely the opposite of what it seems to mean. The soothing simplicity may mask a tortuous confusion, an irresolvable complexity. At the same time, paradoxically, the metaphor meaning confusion also means escape from confusion into clarity, from complexity into the simplicity of death. The paradox insures that neither confusion nor its metaphorical presentation and reversal can prevail. They are pressured into a perilous equilibrium that is itself the most intense experience the reader can have of this part of the poem.

The present text of "Death by Water" has three sites or contexts. It is the end of the French poem, the end of the New England sea adventure in the first draft, and the entirety of part IV of *The Waste Land*. In all three contexts, the lines intrude into an alien context to hide or foreclose confusion and anxiety by transmuting it into a literalized metaphor. In the first-draft version, the lines follow a shipwreck mixed with surreal visions. In both "Dans le Restaurant" and *The Waste Land*, the lines follow evocations of erotic nostalgia and loss. The French poem presents a waiter who speaks of his distant homeland and childhood to a silent diner who resents the intrusion of the waiter's story and the similarity of his burdens to his own. The diner's feeling of simultaneous disgust and self-recognition is clearly associated with guilt and with sexuality in childhood. The Phlebas narrative of death by water intrudes into this world, somehow releasing the diner from the unresolvability of his emotional difficulties. In *The Waste Land*, the feeling of being awash in sexual anxiety is generated by the catalog of sordid couplings in "The Fire Sermon." Again, the intolerable tension is followed by Phlebas and death by water. In both the French poem and *The Waste Land*, the feelings are too subtle to be understood and too common to be evaded. Eliot's use of the metaphor of drowning translates confusion and loss into an image that contains and for the moment assuages what cannot be ignored.

The final section of *The Waste Land*, "What the Thunder Said," enacts an emergence from extinction into a renewal of suffering—suffering that is overt, on the surface, both mental and physical. The attempt to "escape downward" is over once and for all. The rebirth of conscious anguish and desperate searches for ways of interpreting the universe, however painful and insufficient they are, constitute an exhilarating affirmation.

7 / Before and After Meaning

"What the Thunder Said"

Well here again that dont apply
But I've gotta use words when I talk to you.
—Eliot, *Sweeney Agonistes*, "Fragment of an Agon"

"It is a test," wrote Eliot in an essay on Dante (1929), "that genuine poetry can communicate before it is understood."[1] This pronouncement can be taken as a reference to the music of poetry, its *symboliste* suggestiveness, or to some sort of "auditory imagination." It can also be taken as a reference to Bradley's speculations about experiences of meaning at sequential stages of cognitive process. As we noted earlier, Eliot in 1926 referred to the possibility that ritual began "before 'meaning' meant anything at all."[2] As history or anthropology, that speculation has only the vaguest value, but as an expression of skepticism about the validity of interpretation, it is coherent in a precise way with his studies of both Bradley and Buddhism.

Eliot's focus on the nature and limits of interpretation is particularly intense in the last section of *The Waste Land*. The title— "What the Thunder Said"—calls attention to interpretation, to what the thunder meant. In a poem in which the privileged metaphor is that of a desert or waste land, what the thunder says is automatically privileged, for in such a context, thunder announces the possibility or likelihood of rain and, consequently, of revival. This section begins with references to thunder, references which compel the reader toward interpretation, and then moves to the climactic passage about the thunder god, what he says and how he is interpreted. In reading the poem's concluding section, we will build on our previous discussion of the stages of experience (before and after meaning), on our distinction between internal and external interpretation, and on our articulation of the effect we call the hermeneutical loop.

172

"What the Thunder Said" opens with a description followed by an interpretation.

> After the torchlight red on sweaty faces
> After the frosty silence in the gardens
> After the agony in stony places
> The shouting and the crying
> Prison and palace and reverberation
> Of thunder of spring over distant mountains
> He who was living is now dead
> We who were living are now dying
> With a little patience

The narrator is not identifiable here, but the manner in which internal interpretations follow the description suggests that he is an eyewitness of a recent catastrophe. He notes that one person is dead and interprets the situation as one in which "we"—all of us or all of his group—are dying, waiting for the final coup de grace with a little patience. His language, however, does not inspire patience, for it calls immediate attention to interpretation. "We who were living" seems to be a metaphor meaning "we who once had hope." It cannot read as a message from someone already dead because that is denied by "are now dying." Only the living can be in the process of dying, patiently or not.

The internal uncertainty here focuses attention on internal interpretation, stimulating the reader to go forward toward a possible resolution of the difficulties. By pushing the reader forward, the language tends to remove the option of looping back to the textual moment. The complexities we have discussed earlier now have a new dimension. In most instances in the first four parts, the reader can discern a movement of meaning from perspective to perspective. It is possible either to sense movement in a direction of transcendence toward a potential unitive position or to loop backward toward acceptance of the textual moment as fact after meaning. But here at the beginning of "What the Thunder Said" those options are withdrawn by the undecidability of both internal and external interpretations. In brief, the poem now dislocates the reader into meaning. The defeat of the hermeneutical loop means that the option of meaninglessness is withdrawn. As a result, the poem gains maximum emotional power.

What, then, could the opening passage mean? Eliot's note and the text itself point to the Passion of Christ. The opening lines suggest that Christ's suffering in Gethsemane, his betrayal and arrest, and his trial and Crucifixion are recent events; and further-more, since the narrator seems to have lost hope, the lines suggest that the narrator is speaking after the Crucifixion but before the Resurrection. Easter and redemption are not in view. Since nothing in this first level of interpretation resolves the questions about the narrator's metaphors or position within life or death, the reader remains within a mental area dominated by the need to go on interpreting. A second level of interpretation will note that the death of Christ is not the only reference here. Countless figures from myth died in ways that fit the details in the lines, and Eliot's references to Frazer suggest that these figures—Osiris, Adonis, Dionysus, and others—be included in the reading. Eliot's notes seem to suggest that the death of the one "who was living" be taken as an aggregate of all traditions grounded in fertility magic and vicarious atonement through blood sacrifice. Perhaps this passage should be read as an indication that salvation through sacrifice of the hero is itself dead, no longer operative in the modern world.

The obsolescence of the notion of salvation through sacrifice seems to be related to the disappearance of metonymic conscious-ness. The speaker's apparent despair as he waits for death reveals that he does not identify with the victim, that he does not see the victim as a sacrifice that can lift burdens of disease and sin. He sees only that a negation has occurred, not the traditional mythic pattern of salvation for the people through death of their best and met-onymically representative member. If the victim is perceived not simply as "one of us" but as a part that *is* the whole community, then his death gives fresh hope that evil has been conquered. To put it another way, the paradox at the core of mythic or metonymic consciousness has been lost. That paradox is the idea that death for the most godlike person brings new vitality to the survivors who feel a unity with him.

Thus Christ, all the heroes of fertility myth, the tradition of revering such figures, and mythic consciousness itself seem to be dead in the reverberation of spring thunder over distant mountains. This interpretation, however, does not answer all of the questions raised by the passage. Too many signifiers within the passage point in too many diverse directions. For example, the "agony in stony places," "frosty silence," and "gardens" of various kinds point to passages earlier in the poem. At the same time, "thunder . . . over distant mountains" points ahead to the dry journey and to the voice of the thunder god over the high Mount Himavant. The second line—"After the frosty silence in the gardens"—evokes Gethsemane and the sacred grove where the golden bough is used, but it also points back to the hyacinth garden and the lover who "could not/Speak . . ./Looking into the heart of light, the silence." Frost points to the "sudden frost" that might disturb the grave of the corpse buried in Stetson's garden. The third line—"After the agony in stony places"—points to the agony of the tempted Christ in the desert and that of the dying gods and kings in Frazer, but it also recalls the "stony rubbish" and "heap of broken images" where the son of man is told that "fear in a handful of dust" is the only alternative to shadows.

The details of this verse paragraph, then, point to figures outside the poem in myth and, at the same time, to figures inside the poem in a contemporary setting. In following these directions of significance, the reader encounters a reciprocal matrix of meaning. "He who was living" seems to point to the one who went through frosty silences, gardens, and stony places, so the "He" refers to Christ, the dying gods in Frazer, and some commonplace urban figures in the twentieth century. Each referent of "He who was living" is referring to all of the others. Picture each as a multiple pointer aimed at each of the others and also aimed at by them. Interpreting these lines is like entering a hall of angled mirrors, each with multiple facets. This field of reciprocal interpreters and interpretations does not produce the kind of level-by-level shifts that we earlier noted as the first stage of a series leading toward a unitive perspective. The shifts are all on one level of meaning. Someone died, to put it bluntly, but he cannot be identified. His identity thwarts interpretation at the same time that it thwarts any attempt to avoid interpretation. Both meaning and meaninglessness cease to be available as options in reading.

A hermeneutical field of this kind, blocking both closure and open-endedness, places the reader in a center where the experience of being before or after meaning is no longer available. He becomes entangled in interpretative activity and frustrated by an endless array of meanings. Most readers will remember early stages of contact with *The Waste Land* when the difficulty of finding meaning was frustrating. But now it is the opposite difficulty that produces frustration. At the beginning of "What the Thunder Said," the reader is trapped by the poem's methods within reciprocal meanings, much as the characters in "The Fire Sermon" were trapped within relations. The reader, however, knows his condition and feels the need to break out of it, whereas the figures within the poem will always be entangled in relations.

With a little patience, then, the reader undertakes the journey over dry mountains.

> Here is no water but only rock
> Rock and no water and the sandy road
> The road winding above among the mountains
> Which are mountains of rock without water
> If there were water we should stop and drink
> Amongst the rock one cannot stop or think
> Sweat is dry and feet are in the sand
> If there were only water amongst the rock
> Dead mountain mouth of carious teeth that cannot spit
> Here one can neither stand nor lie nor sit
> There is not even silence in the mountains
> But dry sterile thunder without rain
> There is not even solitude in the mountains
> But red sullen faces sneer and snarl
> From doors of mudcracked houses

Arduous, desperate, painful climbing is dramatized in this paragraph, contradicting the clear statement in the previous paragraph that "we" are merely waiting to die. Is the speaker a different person from line 331 onward? Has the reader been permitted to flee the gardens of ambiguity presented a moment earlier? Regardless of one's position on such questions, it is clear that the "road winding above among the mountains" leads to intense suffering. In this landscape, water is unavailable—antisymbolic water (water has been thoroughly demythologized), plain unsacramental H_2O. The traveler is even deprived of sweat and spit. The spring thunder is carried over from the first paragraph, but it has no meaning, carries no rain; it is mere noise, "dry sterile thunder without rain." Both speech and silence are lost along with rest and solitude. The most arresting line, given our direction of commentary, is "Here one can neither stand nor lie nor sit." That sums up our point about entrapment within a field of reciprocal meanings. The reader cannot stand on one meaning, accept them all, or drop out of meanings.

The poem now moves into a lyric passage sometimes called the "water-dripping song." The short, gasping lines provide a new experience for the reader.

> If there were water
> And no rock
> If there were rock
> And also water
> And water
> A spring
> A pool among the rock
> If there were the sound of water only
> Not the cicada
> And dry grass singing
> But sound of water over a rock
> Where the hermit-thrush sings in the pine trees
> Drip drop drip drop drop drop drop
> But there is no water

Eliot points out in his note to these lines that the hermit thrush makes a sound traditionally called a water-dripping song. The bird itself is invisible, but its song is audible and resembles the sound of water dropping on a hard surface. The passage thus portrays a movement from a desire for water to a desire for the sound of water to a desire for the suggestion of the sound of water. If water is not to be found, if the sound of water is not to be heard, then the sound of the hermit thrush will suffice. The speaker's movement in search of hope is desperate in the extreme. He is willing to delude himself into a momentary belief that water is near. The dramatized desire here is for some occasion, however preposterous, for making a favorable interpretation. If the bird would sing, its song could be treated as a signifier even though everyone, even the speaker, knows that it is a false sign, an auditory mirage. But since even the deception of the thrush is absent from the perceptual field, the speaker cannot resort to any desirable interpretation. Here the reciprocal reference effect returns briefly. In "The Burial of the Dead," the "Son of man" is said to know only a heap of broken images in a sun-stricken land where "the dead tree gives no shelter, the cricket no relief,/And the dry stone no sound of water." This is, among other things, a reference to Moses in the wilderness providing water by striking the rock. Now the son of man, his questioner, and Moses are referred to by the traveler to Emmaus, but they in turn point back to the water song.

The absence of the illusion of water's sound is a final stimulus for the onset of hallucinations of a more immediate kind. First, a gliding shadow appears; then another one is noticed suddenly in another position, "on the other side of you."

> Who is the third who walks always beside you?
> When I count, there are only you and I together
> But when I look ahead up the white road
> There is always another one walking beside you
> Gliding wrapt in a brown mantle, hooded
> I do not know whether a man or a woman
> —But who is that on the other side of you?

In a way, the speaker gets his wish. He wanted a sound to misinterpret on purpose—the deception of the hermit thrush—but he received visions of shapes that he is unable to interpret. His uncertainty forces the reader to attend to the problem of internal interpretation. The shadow episode is presented first as a perception known by a rational process to be an illusion, unreal. The speaker explains that he counts only two people including himself, and yet he sees a shadow suggesting a third person. This bizarre mixture of realism and fantasy subverts all rationality. The narrator seems to be taking care not to describe more than he can see—"I do not know whether a man or a woman"—and yet he describes the shadow as "wrapt in a brown mantle." In distinguishing the brown color of the shadow's garment from the shadow itself, he has contrived to see a detail that contradicts his interpretation of the figure as a mere shadow. This careful and restrained description is interrupted by the sudden appearance of a second figure in a different place, "on the other side."

The focus on internal interpretation reveals the sort of reciprocal signification noted at the beginning of part V. The shadows striding behind and rising in front from the "Son of man" passage are pointed to by these new shadows, which in turn point right back. One difference in this passage is that there is no voice promising a different truth, a substance in contrast to shadows, fear as essence within dust. Another difference is that now the shadow is not the speaker's own and not that of the person he addresses. The reciprocal field of significance is losing its self-contained, sealed, closed-system status. Differences between passages begin to be as clear as similarities.

The same interpretative experience occurs when focus is on the issue of whether the figure is male or female. "I do not know whether a man or a woman" points back toward Tiresias and the multitude of associations his mythic background and past role in the poem convey. But again, going back to Tiresias sends the reader back to the uncertainty of sexual identity as stated here. However, differences of a crucial kind do emerge from this moment of reading and rereading. Both in myth and in the poem's contemporaneity, Tiresias is a seer and a revealer of truth. What he sees is substance. But now he himself becomes an insubstantial gliding shape to be seen and not recognized. It is thus not even Tiresias that we have before us but a single quality abstracted from him. That quality is his sexual ambiguity, his "throbbing between" mode of experiencing his body, a body that now no longer exists, a shadow.

The hallucinatory nature of the passage under discussion is qualified by Eliot's note associating this part of the poem with Christ's progress to Emmaus after the Resurrection. If this hallucination occurs on the journey to Emmaus, the hooded shadow, "the third who walks always beside you," must be identified as Christ. The details of the passage are clearly congruous with the biblical account of the resurrected Christ joining his disciples on the road to Emmaus. Lacking faith in the Resurrection, they had not expected Christ to appear as a fellow traveler and thus failed to recognize him. In Eliot's version of the story, he comes wrapped in a brown mantle, a hooded shadow whose face and sexual identity are unclear. Eliot also suggests that the Frazerian perspective be considered here. This perspective associates the shadows with the dying gods of fertility rituals and with the Hanged Man that Madame

Sosostris was unable to find among her cards. Perhaps, as Eliot might say, these figures "melt" into each other, but they do not have the fluidity normally associated with that image. It seems more accurate to say that they flash in and out of the reader's center of attention so that each, for an instant, is a fact and during other instants is a fading peripheral image.

The experience of sexual ambiguity can be related to further interpretations of the poem's several mythic savior figures. If the line "He who was living is now dead" can be said to refer to Christ and the other dying gods, and if this image is sexually ambiguous, it follows that the dead man is a collection of men and women and that this collection is in cubistic fashion abstracted into the hooded shadow. A compound image of this sort would be both male and female at the same time that it would be neither. The experience of sexual uncertainty is even more closely associated with the savior's adjunct figures, such as Tiresias and the "Parsifal" speaker (line 202). These figures, like Mr. Eugenides, add a suggestion of homoerotic desire. Sexual ambiguity is also a part of the portrait of Madame Sosostris. As other commentators have indicated, she seems to have been taken from Aldous Huxley's *Crome Yellow* (1921), where "she" is an old man impersonating a female fortune-teller or modern sibyl to amuse people at a country fair. Beyond these imaginable interpretations and sources, however, lies what seems to be the most important point about sexual uncertainty. Quite simply, it defeats fertility. Whether it is androgyny, homosexuality, transsexualism, or simply ambiguity, the effect is sterility; the effect, in short, is the waste land and the barren body which mythic saviors died to rejuvenate. In the sexual ambiguity of this passage, then, the mythic figures seem to be involved in an objective correlative of the very curse they sought to dispel.

The foregoing reading has suggested that the poem's population has been compressed, rearranged, and compounded into a single but at the same time double image, the shadows which appear to fill the void the speaker feels. The shadow appears to fulfill his wish for an illusion to interpret as water or as its symbolic equivalent. That speculation is thus redrawn as a cubistic structure, layered, faceted, multipaneled, and unrecognizable except from the perspective we have invented in the process of reading. Our interpretation, of course, is one of many, and like all others, ours is limited. What we have tried to demonstrate is an interpretative process that is motivated and energized by the poem's demand for a synthetic point from which it can be perceived. That point of view is conspicuously absent from the poem, but if the poet's philosophical speculations are taken into consideration, the synthetic perspective from which the poem can be understood can be invented. The poem requires this kind of perceptual inventiveness.

If the shadow is the whole poem's population in a cubistic microcosm—or microimage—the hallucinations following it add facets to it and become parts of the same image. The next paragraph is surrealistic, with mundane reality vanishing and being replaced by the sound of lamentation in the air, visions of hooded hordes swarming over endless plains, and a city suspended over the mountains, a position that is literally unreal. The city splits apart, re-forms, and explodes in air that is violet, no longer white with dry heat. The fallout from this explosion consists of towers, three ancient and two recent cities, and a judgment: unreal. A movement toward reexpansion after compression is revealed when it is noted that the hooded shadow of the previous paragraph reappears as hooded hordes swarming over the plains limited only by the horizon.

> What is that sound high in the air
> Murmur of maternal lamentation
> Who are those hooded hordes swarming
> Over endless plains, stumbling in cracked earth
> Ringed by the flat horizon only
> What is the city over the mountains
> Cracks and reforms and bursts in the violet air
> Falling towers
> Jerusalem Athens Alexandria
> Vienna London
> Unreal

The crash of thunder high in the air supplies a vertical dimension to this unreal scene. The sequential cracking apart, re-forming, and bursting of the airborne city, along with the roughly chronological list of cities, add a time dimension. In a context such as this, the word "Unreal" is an affirmative judgment in contrast to its application to London and other cities earlier in the poem. The word

"Unreal" is an acknowledgment that the exploding fragments are hallucinatory, but it can also be read as a desperate attempt to deny the real chaos. In previous paragraphs, Eliot has compressed many figures into first one shadow, then two, and now he expands the hooded shadows into hooded hordes and multiplies this expansion of meaning in the drama of the city that first cracks, then re-forms, then bursts out in all directions. This is dazzling craftsmanship.

The surreal episodes continue, with the hallucinations becoming more personal.

> A woman drew her long black hair out tight
> And fiddled whisper music on those strings
> And bats with baby faces in the violet light
> Whistled, and beat their wings
> And crawled head downward down a blackened wall
> And upside down in air were towers
> Tolling reminiscent bells, that kept the hours
> And voices singing out of empty cisterns and exhausted wells.

These lines relocate the narrator by placing him within the unreal city. A woman draws her hair into strings and fiddles "whisper music" on them, a scene which points to earlier parts of the poem in which women were defined more by their hair than by their faces. The hyacinth girl was said to have wet hair, the affluent woman in "A Game of Chess" brushed her hair into "fiery points" until it glowed into words, and the typist smoothed her hair with automatic hands as she put a record on the gramophone. This reciprocal matrix of references to wet hair, hair spreading out in fiery points glowing into words, hair and gramophone music, and, finally, hair and fiddle music forms an overlapping picture. Water, fire, words, and music emanate from the cubistic woman paying attention to her hair.

Interpreting these incredible references provides a textbook example of the hermeneutical loop effect. Interpretation seems necessary, but most searches for meaning will lead back to the initial compound image that emerges in "A Game of Chess," the image of the faceless woman brushing her hair before the lighted mirror. An interpretative strand can be picked up by noting the striking similarity of Eliot's image to the medieval image of the Hypostatic Christ. In *Ulysses*, which Eliot was reading while writing *The Waste*

Land, Stephen seems to see Mr. Bloom as the figure of the Hypostatic Christ as depicted by medieval churchmen. Hypostasis is the simultaneity of earthly body and heavenly substance, finite and infinite, visible and invisible. The figure in Joyce is described as "leucodermic, sesquipedalian with winedark hair."[3] "Leucodermic" refers to colorless or invisible skin, so we can take the picture as a suggestion that framing hair reveals a presence that would otherwise be imperceptible. A more familiar analogue is the Wellsian story of the invisible man who can be "seen" only when he is covered; naked, he remains invisible.

This line of interpretation can be supported by remembering that Christ is present in the poem as a hooded faceless shadow walking on the road to Emmaus, a compound shadow whose sexual identity is not clear. Christ, then, can be grouped with Eliot's invisible women, the women whose hair is all that can be seen of them. Being hooded now seems relevant to the way of describing women by referring only to their hair. The hyacinth girl, the affluent woman, the typist, and the fiddler are invisible except for hair, words, music, and fire. If fire is a halo and hooded hordes are a proliferation of divinity into a swarming multitude, the women along with everyone else become variants of Christ, each an incarnation of divinity, each a hypostatic union of visible framing exteriors and invisible essences within. The wine-dark hair outlining a blank area where a face should be is the closest medieval thinkers came to imaging this figure, but cubism, with its multiple perspectival shifts of focus, provides a new technique for presenting the absurd simultaneity of physical and metaphysical demanded by the doctrines of the incarnation. This reading, if pushed further, tends to deify humanity, but only as a prologue to showing that humanity is altogether as problematic, vague, dubious, and endangered as deity itself.

This interpretation, we freely admit, is suspiciously inventive and, like most interpretations, is unlikely to survive for long in reading such a complex passage. Another hermeneutical loop has been traversed, and the text reconstitutes itself, recenters itself as a fact of reading. A trace of the foregoing interpretation remains, however, to supply a transition to the surreal image: "And bats with baby faces in the violet light/Whistled, and beat their wings/And crawled head downward down a blackened wall." The whistling serves as a variation on words and whisper music, and the wings suggest a potential for upward movement that is denied, even reversed. Their baby faces produce a vivid picture, vivid enough to arrest us. Is it not conspicuously odd to place an infant's face anywhere, even on hallucinatory bats, in one of the most intense moments of a poem about the consequences of literal and metaphorical infertility? Extremely so; but that placement is more effective for its oddness.

Most readers will see those baby faces not as the images of young bats but as the faces of human infants mounted on bat bodies. Marie, the hyacinth lovers, Madame Sosostris, and the affluent woman are all faceless. The clerk presents a face with carbuncular assurance, and Mr. Eugenides an unshaven one. But these bats have faces, the only vividly clear faces in the whole poem, the generic face of the human baby, the face, say, on the Gerber baby food jar. In the poem's population, there are three other children, Marie and her cousin on the sled and "young George," Lil's son whose birth almost killed her. There is also a fetus, Lil's abortion. The maternal lamentation heard above in the air is a general grief for lost children—and Lil's grief is related to her own lost child. Most important here, however, is the emergence of the infant's face as a gothic image to stand for all human faces that are embedded, trapped, within relational nature. The bats with human baby faces are the formal opposite of earlier suggestions of hypostasis. They show what is only human and only animal, visages framed by grotesque bodies. Taken together, the faceless women with hair and the bats with human faces present the alternative of dying as fading myths or dying as merely natural beings within relations.

The final hallucinations identify the city as the same complex of cursive and recursive cities in which Stetson is asked about a planted corpse. The church of Saint Mary Woolnoth on King William Street with its "dead sound on the final stroke of nine" now becomes one of the towers upside down in the air "Tolling reminiscent bells, that kept the hours." To the oscillating image of London, Paris, and Hell in part I must now be added Jerusalem, Alexandria, Athens, Vienna, and probably every other real and mythic city and even the complex including both Carthage as Augustine's model of the secular city and his City of God. They all crack, re-form, and explode.

Beyond the tolling bells that convey the news about time, only singing voices from dry wells and cisterns can be heard. These final hallucinatory details draw attention to the persistence of music and time in an environment where space has collapsed into a set of undecidable dimensions. Shadows which are at one moment gliding ahead are at the next instant "on the other side of you." The road is replaced by a cracked earth ringed by the horizon, and the vertical direction is established by sounds high in the air only to culminate in a city that is upside down after exploding. Forward, backward, sideways, upward, downward—all spatial directions fail, and with them all geometries—Euclidean, non-Euclidean, and multidimensional—are swept away. Only time and its artistic formalizations—music and poetry—remain. There is space, to be sure, within empty cisterns and exhausted wells, but it is no more reliable than the rapidly collapsing spaces just encountered. Time remains a persistent dimension of reference in the sounds of clocks and singing voices. We will return to the implications of time's and music's continuity when we consider the fragments in the poem's closing stanza.

With the entry into a "decayed hole" where an empty chapel stands, the hallucinations end and commonplace reality reappears. Stable space is here reconstituted where "the grass is singing/Over the tumbled graves, about the chapel." Music serves as one transition from surreal to real locations. Cicadas, hermit thrush, cries in the air, whisper music played on taut hair, bats whistling, and singing voices give way to a naturalistic and literal Aeolian music of grass soon to be provided with a concluding note by a crowing cock.

> In this decayed hole among the mountains
> In the faint moonlight, the grass is singing
> Over the tumbled graves, about the chapel
> There is the empty chapel, only the wind's home.
> It has no windows, and the door swings,
> Dry bones can harm no one.
> Only a cock stood on the rooftree
> Co co rico co co rico
> In a flash of lightning. Then a damp gust
> Bringing rain

185

Although most of this passage consists of description, it does include two interpretations: the chapel is "only the wind's home" and "Dry bones can harm no one." If this is the Chapel Perilous from the grail story, it is empty of peril, empty of occasions for testing the courage of Perceval on his way to question Amfortas the Fisher King. With no test to pass, there is no sanction for the knight's continued journey, no hope that he can restore the king to his land among joyful voices singing praise to God. Here, quite simply, the journey stops at an anticlimactic dead end in common sense. All spirits have departed, given way to their etymological origins in words that mean only wind. Both good and evil, both comforting and terrifying presences have been swept away in favor of dry bones, history's and myth's only legacy. The burial of the dead is thus complete. The cock's crow adds a final assurance that no ghosts—only a gust—are present. The cock's cry is a time-honored signal for spirits to depart, but here no spirits exist to heed the message. With that final redundant exorcism, rain, so desperately desired on the preceding journey, finally arrives. Water is now purified of symbolic and sacramental content, its blunt facticity assured.

Though the promise of redemptive and mythic symbolism is here canceled and erased, backward references continue. The chapel is in a "decayed hole among the mountains." In that description, a suggestion of an earlier line resides: "Dead mountain mouth of carious teeth that cannot spit." Carious teeth are teeth full of decayed holes. Metaphorically, the chapel is in a hole and the mountains are decayed teeth in a dry, dead mouth. Regardless of how this metaphor is understood, it provides a direction of reference pointing beyond the antisymbolic end the passage emphasizes. Is the mountain range somehow the mouth gaping open, chuckle spread from ear to ear, at the place where breath and words once emanated from the world's body? Is wind, in the context recursively added by the metaphor, a sign that life is still continuing, a breath that does not sing but nevertheless causes the door to swing and the grass to make music? No satisfactory answers to such questions are available, but the questions themselves energize an alternative to the hopeless dead end the literal reading has provided. Further, the metaphor directs attention away from the chapel that is no longer perilous and shifts it back to the tavern in "A Game of Chess," where Lil's ruined teeth are a subject of concern. She used money allocated for replacing her teeth on an abortion that ruined her health. Lil, as we have noted, is the most detailed and sympathetic character in the poem, the suffering female figure who *is*, in a conventional literary sense, the symbolic earth in a condition of barrenness and ruin. Now she reappears as the place where the chapel stands. She is miserable but still clinging to life, still breathing the air that is the absence of spirit.

The contrasting directions of reference produced by the poem's various methods lead to an oscillation of negative and affirmative interpretations. External references—allusions to myth, specifically to the questing knight and the impotent king, along with the victims of sacrificial rituals—lead to a complete negation of value. Death continues, but it is nothing but death, plain death without redemptive promise, a purely private end. Crucifixion is as anti-symbolic as water. By contrast, internal references—allusions to other figures in *The Waste Land* itself—lead to affirmations of life, however dim and unpromising that life may be. External references, to put it succinctly, point toward despair, whereas internal references point toward minimal hope. Both sets of references are present, and both must be considered by the reader. Therefore, he must accept the oscillation of these contrary tonalities without attempting to ignore one of them in a search for a closure that is specifically withheld. This point becomes more compelling when it is noted that the mountains, primarily negative in mythic reference and minimally affirmative in reference to Lil in the tavern scene, are clearly affirmative in pointing toward Marie, who as a child overcame fear by consenting to a descent on a sled in winter and who as an adult feels free from fear in the mountains. Within the poem, then, resides a network of analogies that are inescapably affirmative, analogies constituting a parody of redemption through art. We will return to this point in our discussion of the poem's closing array of fragments.

The poem now moves outside of Western culture, to India and the fable of the thunder god Prajapati. The story, as indicated by Eliot's note, is found in the *Brihadaranyaka—Upanishad*, 5, 1. Prajapati, the god who speaks through thunder, says "Da! Da! Da!" and the three orders of beings—gods, men, and devils—interpret this "message" as three cardinal commands, "control, give, sympathize." Eliot, as B. P. N. Sinha notes, alters the sequence to "give, sympathize, control."[4] With the movement to the Ganges River and Mount Himavant, Eliot shifts for the first time to a position outside all of the poem's former scenes. Rapid shifts in time back and forth between contemporary and mythic details, along with shifts in space between England, Germany, and North Africa, now collapse into a unitive pattern when viewed from a perspective outside European culture. India is remote enough to make the Western panorama of futility and anarchy look like a simple, limited fact. India and its religious traditions are a temporary escape from the relational heap of perspectives within Western consciousness. It is a perspective on perspectives.

> Ganga was sunken, and the limp leaves
> Waited for rain, while the black clouds
> Gathered far distant, over Himavant.
> The jungle crouched, humped in silence.
> Then spoke the thunder
> DA
> *Datta*: what have we given?
> My friend, blood shaking my heart
> The awful daring of a moment's surrender
> Which an age of prudence can never retract
> By this, and this only, we have existed
> Which is not to be found in our obituaries
> Or in memories draped by the beneficent spider
> Or under seals broken by the lean solicitor
> In our empty rooms
> DA
> *Dayadhvam*: I have heard the key
> Turn in the door once and turn once only
> We think of the key, each in his prison
> Thinking of the key, each confirms a prison
> Only at nightfall, aethereal rumours
> Revive for a moment a broken Coriolanus
> DA
> *Damyata*: The boat responded
> Gaily, to the hand expert with sail and oar
> The sea was calm, your heart would have responded
> Gaily, when invited, beating obedient
> To controlling hands

This new location, India, is also divided into distances and perspectives. The clouds are "far distant, over Himavant," and the reader seems to be "placed" in a position near the river in the silent jungle. "Speech" from the thunder arrives from this distance, but the space between mountain source of sound and jungle position to hear it is quickly erased by a rapid series of interpretations. This point is relatively minor but must be noted because the following hermeneutical exercises within the poem should be experienced as a replacement of spatial relations by the nondimensional and discursive relations of signs and significances. The passage is not about messages from above but about interpretations.[5]

The first and most important point about the thunder is that it does not say anything at all, and further, it does not mean anything. It is like the birds who "say" twit, jug, and tereu, and the cock who "said" co co rico. As quotations, these words, along with DA, are onomatopoeic contrivances to simulate pure noise, pure insignificance. When such words reveal the presence of birds, cock, or thunder, they have those meanings, but when they are offered as quotations of what the birds, cock, and thunder said, they reveal that nothing whatsoever has been said. The lines "Then spoke the thunder/DA" dramatize vividly the moment before meaning, a moment of pure insignificance. As soon as the word *"Datta"* is supplied, however, the ideal unity of a nonsignifier collapses into the dualism of meaning. The rest of the passage (through line 423) is a multiplication of these dualisms into a full-scale discourse on human relations.

A second basic point, too often missed by critics, is that the distinction between external and internal interpretation is crucial in reading this fable. *The Waste Land,* we have argued, is full of internal interpretations, but here, within the Indian perspective marked by its alienness and exoticism, internal interpretations move to a foreground of concern unique in the poem. Madame Sosostris was, after all, only a halfhearted interpreter of prefabricated signifiers, the cards in the tarot deck. She has vanished from the poem along with all of its earlier figures; they have been compressed into shadows and exploding fragments and their recursive reappearances. But unlike the earlier interpreters, the interpreters of the thunder are not undermined or trivialized. In the jungle, serious interpretative action is foregrounded for the first time. The discourse on the

189

implications and consequences of giving, sympathizing, and controlling is rich in meaning, obviously; but as internal interpretation it is merely a fact to be centered, a field to be enclosed by our perspectives as readers. The internal interpretations must be examined as phenomena in themselves before the reader moves outside the discourse in search of meanings.

A third preliminary point is that several interpreters (or groups of interpreters) are involved in decoding the sound of the thunder. The first interpreter responds to the sound of the thunder ("DA") by supplying the word "*Datta*," and the second responds to "*Datta*" by supplying a commentary on existence. In the *Upanishad* to which Eliot's note refers, the interpreters use a very elementary method for making sense of the sound of thunder. In their language, the syllable *da* is used to convey the noise of thunder, so a word beginning with those letters is their "translation." If the scene were enacted in England or America, those challenged to hear a signifier in the sound of thunder would look for words suggested by "boom" or "kapow." They could suppose that the three messages of the thunder were "bloom," "capon," and "boon." The second group then interprets the interpretation of the first group. In our example, the second group could go on to invent a discourse on blooming to full maturity, abandoning lusts of the flesh like capons, and thereby achieving the moral boon of enlightenment. The process would receive the derision it deserves unless it were carried on in a psychoanalytic session where such interpretative leaps are conventional.

One reason for using an Indian fable, as we have noted, is that India is remote enough to permit a long perspective. Another reason emerges from the process outlined in the previous paragraph. India is a place where the coincidences Eliot desires are built into the language, a language he studied in graduate school at Harvard. Further, interpretative exercises of this kind are part of the training process for novice priests. Prajapati, lord of thunder, provides a mythic mind that intends to convey messages with his voice. In that cultural context, the process of understanding transcendental signifiers is granted an authenticity denied to it in the West, where only ancient prophets could be taken seriously as translators of such messages.

One special point should be underscored before commenting on the specific internal interpretations. The "translations" from thunder into onomatopoeia into Sanskrit—"*Datta*," "*Dayadhvam*," and "*Damyata*"—are Eastern and universal, but the glosses on the translations are European and personal. "*Datta*," "*Dayadhvam*," and "*Damyata*" are as far as the Indian interpretations go. Those words, once supplied, are elaborated by a Western voice. He refers to obituaries, seals, a solicitor, and Coriolanus, references which clearly identify him as European. Actually, there may be one, two, or three Western interpreters, just as there may be several Indian translators. A vast gulf, then, separates the translators of the thunderclap and the interpreters of the translations.

The discourse on "*Datta*" is existentialist; that is, it declares that existence is dependent on irretractable choices, on irreversible surrenders. The moments of surrender are stressful to an extreme, and so, in other ways, is the age of prudent nonsurrender defined by an acute awareness of the irretrievability of past actions. In spite of the evidence of lawyers and estates and obituaries, a person who has not submitted to the "awful daring of a moment's surrender" cannot be said to have existed. The commentary on "*Datta*" contrives a personal and nonmetaphysical concept of essence in contrast to enclosing accidentals. To live a safe life is to live an inessential one. Making dangerous, even calamitous choices bestows individuation. Fear in a handful of dust becomes a positive datum.

This gloss on "*Datta*" suggests a way of evaluating the authenticity of the existences of earlier figures in the poem. Marie surrendered to an irreversible descent in childhood, but after that she lived a life dedicated to evading the seasons and other cycles. It seems that no further painful choices were made, that her essence is disappearing into the environment where complaints about April's cruelty reveal existential minimalization. The hyacinth girl's lover surrendered to a passionate consummation, but a year later he can remember nothing more than the mystical but secular experience that overwhelmed him. The affluent woman in "A Game of Chess" has no authentic existence. She has never known the awful daring of a moment's surrender and can only wait for someone to tell her what to do. In contrast to Marie and Lil, but exactly similar to her companion, she can be said to be unreal, a phantom. Lil has made irreversible choices, but she did so under duress or, as in the case of the abortion, in ignorance of the dangerous side effects. Like Marie, she has a minimal existence. If she could muster the awful daring to free herself from her entrapment within biology, she would become someone, but that is not a possibility within the poem. Similar notations can be made on many of the other characters.

These notations, however, are not appropriate from an outside position, our position as readers. They are appropriate to the figure in the poem who adds his Western commentary to the word "*Datta*." From his perspective, such judgments make sense. From the reader's perspective, he and the ideas he suggests form a fact to be observed. The reader is free to share his notions but is also free to reject them by seeing them as mental movements that make up one part of the poem's design as an object. As we suggested earlier, the idea that individual existence is achieved through emergence from circular nature into rectilinear time, where no repetitions or reversals are possible, has its origins in myth. The gloss on "*Datta*" is thus a reference to the mythic foundations of the poem, a refinement of myth's last residues into a practical philosophy of existence that can imaginably be of some use in a world where mythic consciousness has vanished. Such existentialism—essence achieved by dangerous choice—is a secular trace of a once vital tradition. In the twentieth century, it is a popular way to explain one's life where no transcendent explanations are possible. The discourse is thus both positive and negative, a fragment shored against ruins.

The so-called second command of the thunder is less direct and emphatic. "DA" is interpreted as "*Dayadhvam*" (sympathize), and "*Dayadhvam*" is interpreted with a metaphor of turning a key which modulates into a more complex metaphor culminating in the reference to Coriolanus. Eliot's note to these lines refers the reader to the episode in which Dante meets Ugolino in Hell and listens to his sad tale about being imprisoned in a tower with his children to die of starvation. "And down below I heard the door of the horrible tower being locked" (*Inferno* 33.46). Eliot's note also quotes Bradley's *Appearance and Reality*:

> My external sensations are no less private to myself than are my thoughts or my feelings. In either case my experience falls within my own circle, a circle closed on the outside; and, with all its elements alike, every sphere is opaque to the others which

surround it. . . . In brief, regarded as an existence which appears in a soul, the whole world for each is peculiar and private
to that soul.[6]

Most critics interpret the quotations from Dante and from Bradley
as parallel, both referring to solipsism, that is, to being locked in the
prison of the self. In a detailed discussion of this passage in *Modern
Philology* (1979), Brooker demonstrated that the quotations from
Dante and Bradley are not parallels but contrasts.[7] The Bradley
quotation refers to the precognitive moment of immediate experience, the moment before the self comes into existence as a datum.
The reference to immediate experience is presented not as an equivalent to the situation of being locked in a tower but as a key that can
be used to get out of the tower. The lines in the text of the poem "We
think of the key, each in his prison/Thinking of the key, each confirms a prison" correspond not to immediate experience but to
relational experience. In Bradley's philosophy, as we have pointed
out, thinking is the activity that dissolves unity and generates such
dualisms as self and other, time and space, and mind and matter. It
is impossible to get beyond dualism while one is "Thinking of the
key," for thinking imprisons one in dualism.

The reference to Coriolanus also suggests that conscious attempts
to be sympathetic simply do not work. Shakespeare's *Coriolanus* is
about a conflict between a hero and the general populace. He makes
a conscious effort to sympathize with the crowd, and in the process
he is destroyed.[8] The relation between "thinking of the key" and
"confirming the prison" is evident in Bradley's *Ethical Studies*. Bradley suggests that a conscious intention to sympathize, or a conscious response to a suggestion to sympathize, makes the act of
fusion with the other a process known in advance to be impossible.
The situation here is similar to Bradley's account of the problems
involved in utilitarianism. The intention to pursue happiness turns
it into an infinitely receding condition. At every stage of the process, the speaker must, like Julian Sorel in Stendhal, ask if he is now
happy, and the answer is always "Not yet."

The prison metaphor dramatizes the trap involved in trying to be
empathetic (in contrast to being empathetic unconsciously). The
metaphor seems, in fact, to be generated by the logical and emotional datum of undecidability. To seek empathy is to feel its ab-

sence, and to feel its absence is to intensify the seeking. This circularity must continue in the same way as undecidability must continue in a search for a solution to the problem of the Cretan liar. Russell labored to eliminate the problem prior to completing his part of the *Principia Mathematica*. It is a familiar puzzle. In a village on Crete, a barber says, "Don't believe anything you hear in this town, for everyone in it is a liar." If he is telling the truth, he is telling a lie. If he is telling a lie, he is telling the truth and therefore telling a lie. Russell did not solve this problem satisfactorily, and neither has anyone else. It remains a pure example of the oscillating undecidables that constitute a large segment of our conscious lives.[9]

It is possible to transcend the self, to get out of the tower or prison. And the key for unlocking the door, as Brooker has pointed out, is to be found in Eliot's quotation about immediate experience. Immediate experience is both the judge of solipsism and the guarantor that it can be transcended. Immediate experience dissolves automatically into intellectual consciousness, but it does not actually disappear. As Bradley says, it "both remains and is active."[10] It is a judge because, in continuing to exist as part of a felt or unconscious background, it enables us to know the difference between unity and dualism, to know that we are caught in our own categories. Immediate experience is a key because, in providing a memory of unity, in enabling unity to become an object for reflection, it provides a model of transcendence, a hint that it is possible to move beyond relational experience. As Eliot explains in his dissertation, by reflecting on immediate experience "we are led to the conception of an all-inclusive experience outside of which nothing shall fall."[11]

The gloss on "*Dayadhvam*" is thus a critique of the gloss on "*Datta*." Paradoxically, in trying to give or to surrender oneself to an irreversible series, one inevitably projects oneself into otherness. In consciously abandoning the self, one merely affirms it. The straightforward affirmation of the existential process of achieving authentic existence in the first gloss is transformed into an infinite oscillation of undecidables in the second gloss. Existentialism creates more problems than it solves.

Further, the second commentary encapsulates the poem's dialectic of abstraction and empathy. We have noted that some strategies of presenting character evoke a receding, two-dimensional presence like Mr. Eugenides on a tarot card or the first woman in "A Game of Chess." Other strategies, in contrast, evoke a vividly felt presence in three-dimensional space, such as Marie on her sled or Tiresias describing his breasts. But then again, all figures, both the abstract ones that block empathy and the kinesthetic ones that block abstraction through rounded presence, eventually fade into the most abstract of images, the shadow of someone who is not there on the road to Emmaus. The conflicting glosses of *"Datta"* and *"Dayadhvam"* typify the oscillating patterns of the poem itself.

The response to *"Damyata"* is less a gloss than a statement of regret. Control can be learned and used successfully, as the example of the boat responding to the expert hand explains. But the passage concludes with a statement in the subjunctive mode—"your heart would have responded"—that emphasizes a failure to exercise the same kind of control in a human relationship. Regret and a touch of guilt dominate these lines. The speaker's interpretation reveals his mental state, as do all of the preceding responses. An important aspect of that state of mind is the habit of generating metaphors in attempts to make the Indian interpretations relevant to his situation.

These glosses, then, must be approached first and foremost as internal interpretations, that is, as dramatizations of the action of inventing meaning. The speakers take general instructions—give, sympathize, and control—and turn them instantly into personal, private, limited guidelines for living within human relations. The first gloss is addressed to "My friend," and it continues with plural pronouns. The second also uses both singular and plural pronouns, and the third uses the second-person pronouns and is addressed to an intimate associate. The person addressed is someone who could have been helped if the techniques of control had been known and applied. It is tempting to think here of Eliot's first marriage, of his anguish over his inability to help Vivien and thereby himself by discovering the appropriate method of control. However, it is important to place this reading among less specific glosses, that is, essence through choice, the undecidability of empathy, and the self-reflexive nature of control.

The triad of thunder words and the notions they inspire do not provide us with an authoritative statement of the poem's main ideas

195

or even of some exotic guides to life, no longer common clichés because derived from the alien cultural context of India. In fact, the three glosses are widely divergent, even contradictory. How, for example, can one reconcile the implications of the "heart" responding "Gaily, when invited, beating obedient/To controlling hands" with the real existence that can be achieved only by "The awful daring of a moment's surrender" that can never be reversed? Submission to someone's "controlling hands" might be such a surrender, but the owner of those controlling hands would be excluded from the "awful daring" requisite to essential existence. Further, if the first and third glosses clash with each other, the second clashes in a different way with both. Sympathy produces an oscillation that negates the straight and irreversible emphasis of the first gloss and also denies the possibility on the conscious level of control. Even more difficulty arises if the glosses are read as products of three separate interpreters. They are each prepared to consider human relations in ways that conflict. The three would not be able, using these ideas as guidelines, to establish harmonious relations among themselves.

The thunder episode ends by exposing the inadequacy of the interpretative process in conceiving a coherent plan for contending with the complexity of human relations. Even if the most affirmative modes are contrived in reading the episode, problems will remain. For example, the glosses might be read as follows: The awful, blood-shaking daring of past surrenders has conferred an authentic existence upon the figures involved. Because they are now authentic beings, they are capable of sympathy. At least they share the existentialist mode of being—essence through choice. The process has led to self-control, imposition of a formal order upon the material of selfhood which allows them to share and reinforce that order in their interactions. With such a reading, the difficulties seem to vanish, but only because we have closed our eyes to the self-canceling tendency of the metaphors used in the glosses: key, door, prison, Coriolanus, and boat. Further, Eliot seems to have designed these metaphors to fail and to cancel each other. A person cannot be controlled like a boat—Eliot's contempt for most psychotherapeutic theories is plainly at work here—and sympathy, whether undecidable or not, does not cohere with the metaphor of hearing "the key/Turn in the door once and turn once only." A stripped-down, commonsense notion of empathy would see it as a frequently recurring impulse. Choice as method of validating existence is here presented as a rationalized process of turning catastrophe into victory, a Panglossian optimism that survives only as a way of turning a past failure into a present success.

The thunder legend is usually read as Eliot's "solution" to the problems dramatized earlier in the poem, as the poet's "wisdom" offered for our guidance;[12] it is presented not as a message, however, but as a series of interpretations of interpretations of a message that did not exist at all. The thunder did not speak. The Sanskrit words were arbitrary inventions, and so were the personalized glosses. To shift the focus of attention, this point underscores the arbitrary and purely contingent nature of all language. If the thunder, like the sounds of birds, is mere noise, all utterances are mere noise before meaning is assigned to them. Words in one's own language have references with long histories, traditional and individual histories of definition and usage. Words in an unknown language, however, have meanings only after a glossary is consulted. These meanings pulled from a glossary have short histories and special classes of meaning that can exist only after a translation into a known language. We can explain and philosophize about the implications of our words "give," "sympathize," and "control," but in regard to *"Datta," "Dayadhvam,"* and *"Damyata"* we can only look up our equivalent words.

A crucial implication emerges from these observations. *The Waste Land* is in part a commentary on the contingency of language. Readers are presented with a text in several languages, a text which involves the experience of comparing their experience of their own linguistic environment with their experience of others. Even those rare readers who do not need footnotes, who can read Italian, Latin, Greek, German, French, and Sanskrit, know those languages to various degrees. Even polyglot readers, seeing that the poem is in English, will center that language and understand the other languages as peripheral sounds that should be decoded into English before they can be understood. Such readers may well dispute this assertion, but they will do so in English and their argument will thereby lose much of its force.

For most readers, however, there is no dispute. Their own language is organic, continuous, and internally significant, whereas other languages are, at least until they are translated, only noise. Eliot's use of birds, cock, and thunder supports the idea that he was aiming directly at this kind of linguistic effect. "Co co rico co co rico" is a quotation of an alien word, and *"Datta"* is a quotation of an alien word from a different class of alienness. Both stimulate the reader to search for translations and ways of placing them into their contexts. The process of translating and placing turns noise into signals. One of the effects of including alien words in a text is to remind the reader that his native language is also mere noise from the linguistic points of view referred to by the alien words. A reader who knew only Sanskrit, for example, would regard four words in the poem as organizing signifiers. He would have to translate every other word into Sanskrit before he could feel that he had read the poem. Further, the reminder that one's own language is, from other points of reference, only noise stimulates an awareness of points of reference within one's own experience from which language is also only noise. Infancy, which is largely forgotten because memory is mediated by language as much as by imagery, is a common position in a realm of pure insignificance, pure noise. There the sounds of speech are indistinguishable from the sounds of roosters, thunder, horns, and motors. Also, moments of inattention, alternative states of consciousness, like that of the hyacinth girl's lover, are positions from which meaning in language does not exist.

The differences between signals and ambient noise must therefore be understood to oscillate in the poem as ergon and parergon do. At one moment, English is central and other languages are peripheral. In other moments of thought, the positions reverse and then rereverse. Other reversals are also generated. For example, "Da" signifies thunder, but, once that is understood, actual thunder, heard perhaps by coincidence in a classroom where "What the Thunder Said" is under discussion, can easily signify "Da." In the same way, a rooster's crowing, though not likely to sound like "Co co rico co co rico" to any ear, may well signify that sound. A dog, simply put, signifies the word "dog" if he lives in an English-speaking country.

The ultimate importance of the thunder passage, then, is in its dramatization of the inauthenticity of interpretation, the contingency of language, and the function of language in the sequential cognitive stages constructed in Bradley's philosophy and reinterpreted by Eliot in his dissertation. It is not a matter of noting that "Words strain,/Crack and sometimes break, under the burden" ("Burnt Norton," part V). A much more elementary and fundamental failure of language is at issue here. Specifically, in Bradley's view, language is a part of the world of appearance, the dualistic realm of relational knowing. It does not exist in immediate experience and does not exist in transcendent experience. Language must fail, then, because words function only in the relational center where no authentic given bondings of signifier to signified are possible. Such relations are as unstable, as dependent on point of view, as all other relations. One might suppose, with some older believers in salvation through clear language,[13] that the social, moral, and spiritual problems Eliot presents in *The Waste Land* are caused by the absence of a vocabulary of communion. But that supposition is almost certainly not Eliot's. His work on Bradley makes it likely that he regarded language as the most important mediator of unstable relations. The ideal unity of immediate experience, however, excludes mediation by definition; that is, immediate means not mediated. And the ideal unity of transcendent experience is on the far side of all relations, including language; transcendent experience is not mediated by and not reachable through language. Between signifier and signified falls the shadow, the reminder of their duality. Only by ceasing to exist can they become one. It is of no consequence, then, that thunder can be supposed to speak and provide a guide to life. Language exists only in the radically unstable relational realm and has meaning only in reference to the nonrelational constructs that precede and sometimes follow it. Transcendence to the Absolute is the only answer, and that answer cannot be accepted without a leap beyond philosophy into faith. Something after meaning is needed before meaning can be found in a coherent form.

Our reading of the thunder passage is corroborated to some extent by the fact that it offers immediate help in the poem's final paragraph, one of the most notorious passages in the history of English poetry. The most important lines in the last stanza are "Shall I at least set my lands in order?" and "These fragments I have shored against my ruins." These lines signal a shift from the motifs of searching to a motif of pragmatic accommodation to circumstance. They have an effect like Candide's final answer to Pangloss: "Let us cultivate our garden." This may or may not be an allusion to Voltaire; be that as it may, there is without doubt an analogous concluding shift of emphasis.

More important, the movement to pragmatics signals a rejection of both meaning and the varieties of guideline ideas generated by the Western interpreter(s) of the Sanskrit words. As a rejection of interpretation, the passage also suggests an abandonment of the perspectives required by the mythic method. Myth is a source of meaning, value, and order, a contrived perspective taken from Frazer and Weston, which suggests transcendence to a position beyond all the positions within the world. That position is not real, because it cannot be said to exist, and is also not ideal, because it is by definition outside the possible realms of thought. All we have is the sense of movement toward an ever-receding point from which to view the modern world in the poem—and the poem itself—as a unitive order. This is one reminder among many in the poem that order through perspective is only the familiar illusion of supposing that a galaxy is a single star because it is so far away that its internal diversity cannot be perceived. Here, in the final paragraph, the poem abandons the notion of the perspectival order and moves toward a fragile conclusion.

The abandonment of the quest for meaning is evident in the structure of the stanza itself.

> I sat upon the shore
> Fishing, with the arid plain behind me
> Shall I at least set my lands in order?
> London Bridge is falling down falling down falling down
> *Poi s'ascose nel foco che gli affina*
> *Quando fiam uti chelidon*—O swallow swallow
> *Le Prince d'Aquitaine à la tour abolie*
> These fragments I have shored against my ruins
> Why then Ile fit you. Hieronymo's mad againe.
> Datta. Dayadhvam. Damyata.
> Shantih shantih shantih

In the opening lines of this passage, the speaker enacts a rejection of the quest by turning his back to the wasted land. There will be no more agonies in stony places, no more shadows, no more movements over psychic terrains of distress. His back is turned. Further, we can hardly fail to think of the speaker as some version of the Fisher King. When the impotent king of a barren land wonders— after the failure of the questing knight to arrive and prepare him for a ceremonial death to rejuvenate his realm—if he should at least set his lands in order, his message is clear beyond mistake. Now, he implies, I can only take care of myself. Kings are not metonymically one with their lands, so kings and subjects alike may go their separate ways, each responsible only for himself. If the Fisher King takes Candide's advice, his private cultivation, or setting in order, is a recognition that he is set free from the burden of being the king. From now on, it is everyone for himself. Community no longer exists.

The speaker, then, moves toward a private rather than a communal order. His method involves using fragments of poetry to shore up his ruins. Removed from their contexts in various poems, and also from the contexts in which they conveyed some kind of meaning, the fragments are, from the speaker's point of view, virtually meaningless. They illustrate a position of exhaustion "after" meaning, a position of refuge not only from surrounding ruins but from the need to interpret, the compulsion to make sense of fragments. We must emphasize, however, that the fragments are after meaning only from the speaker's point of view. From an external position, that is, from the reader's point of view, these fragments are rich in meaning.

From the point of view of the exhausted Fisher King, the meaning of the fragments does not matter, and the order of the fragments is of no consequence. The fragments simply coexist. Thus the fragment from *The Spanish Tragedy*, the three thunder words, and "Shantih" merely coexist with the other fragments. But from the reader's point of view an obvious problem exists. The problem is related to the placement of the line, "These fragments I have shored against my ruins." It makes perfect sense to say "I will shore the following items against my ruins" and then go on to present an inventory of timbers, sandbags, and other props. But here the statement comes in the middle of the inventory. This is clearly more than the use of collage as an emergency procedure for preventing the collapse of ruins. Eliot's structure suggests some special complexity is at work here.

Another signal of complexity is the repetition of the word "shore." Eliot's original draft has the line "These fragments I have spelt into my ruins," a line which alludes to the Sibyl of Cumae, who prophesied by spelling messages into palm leaves. Before showing the poem to Pound, Eliot revised the line, changing "spelt into" to "shored against."[14] His original choice, actually, is fascinating. It means, for example, that the Sibyl of Cumae was in the poem before Eliot put her in the epigraph and provides an argument that the Sibyl is the controlling narrator. He could not have substituted "shored against" for "spelt into" thoughtlessly. And yet, he did make the substitution, causing the speaker to sit upon the shore and "shore" his fragments. Shore is thus a deliberate and striking repetition which makes a difference in the way the entire poem is read. As a noun, shore indicates the margin where land and sea meet, but as a verb, it denotes the effort to set things in order. The wordplay here has the effect of placing the process of setting things in order ("shoring") on a precarious margin (a "shore"). "Shore" and "shored against" join forces to place this final stanza squarely on a dividing line where no closure through choice of one side or the other can become a valid end of the reading process.

Eliot's purposes in this collection of concluding fragments can be clarified to some extent by looking at his manuscript. Most critics focus on Eliot's typed draft because it shows the extent to which he took Pound's advice on cutting. But the handwritten draft is much more important, because it shows crucial decisions Eliot made after the first writing but before typing it and showing it to Pound. In the handwritten draft, the line about using fragments to prevent ruin is followed only by the Sanskrit commands and benediction. But in Eliot's handwritten revision, one of the fragments "Why then Ile fit you. Hieronymo's mad againe" is moved to its present position, *after* the statement of purpose for the fragments.[15] This has the effect of positioning the statement of purpose in the midst of rather than at the end of the fragments and also of separating it from the solemn thunder words and the benediction.

This change provides a clue to what Eliot is doing in the concluding sequence. Hieronymo and his madness are plainly in conflict with the other quotations. All of the others can be interpreted in a positive way, but the reference to Hieronymo is a reference to unspeakable horror, to betrayal, revenge, madness, murder, and mutilation. Splitting it from the affirmative fragments and placing it after the statement about shoring ruins turns it into a counterstatement, a negation. If a nursery rhyme, Dante, the *Pervigilium Veneris*, and Nerval are seen as shoring something up, *The Spanish Tragedy* can only be seen as tearing it down again. To test this possible reading, let us consider what, if anything, the fragments have in common. This project involves reinserting the fragments backward into their contexts in the works from which they were taken, and thus backward into the realm of meaning. In this undertaking, we are doing precisely what the exhausted internal speaker, who has reached a state of passive accommodation, appears not to want. As readers, however, we must go forward. The poem gives us no other choice.

In one way or another, all of the concluding fragments have to do with song and poetry, with singing that persists through and transforms disaster. The first fragment—"London Bridge is falling down falling down falling down"—is a refrain from a children's song, a line paradoxically associated with fun and games. The line provides an example of the metamorphosis of catastrophe into innocent and mindless art. The second fragment, in Italian, is one of Eliot's favorite lines from the *Purgatorio*. It refers to Arnaut Daniel's joyous purgatorial suffering and can be translated "Then he dived back into the refining fire." Just before he leaps, he describes himself as one who goes singing. This fragment also has to do with the transformation of suffering into music. The next line contains two fragments, both having to do with transformation, suffering, and music. The first—which can be translated "When shall I be as the swallow?"—is from an ancient Latin poem and the second—"O swallow swallow"—is from poems by both Tennyson and Swinburne. As Eliot points out in his note, this line alludes to Philomela's rape and torture and her consequent transformation into the nightingale, a story alluded to several times in *The Waste Land*. The next fragment, from Nerval's sonnet "El Desdichado," can be translated "The Prince of Aquitaine, to the ruined tower." The poem is about a disinherited prince who turns his desolation into the music of poetry. These fragments have in common the motif of singing which persists through loss and transforms disaster into art. They are followed by the statement that they are being used to shore up the ruins of the narrator, another disinherited and desolate figure trying to use remnants as building blocks for art.

A closer look at the fragments reveals that they are carefully presented in symmetrically opposed pairs. A children's song is matched—or answered—by a description of a poet hiding himself in the refining fire after urging us to be ever mindful of his pain. The symmetry appears when we see that the first fragment is a voice from earliest childhood, whereas the second refers to a condition after death. Further, "London Bridge is falling down falling down falling down" uses the conventions of poetic repetition and rhythm to divert attention from the song's plain meaning. Countless people know that line without it ever occurring to them that it says something horrendous. The old lullaby "Rock-a-bye-baby on the tree top" is an identical example. That song goes on to sing cheerfully and soothingly about a disaster, "When the wind blows the cradle will rock,/When the bough breaks the cradle will fall,/Down will come baby, cradle and all." These nursery songs are part of experience before consciousness of meaning, that is, before experience is filtered through the mind, before interpretation. In symmetrical contrast, the song of the poet leaping into the purgative fire is part of experience that comes after meaning, after surrendering interpretations, and indeed after having sung his final, meaning-charged song, "Now I pray you, be ever mindful of my pain." This line is as clearly after meaning—and after life—as the children's song is before meaning and awareness of catastrophe.

The second set of fragments is designed as an equivalent symmetry. In the passage from the anonymous Latin *Vigil of Venus*, a poet in springtime laments that, unlike the squawking swans and the singing swallow, he cannot find his voice and cannot sing. He then asks when his spring will come, "When shall I be as the swallow

204

and my silence cease?" By contrast, the troubadour from Aquitaine, province of great singers, merely stands before the ruined tower and remembers all that has been and is no more. Springtime, the beginning, is balanced by the ruined tower, the end of a tradition. The contrast between before and after meaning is continued in the single short fragment "O swallow swallow." It alludes to a poem by Tennyson in which a poet laments his inability to fly to his beloved with a song of love and instructs the swallow to go for him. It also alludes to a poem about Philomela and Procne by Swinburne, a poem in which the nightingale chides her sister, the swallow, for singing in ignorance of the grief that should make her tongue cleave to the roof of her mouth, "the small slain body, the flower-like face" of her firstborn child. Instead of grieving, the swallow sings through a thousand springs and summers and, even in winter, flies south and continues her song. The Tennyson swallow is before meaning, and the Swinburne swallow is after meaning. The nightingale with her consciousness of wrong and her song of grief is caught in the middle; unable to let go of meaning, she is forced continually to interpret her experience. The five fragments are poised against each other in a precarious equilibrium.

Seen in these ways, the first fragments really do illustrate a shoring-up process. They affirm order and art as potent answers to collapse, pain, depression, and even the dissolution of a tradition of order and art. If *The Waste Land* had ended with "These fragments I have shored against my ruins," we could have read a final message to the effect that poetry can act as a saving consolation in times of hopelessness. Matthew Arnold's statement that poetry is capable of saving us would prevail. But that is not the way the poem ends. The mocking words from *The Spanish Tragedy* intrude and destroy any notion that salvation is available through art. They negate even a temporary shoring up of ruins through art. Their placement, a deliberate choice by Eliot, clearly contradicts the implications provided by the first fragments. "Why then Ile fit you. Hieronymo's mad againe" contains its own implications about the function and possible uses of art. Hieronymo has a play performed for his enemies, in order to entrap them and carry out his bloody revenge. His poetic and dramatic efforts culminate in a scene in which he avoids speech under torture by biting off his tongue and spitting it at his captors. The Philomela myth is part of the web of allusions here, for Hieronymo does to himself what King Tereus did to Philomela. The result of the first mutilation is the use of terrible wrong in the service of music, but the result of the second—Hieronymo's—is the use of poetry in the service of madness and silence.

So much for redemption through art. All solutions, all affirmations generate their formal opposites. The poem ends on the margin between secular hope and secular damnation, between order and madness. On that margin, that shored-up shore, "Datta. Dayadhvam. Damyata" return as mere shells of signifiers. They are stripped of their glosses, their ambitions toward being guides, like poetry, to life. The appropriate end is the repeated benediction, "Shantih shantih shantih." It is only because peace is out of the question on this precarious margin that peace must be stated. Understanding has brought us to a margin between minimal affirmation and maximal calamity, so the only peace thinkable is that which passes (transcends, in the Bradleian sense) understanding.

We can now take a look from the perspective of its ending at the entire poem. "These fragments I have shored against my ruins" can be understood to refer to all of *The Waste Land*, all its methods, all its directions of suggestion. Its cast of characters can be seen as fragments of a whole population, but they can also be seen as unique, isolated persons. The reading process has instructed us in how to see them, and the primary instruction is that we are not to see them in any single way available to us. They are at once parts of a whole and wholes in themselves. Similarly, its array of methods, techniques, and styles, along with its differing languages and variations on interpretation as action, must be seen as parts and as isolated moments of expression.

The traditional term in rhetoric that best describes the poem's method is parataxis. Simply stated, parataxis is the absence of transitions. A simple inventory of persons and perspectives is paratactic. In ordinary texts, relative importance is stated through the use of subordinating connectors, but these along with other transitions have been omitted. It seems plain that they have been omitted because they do not exist in the world. They are among the amenities demanded by language. Our medium of expression and description makes these transitions available, and convention requires their use. That medium, language, thus pushes us toward a coherence that does not exist in the world, a syntax that we desire because we want the subjects of discourse to have forms like the codes we use in stating such discourses. *The Waste Land* has succeeded in resisting the temptation to insert the coherence of language into the panoramas of myth, history, and modern urban crowds, despite its medium's pressure to do so. Like *Ulysses* and the *Cantos, The Waste Land* remains triumphantly paratactic, and that is the hallmark of its modernism.

We can also sum up and survey the poem by returning to its fragments as signals of the need to cherish and revere the very problems they cause. For example, the thunder passage tells us that neither internal nor external interpretations can stand alone. Neither positive nor negative readings suffice. Just as the mind of Europe cannot comprehend Asia, the mind of Asia cannot serve as a unifying point of view on Europe. Rubies can be found by the Indian Ganges, but they are of no use to the waiting king who complains by the dull canal behind a London gashouse. The DAS— thunder words—and shantih join the other fragments merely to coexist with them, not to sum them up from the outside. There is no outside; all perspectives are inside the closed systems of space and time. The final stanza indicates that neither shoring up nor tearing down will achieve closure. Art does and does not help. The Indian words do and do not help. The finale is a balance of positive and negative values. They add up to zero.

The value of the poem comes in the process of reading it and of collaborating with Eliot in making it. We have tried to work with him in ways that cohere with his habits of thinking and feeling, insofar as that project is possible. The final result of intense reading is an awareness of having been involved in creating. We do not imagine that our readings are the only (or even the best) ways of collaborating in reinventing the poem. We have only offered some samples of what can be done in reading *The Waste Land*.

A Speculative Postscript

Infancy and Immediate Experience in Reading

The Waste Land

We shall not cease from exploration
And the end of all our exploring
Will be to arrive where we started
And know the place for the first time.
—Eliot, "Little Gidding," V

We now wish to add a brief postscript to our reading of *The Waste Land*. In full awareness of the limits of interpretation, in full awareness that Eliot's mind and intentions are irrecoverable, we wish to point to some studies from the field of infantile epistemology that suggest parallels to the materials we have discussed in Bradley and in Eliot. We do not claim that either the philosopher or the poet was aware of the studies we will mention; on the other hand, we know that they held certain positions that are parallel to positions in other fields, especially in psychology. Furthermore, we have found that an awareness of these studies in psychology is helpful in reading modernist texts in general and particularly suggestive in reading *The Waste Land*.

Bradley's philosophy and Eliot's method stimulate a search for a final perspective, a metaphysical "outside" from which history and the poem can be viewed as a simple, organic unity. That perspective can be called heaven or nowhere or the Absolute, but it is by any name a place that cannot be reached. The outside perspective can be imagined, however, and in this postscript we wish to speculate on one version of the view from outside. We do not aspire to reveal a final perspective, but we do hope to add another dimension to our reading of *The Waste Land*.

Bradley's Absolute cannot serve as a platform from which unity would be evident, for it is unreachable, by definition. His concepts of immediate and transcendent experience coming before and after the dualistic everyday realm of relations, on the other hand, constitute possible perspectives for perceiving *The Waste Land* as a

208

unity. Transcendent experience, however, is available only in isolated moments and only to a limited extent; both as a concept and as a hope, Eliot considered it highly problematic. At any rate, moments of transcendence are too unconscious and too fleeting to serve as positions from which to gain the comprehensive view that would reveal unity.[1] Immediate experience remains, on the other hand, not as something to hope for but as something known and lost and yet not lost. It was from the beginning, is now, and ever shall be. It manifests itself over and over again in instances of coming to awareness, and although it is constantly being lost as the intellect assumes dominance, it remains throughout as the foundation and the judge of conscious life. As such, it is the starting point for our concluding speculations about a perspective from which unity may be discovered.

Immediate experience, as discussed by both Bradley and Eliot, has striking similarities to the condition of infancy, as described in the writings of Jean Piaget. Infancy, in fact, provides a nonmetaphysical perspective from which an enactment of contingency such as we find in *The Waste Land* can be perceived as an organic unity. Like Bradley's Absolute, infancy cannot be reached to be used as such a perspective, but unlike Bradley's version of the Absolute, unlike all versions of the Absolute, infancy can be felt as a potential area of psychological truth buried in every person's unconscious mind. Moreover, Piaget's theoretical descriptions of infancy are remarkably close to Eliot's description of immediate experience in the first chapter of his dissertation. Infancy, in fact, seems to be a special and universally shared instance of immediate experience. Of course, as a stage of cognition that occurs over and over again throughout life, immediate experience is not identical to the stage of infancy. Early infancy, nonetheless, is a clear approximation of immediate experience. The fact that, unlike immediate experience, it is a condition that persists for some time makes it even more useful for our purposes. We now turn to Piaget's speculations about infantile cognition and perception, which Joseph Bentley has related to the work of Joyce,[2] for our retrospective speculations about reading *The Waste Land*.

Specifically, we wish to entertain the possibility that *The Waste Land* implies a partial retrieval of infantile states of mind. Several problems must be cleared away before proceeding. The first is related to the fact that terms like "infantile" and "regression" have negative meanings in common speech. In our usage, however, they have no such connotations and should not be taken as a disparagement of *The Waste Land* or of any other work (*Ulysses*, for example) that can be approached in the same way. The word "infantile" simply means "of or related to infants or infancy," and the word "regression" means "the act or the privilege of going back." Any value judgment implied by these terms is positive, in our usage. If a work is regressive to the point of being infantile, it is for that reason more profoundly successful in probing deeply into the layered residues of the past—our past—than even the most spiritually ambitious art works and philosophies.

A second problem resides in the tradition of psychoanalytic literary criticism. Many students of literature are weary of talk about such matters as birth trauma, return to the womb, incest, and the Oedipus complex. The difficulty is not that these matters have been proved useless but that they seem facile, too easily invoked, too handy to prove everything and therefore nothing. One advantage of Jean Piaget's account of infantile experience is that it does not arise from the need to develop or to support a theory of mind. It is a by-product of his observations of infants responding to stimuli. He is simply not interested in a big question like "How does the human mind work?" He deals with isolated questions like "What does an infant see when a red ball is put before him?" Eventually, large theories emerge, but Piaget remains a summarizer of isolated and tentative answers to such small questions. From our point of view, the most remarkable aspect of Piaget's summations and reflections is his neglect of aesthetics. As far as we know, neither Piaget nor anyone else has pursued the implications of genetic epistemology in theories of art.

In order to be clear in explaining our speculations on these matters, we must first answer in summary form two basic questions. What is the principal theme of *The Waste Land*, and how does that theme relate to its techniques of presentation? The first question can be approached by noting that the characters and the episodes of the poem have in common an experience of loss. *The Waste Land* is, in a basic way, a lament for lost community. Its allusions are probes sent in search of that community in past traditions. The allusions guide the reader toward those lost communities as reference points against which to understand the degree and the nature of contemporary loss. But when the reader arrives at those biblical, Greek, Indic, Germanic, and English mythic sites, he will find in each of them a failure of communion and will discover no place better suited for communion than a public bar near Magnus Martyr.

The poem's central subject, then, is loss, displacement, deprivation. In a profound way, the loss it evokes is not just a twentieth-century urban condition. The poem's references reveal that this sense of loss has been pervasive throughout history. The idea that mythic consciousness has at times made recovery of community an intense experience does not alter the perception that the feeling of loss has pervaded cultures at all times in the history of civilization. If it had been otherwise, there would not be such a full record of religious strategies for dealing with that sense of lost community, for regaining a vanished unity. The very word "religion" comes from roots meaning rebinding, retying, transcending brokenness and regaining a primal condition of harmony. Although the twentieth-century waste land is a place of intense awareness of disunity, it is only a recent version of a constantly recurring condition. Eliot's nostalgia is for a community that he knows has not existed in history.

The second question is: How do the poem's techniques cohere with its themes? The poem's dominant rhetorical technique, as we have pointed out, is parataxis or the absence of connectors. The process of reading the poem, then, is inevitably an experience of loss involving repeated moments of unresolvable uncertainty. It is inseparable from a constantly repeated loss of the text's immediate past. For example, the opening sequence of "The Burial of the Dead" orients the reader in a precise way. He is presented with a commentary on the seasons, and then with a scene in Germany and a central character named Marie. After hearing a little of the conversation in the Hofgarten and learning a little about Marie's views and habits, the reader finds that this initial orientation has been stripped away. Going on to the following passage, he finds that the first one has vanished. This experience of loss is a denial of continuity, stability of setting, and expectation of transition. The same loss is repeated throughout the poem. Each section displaces its predecessor and is in turn displaced. The feeling of loss and displacement experienced by readers is inseparable from the absence of linguistic sequence, from parataxis. To read *The Waste Land*, then, is to find oneself enacting its subject matter. We will return to this analogy between loss of community and loss of transitions soon.

Before turning to Piaget's findings on early infancy, the time which is analogous to Bradley's cognitional level of immediate experience, we wish to describe a paradoxical situation in late infancy and to note its implications for modernist texts such as *The Waste Land*. In later infancy, the child begins the twin tasks of learning to talk and learning to walk. He begins to crawl and attempts to walk at the same time that he begins to communicate with words. In *Desire in Language*, Julia Kristeva discusses the crucial consequence of this normal coincidence of locomotion and speech. When the child moves on his own initiative, he begins the process of separating himself from his mother. The independence is desirable because it confers power, but in that it involves loss of the security and warmth of contact with the mother, it is tinged with ambivalence. The child is himself responsible for this increasing remoteness from the mother, but in slowly developing linguistic skills, he is able to communicate with her at a distance; he is able, in a sense, to compensate for the loss of physical contact. The ambivalence associated with movement and speech in infants remains as part of the felt background of language as behavior in adults. Language is simultaneously related to both gains and losses.[3]

Insofar as language is a substitute or compensation for loss of physical closeness, language in its earliest stages is associated with the experience of intimate physical contact. Freudians like Kristeva insist on a vocabulary that calls this association incestuous. Speech is symbolic incest because it is a substitute for contact with the mother. The argument that language is related to incest suggests that the residua of the original associations of language continue to impinge on consciousness after childhood and that those surviving fragments of linkage add feelings of incestuous relations to verbal activity. It follows that using language in ways that subvert direct communication can constitute a strategy for avoiding physical contact. Literary, ironic, and figurative language can be seen, if we wish to pursue these speculations further, as evasions of incest. In fact, any kind of deflection of language into autotelic or self-referential modes will diminish its symbolic incestuousness. Language games, for example, can be seen as ways of facilitating contact without intimacy. The term "incest" and the question of guilt are not necessary for our argument; the inevitable linkage between speech and intimate physical contact, on the other hand, is basic. Speech always begins in the context of separation and loss. Language is a skill permanently associated with both isolation and reunification; it is a signal system that at once confirms and overcomes loss.

We do not wish to suggest that Eliot had any incestuous motives; rather, we wish to note that his typical linguistic structures indicate that, probably unconsciously, he was moved by some kind of variation on these theories that associate speech with intimacy; to be more precise, he seems to have been intrigued with speech as a means of simultaneously establishing and preventing contact. It is well known that he devoted his life to opposite poles of language— the clear and elegant prose of his criticism on one end, and the kind of poetry that blocks and even derides explanation on the other. This pattern is useful in approaching a reading of his poetry as a dramatization of the dialectic of the presence of language and the absence of communication.

Parataxis, to return to one of Eliot's basic technical commitments in *The Waste Land*, can be a defensive gesture for those whose vocation is language. To take language as a vocation tends to make the need for intimacy the center of one's life and work; that is, to choose to be a philosopher or poet is to declare one's dependence on language and thus one's need to recover lost physical contact. The deliberate rejection of sequence, signals, connectors, and transitions within language is an advanced strategy for draining intimacy out of the system of discourse. It removes those aspects of language that deal most directly with linkage, merger, and continuity within the code system itself. Parataxis, then, is peculiarly appropriate for a poem taking the loss of community as its central subject, a poem evoking wasted lands, failed loves, and bereft mothers as its central symbols.

The principal shortcoming of this neo-Freudian approach is its lack of specific reference. As a theory, it predicts that all poets will be anxious to regard poetry as an evasion of communication. All poetry, if the theory had universal validity, would enact Rimbaud's desire to escape the indignity of being understood. The theory does not have general validity, but in a special way it does apply to most modernist writing. In regard to Eliot, it is more interesting as a supplementary comment on the speculation that to some extent he was involved in retrieving infantile modes than as an account of why he might have written as he did.

A major task facing the reader of *The Waste Land* is a unification of the twin facets of theme and technique. The main theme, we have argued, is lost community, and the main method is parataxis or lost coherence. To leave the matter at this point and conclude that the two facets are mere analogues of each other would be to bring back all of those arguments typified by Yvor Winters's notion of the "fallacy of imitative form." In his *In Defense of Reason*, Winters argued that chaos as subject does not justify chaos as method.[4] Similarly, multiperspectivism as subject does not justify disconnected perspectives as a work's principle of form. Although unconvincing to most admirers of modernist poetry, Winters's anatomy of nonsense has the considerable merit of warning against an uncritical acceptance of disunity. The fallacy of imitative form, however, is not the only alternative to chaos. Piaget's work suggests a perspective from which *The Waste Land* and a number of other modernist texts can be understood as organically unified.

In *The Construction of Reality in the Child*, Piaget summarizes many experiments conducted with infants during the first two years of life. His description of what the child perceives has much in common with many descriptions of works like *The Waste Land*, *Ulysses*, the *Cantos*, and paintings using cubistic techniques. Piaget seems to have known little about modernist literature and art, but he appears to have discovered its key, its inner subject matter. We speculate that a primary aspect of the inner subject matter of modernist literature is the presence of our first world as a ground on which everything else is constructed. Another way of putting this is to say that the inner subject matter is inseparable from the varying epistemological modes of infancy.

Piaget calls the first two years of a child's life the "sensorimotor phase" and divides this phase into six sections. In the first section, the child perceives a flat, two-dimensional space and a discontinuous time. In the last section, the child perceives the same space and time relations that adults use in conducting their lives. Between the first and last stages, the child is in a sequence of fluctuating perceptual modes which cause him to move through various ways of structuring his environment from moment to moment. The coincidence of learning to speak and to move that might produce a symbolization of language as incest occurs during these intermediate phases.

In the sensorimotor phase, then, infants process sensations in a double way. They perceive the world as both free-floating flat image and substantial object. When they see the world as a congeries of flat images—as they do exclusively in the first six months and intermittently during the remainder of their first two years—children are unable to conceive of themselves as objects among other objects occupying and thus creating space. They are so egocentric that, paradoxically, they have no egos. Their inability to perceive three-dimensional objects in a continuous time sequence prevents them from locating themselves in a stable context. The world is a kaleidoscope with an emptiness at its center where the self should be. Infants, to put it in a way Piaget does not mention, are exceptions to the Cartesian *cogito*. They think, but that activity does not permit the affirmation "I am." They process information, but since that information lacks substance, they cannot perceive of themselves as substantial separate persons.

Piaget applies the term "magico-phenomenalistic" to this early condition. It is phenomenalistic because, from a spatial perspective, it consists of qualities—free-floating adjectives of "broken images"—not yet configured into objects. It is magical because, from a temporal perspective, it consists of incoherent events. Magic, in Piaget's usage, refers to the absence of imaginable causal connections between events in a series. In the primal universe, sequences are totally random. Parataxis is an irrelevant term because no defining alternative to its transitionless nature exists. In a special sense, of course, and for the same reason, magic is itself an irrelevant term. Be that as it may, the imagistic space and magical time that Piaget associates with early infancy are extremely similar to the radical incoherence of much modernist art.

Joyce, it may be remembered, used the term "magic" to describe his technique in the "Circe" episode of *Ulysses,* and Eliot reported his admiration for the episode when he read it in typescript before publication in 1921.[5] Though Eliot does not apply the word "magic," he too saw interesting possibilities in making events leap in and out of existence in a fictional world where space and time are different from space and time in the everyday world. In *The Waste Land,* each loss of a clear image or object is followed by a "magical" entry of its replacement. Loss and gain mutually define each other as the poem proceeds.

Piaget's description of the primal, or magico-phenomenalistic, period is worth quoting extensively, for no paraphrase can match its precision. The infant, he argues, is unaware of himself.

> Through an apparently paradoxical mechanism, it is precisely when the subject is most self-centered that he knows himself the least, and it is to the extent that he discovers himself that he places himself in the universe and constructs it by virtue of that fact. In other words, egocentrism signifies the absence of both self-perception and objectivity, whereas acquiring possession of the object as such is on a par with the acquisition of self-perception.[6]

Infancy is a condition, then, characterized by the Edenic unity of being sought in various kinds of religious, philosophical, and literary quests. Construction of objects and a self in later phases is a fall from unity of being into separation, selfhood, and problematic relations. Piaget's "acquiring possession of the object" and "acquisition of self-perception" can be thought of, to use a religious vocabulary, as "original sin" and the loss of Eden. In Bradley's philosophic vocabulary, Piaget's "acquiring possession of the object" corresponds to the fall into dualism (into relational experience, into language) and to the loss of immediate experience. In the literary analysis we have just concluded, Piaget's phrases correspond to the loss of community, dispossession, and entrapment which we have identified as *The Waste Land*'s thematic center.

Piaget's discussion of infant epistemology is helpful in understanding the problem of solipsism. Bradley is often accused of being a solipsist, that is, one who maintains that the self can know nothing but its own modifications and states. In his dissertation,

Eliot denies that Bradley's philosophy is solipsistic. A number of literary critics, notably J. Hillis Miller in *Poets of Reality*, have argued that Eliot's early poetry indicates that he himself was a solipsist.[7] These critics typically bring as their proof text the quotation from Bradley's *Appearance and Reality* in the notes to *The Waste Land*, the quotation about every soul being in its own opaque sphere.[8] From the perspective of infancy, however, the solipsism question vanishes. In the primal phase, everyone is a solipsist, and that is the only time, except for extreme schizophrenic states, in which it is possible to be a solipsist. The person who believes that he is the only mind in the universe holds that belief only when he knows nothing of objects in the outside universe. And since perception of objects must precede or coexist with perception of self, the solipsist cannot be aware of himself either. Knowledge of self is a function of knowledge of the not-self. Solipsism, then, is a pseudoproblem. Or, rather, it is a name for the lost primal condition, a term to be transvalued as the unreachable ideal of unity before the fall.

Piaget constructs careful terminologies to describe the exotic and marvelous world of the solipsistic infant. This strange universe "presents neither permanent objects nor objective space, nor time interconnecting events as such, nor causality external to the personal actions." Further:

> A universe without objects . . . is a world in which space does not constitute a solid environment but is limited to structuring the subject's very acts; it is a world of pictures, each one of which can be known and analyzed but which disappear and reappear capriciously. From the point of view of causality, it is a world in which the connections between things are masked by the relations between the action and its desired results. . . . As far as the boundaries between the self and the external world are concerned, a universe without objects is such that the self, lacking knowledge of itself, is absorbed in external pictures for want of knowing itself. Moreover, these pictures center upon the self by failing to include it as a thing among other things, and thus fail to sustain interrelationships independent of the self.[9]

Virtually every point made in this description fits *The Waste Land's* thematics and methods. The poem, like the condition of infancy, is a world of pictures where space is only intermittently a solid environment. It is also a sequence of parts that appear and reappear capriciously, where connections of parts to each other are subordinate to their connections to external directions of meaning. Its external and internal allusions cancel each other. For example, in the Chapel Perilous passage, external allusion points to one meaning while internal allusion points to an opposite meaning. The effect is a masking of reference through proliferation of references.

To sum up these descriptions: infancy is a world where there is no space, time, self, or continuity. The fundamental reason for their absence is that the brain is not yet able to construct solid objects from a single point of view and hold them in memory long enough to provide a sense of permanence for those solid objects. The infant is a pure example of a perspectivist. He sees things from one point of view at a time and then forgets them before seeing things again. If adults lost their ability to construct a present out of short-term memory, they would experience each perception as unique and as isolated from all past perceptions. The world would jump in and out of existence with no transitions between the different worlds thus produced. They would know Being; they would know Nothingness or Non-Being; however, they would not have any experience of Becoming. Reality would be a slide show of unrelated flat pictures. The slides would be separated by mere blanks, and cinematic continuity would be unimaginable.

As an infant progresses toward possession of the object, he alternates between primal and developed perceptions. In these intermediate stages, reality enacts a dialectic of abstraction and empathy. The magico-phenomenalistic phase of perception yields only abstract, two-dimensional images. The late phase, by contrast, provides the solidity and depth necessary for empathetic perception. This is another way in which *The Waste Land* seems to function as a mimesis of infantile ways of seeing. Its styles, themes, and organization oscillate between abstraction and empathy, and though this oscillation is bewildering from most perspectives, it coalesces into a unity when seen from the point of view provided by Piaget's conclusions on infantile "genetic epistemology."

Without claiming that Eliot consciously used theories of infancy in constructing his poem, we would like to suggest that it is likely that he drew on infantile experience in two special ways. First, he could have intuited the propriety of his structure unconsciously through the impingement of buried memories on his conscious mind. This possibility can be supported only in a general way. It depends on an assumption that the structures the world has in infancy are stored in the unconscious and that, under some circumstances, they can come close enough to awareness to cause an adult to sense a hidden decorum, an inexplicable rightness in analogous structures. Eliot was aware of cubism, futurism, *Ulysses*, and other exciting examples of paratactic structure. He felt, and knew others felt, that such structures were typical of what made the arts unique in his time. *The Waste Land* remained in his mind as a developing set of ideas for a long poem for several years. During that period, he came to know beyond all doubt that his structure was somehow right and organically unified, despite its violent repudiation of the appearance of unity. Perhaps his own infancy, functioning unconsciously, enabled him to see unity in disunity. In the years after *The Waste Land*, particularly the years close in time to his conversion (one kind of return), he drew on the imagery of a "first world" of unity. The fleeting remembrance of mystical unity in childhood is part of the context of the Ariel poems, the Landscape poems, and "Burnt Norton." And in a 1930 essay he argues that Thomas Traherne's "chief inspiration is the same curious mystical experience of the world in childhood which had also touched Vaughan."[10]

A second way that Eliot could have used infancy as the ultimate perspective in *The Waste Land* is related to the obvious and clear overlap between Bradley's concept of immediate experience and Piaget's concept of infantile epistemology. In his dissertation, Eliot quotes Bradley's statement that immediate experience is "not a stage which shows itself at the beginning and then disappears, but it remains at the bottom throughout as fundamental." Eliot goes on to explain that

> Immediate experience is not at any stage of consciousness merely a presentation which can be isolated from other elements also present or subsequent in consciousness. It is not "sense-data" or sensations, it is not a stream of feeling which, as merely felt, is an attribute of the subject side only and must in some way be "related" to an external world. And it is not, lastly,

> more pure or more immediate in the animal or the infant mind than in the mind of the mathematician engaged upon a problem.[11]

Eliot maintains that immediate experience is not a separate stage of a mind's development. It is always present as a ground upon which other cognitive phases are constructed.

In denying that the "animal or the infant mind" is more immediate than that of the mathematician, Eliot is preparing his argument that immediate experience functions as a psychological constant foundational to consciousness. He goes beyond Bradley by removing the phases of cognition from pure philosophy and relocating them in a theory of the psychological and physiological unconscious. In *The Philosophy of T. S. Eliot*, William Skaff makes a convincing case that Eliot's dissertation integrated Bradley's ideas into those of scientific psychology, primarily by noting the implications of Pierre Janet, who had introduced Pavlov's work to the West, and Carl Georg Lange, who had worked with William James in the 1880s.[12] The unconscious, as Eliot conceived it, was based on ideas prior to Freud and Jung, ideas that aspired to scientific rigor.

Bradley did not go as far into psychology as Eliot was to go, but he did occasionally deal with the question of whether an unconscious is possible. As Skaff points out, Bradley at times responded to Eduard von Hartmann's *Philosophy of the Unconscious* (1869).[13] Bradley speculates that the unconscious is a mental state in which we are not "aware of any distinctions between that which is felt and that which feels." In this preconscious state "there are no distinctions in the proper sense, and yet there is a many felt in one."[14] Though children, he feels, are more likely to experience this sense of unity, adults clearly have moments of the same kind of feeling. Bradley then states what must be for us a climactic argument.

> Was there and is there in the development of the race and the individual a stage at which experience is merely immediate? And, further, do we all perhaps at moments sink back to such a level? . . . For myself I think it probable that such a stage of mind not only, with all of us, comes first in fact, but that at times it recurs even in the life of the developed individual.[15]

Skaff quotes this passage too, but he does not notice infancy as the period referred to by Bradley. He is concerned with Eliot's version of the collective unconscious as a way of understanding myth and the primitive mind.[16] That understanding can come more easily after assuming that we and primitive people have infancy in common. The early phase of the individual is there for Piaget and others to observe. Cultural variations do not affect the infant in his first stage. He inhabits the same magico-phenomenalistic universe, whether he lives in a Paleolithic cave or in a postmodern nursery. As a continuing component of the unconscious, infancy can be seen as the source of intuitions of unity, the soul, mystical experiences, and even the "still point of the turning world." *The Waste Land* points us toward this first and deepest place as a perspective that might reveal its artistic unity. The end of a metaphysical quest is the recognition that metaphysics itself is only nostalgia for the place where we started.

These reflections lead us to our final speculation. Cubists, vorticists, surrealists, futurists, and so on, published a variety of theories on why the new forms were valid. As we noted in our first chapter, some of them were heavily dependent on geometrical concepts involving curved space and the fourth dimension. Such theories, typified by the ideas of Marcel Duchamp, justified images by arguing that the world would look that way if seen from the perspective of a fourth dimension. Our suggestion is that such theories may have been invented because the perspective of infancy was not considered. Even if the perspective of infancy had been considered, of course, it might have been discounted in favor of the views associated with mathematics and the natural sciences. The latter were more exciting and, in a meretricious way, more respectable. We remain somewhat dubious about using infancy as a grand theory of modernism; at the same time, we believe that early twentieth-century theories of the avant-garde would have assumed a different shape if their advocates had perceived the unconscious regression involved in the new structural experiments.

It is beyond dispute that Eliot was preoccupied with questions about the unconscious as it affects conscious decisions and also with speculations about primal components within the unconscious. He focused on these very subjects in his graduate studies, and in the early London years he reviewed seminal books on psychology, philosophy, and sociology. He was more highly informed about primal states of mind than any of his contemporaries who issued theories of modern art. It is not necessary, of course, to suppose that he wrote *The Waste Land* with the conscious intention of simulating the structures of infancy. At the same time, it is reasonable to point out that the theme of lost origins in unity, the techniques of referential and sequential loss, the sense of the need to dramatize the loss of self, and the dialectic of abstraction and empathy are consistent with Piaget's descriptions of infancy. Nothing indicates that Eliot said to himself, "I must now write a poem about the troubles of secular life without myth, make it a hodgepodge, and use immediate experience or the infantile mind as the perspective from which it has organic unity." Many things suggest, however, that that is precisely what he did.

The reader is left with a choice. He can suppose that *The Waste Land* is a simple set of variations on lost unity with no unifying perspective this side of a metaphysical absolute. Or he can suppose that it is a deep intuition of the alien patterns of perception that prevailed in his first world. We tend toward the second choice, in part because it associates the poem's overwhelming power and life with a primal source. *The Waste Land* evokes a perfect, wordless love that existed before all language and all meaning. That is the primary reason it is a great and lasting work of art.

Notes

Introduction

1. T. S. Eliot, *The Waste Land: A Facsimile and Transcript of the Original Drafts Including the Annotations of Ezra Pound*, ed. Valerie Eliot (New York: Harcourt Brace Jovanovich, 1971); hereafter cited as *The Waste Land Facsimile*.

2. Cleanth Brooks, "*The Waste Land*: An Analysis," *Southern Review*, Summer 1937, 106–36. A revised version of this essay is included in *Modern Poetry and the Tradition* (Chapel Hill: University of North Carolina Press, 1939).

3. Grover Smith, *T. S. Eliot's Poetry and Plays: A Study in Sources and Meaning* (Chicago: University of Chicago Press, 1956; 2nd ed., 1974). For an exhaustive study of the sources of *The Waste Land*, see Grover Smith, *The Waste Land* (London: George Allen & Unwin, 1983).

4. William Arrowsmith, "The Poem as Palimpsest: A Dialogue on Eliot's 'Sweeney Erect,'" *Southern Review* 17 (January 1981): 17–69.

5. John D. Margolis, *T. S. Eliot's Intellectual Development, 1922–1939* (Chicago: University of Chicago Press, 1972).

6. T. S. Eliot, *Knowledge and Experience in the Philosophy of F. H. Bradley* (New York: Farrar, Straus, 1964). See also Anne C. Bolgan, *What the Thunder Really Said: A Retrospective Essay on the Making of "The Waste Land"* (Montreal: Queen's University Press, 1973).

7. *Josiah Royce's Seminar, 1913–1914, as Recorded in the Notebooks of Harry T. Costello*, ed. Grover Smith (New Brunswick, N.J.: Rutgers University Press, 1963).

8. Lewis Freed, *T. S. Eliot: Aesthetics and History* (La Salle, Ill.: Open Court, 1962). Lewis Freed, *T. S. Eliot: The Critic as Philosopher* (West Lafayette, Ind.: Purdue University Press, 1979).

9. Piers Gray, *T. S. Eliot's Intellectual and Poetic Development, 1909–1922* (Atlantic Highlands, N.J.: Humanities Press, 1982).

10. William Skaff, *The Philosophy of T. S. Eliot* (Philadelphia: University of Pennsylvania Press, 1986).

11. Jeffrey Perl, "The Language of Theory and the Language of Poetry," *Southern Review* 21 (October 1985): 1012–23.

12. Cleo McNelly Kearns, *T. S. Eliot and Indic Traditions: A Study in Poetry and Belief* (Cambridge: Cambridge University Press, 1987).

13. Jacques Derrida, "Structure, Sign, and Play in the Discourse of the Human Sciences," in *Writing and Difference*, trans. Alan Bass (Chicago: University of Chicago Press, 1978), 278–93.

14. Richard Wollheim, "Eliot and F. H. Bradley: An Account," in *Eliot in Perspective: A Symposium*, ed. Graham Martin (Atlantic Highlands, N.J.: Humanities Press, 1970), 169–93.

15. Marianne Thormählen, *"The Waste Land": A Fragmentary Wholeness* (Lund: C. W. K. Gleerup, 1978).

16. Gregory S. Jay, *T. S. Eliot and the Poetics of Literary History* (Baton Rouge: Louisiana State University Press, 1983).

17. Harriet Davidson, *T. S. Eliot and Hermeneutics: Absence and Interpretation in "The Waste Land"* (Baton Rouge: Louisiana State University Press, 1985).

18. Calvin Bedient, *He Do the Police in Different Voices: "The Waste Land" and Its Protagonist* (Chicago: University of Chicago Press, 1986).

19. Davidson, *Eliot and Hermeneutics*, 3.

20. For a discussion of the important principle of the systematic nature of truth and judgment in Bradley and Eliot, see Jewel Spears Brooker, "The Structure of Eliot's 'Gerontion': An Analysis Based on Bradley's Doctrine of the Systematic Nature of Truth," *ELH* 46, 2 (1979): 314–40.

21. All quotations of lines from Eliot's poems are from *The Complete Poems and Plays, 1909–1950* (New York: Harcourt Brace & World, 1952).

22. Jean Piaget, *The Construction of Reality in the Child*, trans. Margaret Cook (New York: Basic Books, 1954).

1. A Wilderness of Mirrors

1. Eliot, *Knowledge and Experience*, 154–55.

2. Ibid., chaps. 3, 4, 5.

3. Michel Foucault, *The Order of Things: An Archaeology of the Human Sciences*, trans. Alan Sheridan-Smith (New York: Random House, 1970), xxii (*Les Mots et les choses*, 1966).

4. Ibid., xi.

5. Ibid., 359–60.

6. J. Bronowski, *The Common Sense of Science* (Cambridge, Mass.: Harvard University Press, n.d.).

7. Thomas S. Kuhn, *The Structure of Scientific Revolutions*, 2nd ed. (Chicago: University of Chicago Press, 1970). Gerald Holton, *Thematic Origins of Scientific Thought: Kepler to Einstein* (Cambridge, Mass.: Harvard University Press, 1973). Arthur O. Lovejoy, *The Revolt against Dualism: An Inquiry Concerning the Existence of Ideas* (1929; rpt. La Salle, Ill.: Open Court, 1955).

8. Holton, *Thematic Origins*, 35.

9. Lovejoy, *Revolt against Dualism*, 3.

10. José Ortega y Gasset, *Man and Crisis*, trans. Mildred Adams (New York: W. W. Norton, 1958).

11. Ibid., 86.

12. Ibid.

13. Ibid., 119.

14. Martin Heidegger, "Holderlin and the Essence of Poetry," trans. Douglas Scott, in *Existence and Being* (Chicago: Henry Regnery, 1949), 289.

15. Sigmund Freud, *The Future of an Illusion*, trans. James Strachey (New York: W. W. Norton, 1961). Jewel Spears Brooker, "The Dispensations of Art: Mallarmé and the Fallen Reader," *Southern Review* 19 (January 1983): 17–38. Jewel Spears Brooker, "T. E. Hulme," in *British Poets, 1880–1914*, ed. Donald E. Stanford, *Dictionary of Literary Biography* (Detroit: Gale Research, 1983), 19:227–36. Oswald Spengler, *The Decline of the West*, trans. C. F. Atkinson (London: George Allen & Unwin, 1932). Hugh Kenner, *The Pound Era* (Berkeley: University of California Press, 1971). Jeffrey

M. Perl, *The Tradition of Return: The Implicit History of Modern Literature* (Princeton, N.J.: Princeton University Press, 1984). Timothy Materer, *Vortex: Pound, Eliot, and Lewis* (Ithaca, N.Y.: Cornell University Press, 1979).

16. Wilhelm Worringer, *Abstraction and Empathy: A Contribution to the Psychology of Style*, trans. Michael Bullock (1908; rpt. New York: International Universities Press, 1953).

17. José Ortega y Gasset, "The Dehumanization of Art," in *The Dehumanization of Art and Other Essays on Art, Culture, and Literature*, trans. Helene Weyl (1925; rpt. Princeton, N.J.: Princeton University Press, 1968), 3–56.

18. Ortega y Gasset, "On Point of View in the Arts," in *The Dehumanization of Art*, 105–30.

19. Gotthold Ephraim Lessing, *Laocoön* (1766), in *Laocoön; Nathan the Wise; Minna von Barnhelm*, trans. William A. Steel (London: J. M. Dent, 1967).

20. Joseph Frank, "Spatial Form in Modern Literature," in *The Widening Gyre: Crisis and Mastery in Modern Literature* (Bloomington: Indiana University Press, 1968), 2–63.

21. Jo-Anna Isaak, "James Joyce and the Cubist Esthetic," *Mosaic* 14 (1981): 61–90.

22. Guillaume Apollinaire, "The Beginnings of Cubism" (1912), and "The Cubist Painters" (1913), in *Theories of Modern Art: A Source Book by Artists and Critics*, ed. Herschel B. Chipp (Berkeley: University of California Press, 1968), 216–47. André Salmon, "Anecdotal History of Cubism" (1912), in Chipp, *Theories*, 199–206.

23. Albert Gleizes and Jean Metzinger, "Cubism" (1912), in Chipp, *Theories*, 207–15.

24. Linda Dalrymple Henderson, *The Fourth Dimension and Non-Euclidean Geometry in Modern Art* (Princeton, N.J.: Princeton University Press, 1983). We wish to thank Susan Sutliff Brown for bringing this book to our attention.

25. Apollinaire, "The Cubist Painters," 224.

26. Metzinger, quoted by Chipp, in ibid., 223 n.l.

27. Eliot, "Ben Jonson," in *The Sacred Wood: Essays on Poetry and Criticism* (1920, 1938; rpt. London: Methuen, 1960), 115.

28. Ibid., 117.

29. Jacob Korg, "Modern Art Techniques in *The Waste Land*," in *A Collection of Critical Essays on "The Waste Land,"* ed. Jay Martin (Englewood Cliffs, N.J.: Prentice-Hall, 1968), 87–96.

30. Jacob Korg, "*The Waste Land* and Contemporary Art," in *Approaches to Teaching Eliot's Poetry and Plays*, ed. Jewel Spears Brooker (New York: Modern Language Association, 1988), 121–26.

31. Wylie Sypher, *Rococo to Cubism in Art and Literature: Transformations in Style in Art and Literature from the 18th to the 20th Century* (New York: Random House, 1960). Roger Shattuck, *The Banquet Years: The Origins of the Avant-Garde in France, 1885 to World War I* (New York: Random House, 1955). Marjorie Perloff, *The Futurist Moment: Avant-Garde, Avant Guerre, and the Language of Rupture* (Chicago: University of Chicago Press, 1986).

32. Gertrude Patterson, *T. S. Eliot: Poems in the Making* (New York: Barnes & Noble, 1971).

33. David Tomlinson, "T. S. Eliot and the Cubists," *Twentieth Century Literature*, 1980, 64–81.

34. Gleizes and Metzinger, "Cubism," in Chipp, *Theories*, 211.

35. Albert Gleizes and Jean Metzinger, "Cubism" (1912), in *Modern Artists on Art*, ed. Robert L. Herbert (Englewood Cliffs, N.J.: Prentice-Hall, 1964), 15.

36. Grover Smith, in letter to the authors, November 18, 1987.

2. Unifying Incompatible Worlds

1. Joseph Conrad, *Heart of Darkness*, in *Heart of Darkness; Almayer's Folly; The Lagoon* (New York: Dell, 1960), 70–71.

2. For a more detailed review of Eliot's education and book reviewing, see Gray, *Eliot's Development*; Skaff, *Philosophy*; and Lyndall Gordon, *Eliot's Early Years* (Oxford: Oxford University Press, 1977).

3. For a different view of Eliot's relation with Bertrand Russell, see Richard Shusterman, *T. S. Eliot and the Philosophy of Criticism* (New York: Columbia University Press, 1988).

4. Eliot, *Knowledge and Experience*, 153.

5. For a more detailed discussion of the limitations of the relational level in Eliot and Bradley, see Brooker, "Structure of 'Gerontion.'"

6. Eliot, "The Metaphysical Poets," in *Selected Essays* (1932, 1950; New York: Harcourt Brace & World, 1964), 247.

7. F. H. Bradley, "On Our Knowledge of Immediate Experience," in *Essays on Truth and Reality* (Oxford: Oxford University Press [Clarendon Press], 1914), 159–91.

8. Eliot, *Knowledge and Experience*, 17.

9. Bradley, *Essays on Truth and Reality*, 159–60.

10. Eliot, *Knowledge and Experience*, 20.

11. Jewel Spears Brooker, "F. H. Bradley's Doctrine of Experience in T. S. Eliot's *The Waste Land* and *Four Quartets*," *Modern Philology* 77, 2 (November 1979): 146–57.

12. Bradley, *Essays on Truth and Reality*, 161.

13. Ibid.

14. F. H. Bradley, *Appearance and Reality*, 2nd ed. (Oxford: Oxford University Press [Clarendon Press], 1897), 462.

15. Eliot, *Knowledge and Experience*, 31.

16. Ibid.

17. Ibid., 22.

18. Bradley, *Essays on Truth and Reality*, 174.

19. Eliot, *Knowledge and Experience*, 16–17.

20. Skaff, *Philosophy*, chap. 3.

21. Eliot, *Knowledge and Experience*, 28.

22. Perhaps, as Grover Smith has suggested, this epigraph had a personal significance for Eliot. See Smith, *The Waste Land*, xiii. Like Kurtz, Eliot was an idealist and, to use Eliot's own language in a later essay, he was also an explorer of frontiers of consciousness where words fail but meanings exist. Ronald Schuchard has argued that Eliot was preoccupied with horror in art. See Schuchard, "Eliot and the Horrific Moment," *Southern Review* 21, 4 (August 1985): 1045–56.

23. Conrad, *Heart of Darkness*, 114.

24. Eliot, in *The Waste Land Facsimile*, 125.

25. Eliot, *Knowledge and Experience*, 147–48.

26. Eliot, Introduction to Charlotte Eliot, *Savonarola: A Dramatic Poem* (London: R. Cobden-Sanderson, 1926), vii–viii.

27. Smith, *The Waste Land*, 88–91.

28. James George Frazer, Preface to *The Golden Bough*, 3rd ed. (London: Macmillan, 1911).

29. *Josiah Royce's Seminar*, 78.

30. Eliot, "A Prediction in Regard to Three English Authors, Writers Who, Though

Masters of Thought, Are Likewise Masters of Art," *Vanity Fair* 21, 6 (February 1924): 29.

31. Ibid.

32. Eliot, Introduction to *Savonarola*, viii.

33. *Josiah Royce's Seminar*, 193–94.

34. Eliot, Seminar Paper, Hayward Collection, King's College Library, University of Cambridge.

35. Eliot, "*Ulysses*, Order and Myth," *Dial* 75, 5 (November 1923): [480]–83.

36. Eliot, Introduction to *Savonarola*, vii.

37. Eliot, "Tradition and the Individual Talent," in *Selected Essays*, 3–11.

38. Sophocles, *Oedipus Rex*, in *The Oedipus Cycle*, trans. Dudley Fitts and Robert Fitzgerald (New York: Harcourt Brace, 1967), 78.

39. Thomas Gould, "The Innocence of Oedipus," *Arion* 4, 3 (Autumn 1965): 363–86.

40. See Hannah Arendt, *The Human Condition* (Garden City, N.Y.: Doubleday, 1959), 192–93.

41. F. Nietzsche, *Twilight of the Idols*, in *The Portable Nietzsche*, ed. and trans. Walter Kaufmann (New York: Viking, 1964), 474.

42. F. H. Bradley, "On the Critical Presuppositions of History," in *Collected Essays* (Oxford: Oxford University Press [Clarendon Press], 1935), vol. 1.

43. For an analysis of "Gerontion" based on the structural use of the house image, see Brooker, "Structure of 'Gerontion.'"

44. Jewel Spears Brooker, "The Case of the Missing Abstraction: Eliot, Frazer, and Modernism," *Massachusetts Review* 25, 4 (Winter 1984): 539–52.

45. Bolgan, *What the Thunder Really Said*.

46. Eliot, Unpublished Paper, Houghton Library, Harvard University.

47. William Blake to Thomas Butts, November 22, 1802, *The Letters of William Blake*, ed. Geoffrey Keynes (London: Rupert Hart-Davis, 1968), 62.

3. Relational Consciousness and Transcendent Reading

1. Jewel Spears Brooker, "When Love Fails: Reading *The Waste Land* with Undergraduates," in *Approaches to Teaching Eliot*, 103–8.

2. Bertrand Russell and Alfred N. Whitehead, *Principia Mathematica* (1913; rpt. Cambridge: Cambridge University Press, 1957), 1:231–37.

3. Bradley, *Appearance and Reality*, 28.

4. Eliot, *Knowledge and Experience*, 99. For an extended discussion of Eliot's treatment of subjects and objects in the dissertation, see Sanford Schwartz, *The Matrix of Modernism: Pound, Eliot, and Early 20th-Century Thought* (Princeton, N.J.: Princeton University Press, 1985), chap. 4.

5. Bradley, *Appearance and Reality*, 28.

6. Ibid.

7. *The Waste Land Facsimile*, xxxiii.

8. The unpublished text of this poem is in the Berg Collection of the New York Public Library. The poem is discussed in Gordon, *Eliot's Early Years*, chap. 1.

9. *The Waste Land Facsimile*, 8–9.

10. Arthur Koestler, *The Roots of Coincidence* (New York: Random House [Vintage Books], 1973).

11. James Joyce, *Ulysses* (1922; rpt. New York: Random House [Vintage Books], 1961), 185.

12. Percy Bysshe Shelley, "Peter Bell the Third," *Poetical Works*, ed. Thomas Hutchinson (London: Oxford University Press, 1967), 350.

13. Charles Baudelaire, "Seven Old Men," trans. David Paul, in *Poison and Vision: Poems and Prose of Baudelaire, Mallarmé, and Rimbaud* (New York: Random House [Vintage Books], 1974).

14. In *What the Thunder Really Said*, Bolgan remarks that "[The reader] has some difficulty in accepting the allegations and in understanding just what he has done to deserve them" (p. 51). Like a number of other readers of the poem, Bolgan seems to have taken offense at Eliot for calling all of us hypocrites, twins, and brothers.

15. Smith, *Eliot's Poetry and Plays* and *The Waste Land*.

16. Bedient, *He Do the Police*, ix.

17. George L. K. Morris, "Marie, Marie, Hold on Tight," *Partisan Review* 21 (March–April 1953): 231–33. *The Waste Land Facsimile*, 125–26.

4. Amalgamating Disparate Experience

1. Eliot, "The Metaphysical Poets," in *Selected Essays*, 247.

2. Eliot, "Four Elizabethan Dramatists," in *Selected Essays*, 93.

3. Eliot, "*Ulysses*, Order and Myth," 482.

4. *The Waste Land Facsimile*, 126.

5. See, for example, D. G. Rossetti's translation of this passage from the *Satyricon*, in Rossetti, *Works* (London, 1911), 240.

6. Joyce, *Ulysses*, 207.

7. Conrad, *Heart of Darkness*, 27.

8. Ibid., 30.

9. Bedient, *He Do the Police*, 29. *The Waste Land Facsimile*, 19.

10. *The Waste Land Facsimile*, 19.

11. Ibid., 17.

12. Smith, *Eliot's Poetry and Plays*, 82.

13. *The Waste Land Facsimile*, 126.

14. Morse Peckham, *Man's Rage for Chaos: Biology, Behavior, and the Arts* (Philadelphia: Chilton Books, 1965).

15. Smith, *The Waste Land*, 123.

16. Eliot's paper on the interpretation of primitive ritual is in the Hayward Collection, King's College. Much of it is quoted in Gray, *Eliot's Development*, chap. 4.

17. Gray, *Eliot's Development*, 130.

18. Eliot, Introduction to *Savonarola*, viii.

19. Eliot, *Knowledge and Experience*, 60.

20. Ibid., 60–61.

5. Transcending the Moral Point of View

1. Henry Clarke Warren, *Buddhism in Translation: Passages Selected from the Buddhist Sacred Books and Translated from the Original Pali into English*, Harvard Oriental Series, vol. 3 (Cambridge, Mass.: Harvard University Press, 1896), 351–53.

2. Ibid.

3. For an authoritative and detailed discussion of Eliot's Indic sources, see Kearns, *Eliot and Indic Traditions*.

4. *The Confessions of St. Augustine*, trans. Edward B. Pusey (New York: Washington Square Press, 1960), 30.

5. Smith, *Eliot's Poetry and Plays*, 84, 88, 90.

6. Augustine, *Confessions*.

7. Baudelaire, "Fusées," in *Poison and Vision*, 101.

8. Eliot, "Baudelaire," in *Selected Essays*, 380.

9. For an intriguing discussion of Escher's art, see Douglas R. Hofstadter, *Gödel, Escher, Bach: An Eternal Golden Braid* (New York: Random House [Vintage Books], 1980).

10. Eliot, *Knowledge and Experience*, 31.

11. Ibid.

12. Bradley, *Essays on Truth and Reality*, 188.

13. Smith, *The Waste Land*, 111–12.

14. Smith, *Eliot's Poetry and Plays*, 86.

15. Baudelaire, "Get Drunk," in *Poison and Vision*, 141.

16. Bradley, *Appearance and Reality*, 26.

17. *The Waste Land Facsimile*, 35.

18. Meyer H. Abrams, *The Mirror and the Lamp: Romantic Theory and the Critical Tradition* (New York: W. W. Norton, 1953) 272–85.

19. Eliot, "Francis Herbert Bradley," in *Selected Essays*, 398.

20. Ibid.

21. F. H. Bradley, *Ethical Studies*, 2nd. ed. (Oxford: Oxford University Press [Clarendon Press], 1927) 90–91.

22. Ibid., 88.

23. Ibid., 142.

24. Ibid., 168.

25. Ibid., 313.

26. Ibid., 197 n.

27. Ibid., 314.

28. David Bell, "The Insufficiency of Ethics," in *The Philosophy of F. H. Bradley*, ed. Anthony Manser and Guy Stock (Oxford: Oxford University Press [Clarendon Press], 1984), 53–76.

6. Annihilation and Utter Night

1. Eliot, Introduction to *Savonarola*, viii.

2. Ibid., ix.

3. *Josiah Royce's Seminar*.

4. Gray, *Eliot's Development*, chap. 4.

5. Ibid.

6. Eliot, *Knowledge and Experience*, 60.

7. Emile Durkheim, *The Rules of Sociological Method*, trans. S. A. Solovay and J. H. Mueller, ed. G. Catlin (New York, 1938), xliii.

8. The term "hermeneutical loop" is our own coinage, with our own special meanings. It is not the same as Wilhelm Dilthey's "hermeneutical circle."

9. *The Waste Land Facsimile*, 129.

10. 1 Peter 3:21.

11. Frazer, *The Golden Bough*, pt. 4.

12. Jules Laforgue, *Oeuvres Complètes*, 4 Vols. (Paris, 1901–03).

13. *The Waste Land Facsimile*, 128.

14. Ibid.
15. Francis Noel Lees, "Mr. Eliot's Sunday Morning Satura: Petronius and *The Waste Land*," in *T. S. Eliot: The Man and His Work*, ed. Allen Tate (New York: Dell, 1966), 346.
16. Smith, *The Waste Land*, 108.
17. Ibid., 107.
18. *The Waste Land Facsimile*, 55–61, 128.
19. William Arrowsmith, "Daedal Harmonies: A Dialogue on Eliot and the Classics," *Southern Review* 13, 1 (1977): 1–47.
20. *The Waste Land Facsimile*, 55.
21. Ibid., 115.

7. Before and after Meaning

1. Eliot, "Dante," in *Selected Essays*, 200.
2. Eliot, Introduction to *Savonarola*, viii.
3. Joyce, *Ulysses*, 689.
4. B. P. N. Sinha, "The Second Voice," unpublished essay in Hayward Collection, King's College Library, University of Cambridge; quoted in Kearns, *Eliot and Indic Traditions*, 220.
5. For a different reading of the thunder legend, see Kearns, *Eliot and Indic Traditions*, 220–24.
6. Bradley, *Appearance and Reality*, 346.
7. Brooker, "Bradley's Doctrine of Experience," 146–57.
8. William Shakespeare, *Coriolanus*, ed. Philip Brockbank (London: Methuen, 1922); see esp. 5.3.
9. Bertrand Russell, *The Autobiography of Bertrand Russell*, 3 vols. (Boston: Little, Brown, 1951), 1: 236.
10. Bradley, *Essays on Truth and Reality*, 161.
11. Eliot, *Knowledge and Experience*, 31.
12. See, for example, Derek Traversi, *T. S. Eliot: The Longer Poems* (London: Bodley Head, 1976), 51–52.
13. See, for example, Wayne Booth, *A Rhetoric of Irony* (Chicago: University of Chicago Press, 1974).
14. *The Waste Land Facsimile*, 81.
15. Ibid.

A Speculative Postscript

1. Eliot, *Knowledge and Experience*, 153 ff.
2. Joseph Bentley, "*Ulysses* and the Stylistics of Regression," in *Joyce and His Contemporaries*, ed. Maureen Murphy and Diana Ben Merre (Westport, Conn.: Greenwood Press, 1989).
3. Julia Kristeva, *Desire in Language*, ed. Leon S. Rodiez, trans. Thomas Gora (New York: Columbia University Press, 1980).
4. Yvor Winters, *In Defense of Reason* (Denver: University of Denver Press, 1943).
5. Richard Ellmann, *Joyce* (Oxford: Oxford University Press, 1959), 542.
6. Piaget, *Construction of Reality*, x–xi.
7. J. Hillis Miller, *Poets of Reality: Six Twentieth-Century Writers* (1965; rpt. New York: Atheneum, 1974), 159–60.

8. The common misreading of the Bradley quotation is discussed in Brooker, "Bradley's Doctrine of Experience," 148 ff.

9. Piaget, *Construction of Reality*, 2.

10. Eliot, "Mystic and Politician as Poet: Vaughan, Traherne, Marvell, Milton," *Listener* 3 (April 2, 1930): 590.

11. Eliot, *Knowledge and Experience*, 16.

12. Skaff, *Philosophy*, 45–46.

13. Ibid., 58.

14. Bradley, *Essays on Truth and Reality*, 114.

15. Ibid., 174.

16. Skaff, *Philosophy*, 58.

Index

Index

Index

Index

Index

Index

239